THE GUINNESS AFFAIR

THE GUINNESS AFFAIR

Anatomy of a Scandal

Nick Kochan
and
Hugh Pym

CHRISTOPHER HELM
London

To Lionel and Miriam Kochan
and Susan Pym

© 1987 Nick Kochan and Hugh Pym
Christopher Helm (Publishers) Ltd,
Imperial House,
21–25 North Street,
Bromley,
Kent BR1 1SD

British Library Cataloguing in Publication Data

Kochan, Nick
 The Guinness affair; anatomy of a scandal.
 1. Guinness Group — History 2. Brewing industry
 – Great Britain — Corrupt practices
 I. Title II. Pym, Hugh
 383.7'6633'0941   HD 9397.G72G8

ISBN 0–7470–2605–X
ISBN 0–7470–2610–6 pbk

Typeset by Opus, Oxford
Printed and bound in Great Britain by
Billing and Sons Ltd, Worcester

CONTENTS

ACKNOWLEDGEMENTS

We would like to thank all the people we have interviewed about their recollections of the Guinness Affair, either on or off the record. All of them are busy people but almost all gave us much of their valuable time, sometimes several hours.

We must thank our employers, who were tolerant and willing to give us the time to write this book. Ruth Greene deserves special praise for patiently transcribing hours of interview material. Susan Pym was a helpful critic and constant supporter even while her husband was absent for long periods at his word processor. Wendy Leibowitz also made constructive criticisms about the manuscript.

Thanks are due to those who helped in other ways with research and information gathering: Suzie Rogoff, Debbie Goodwin, and Joan Neill. Thanks also to Margaret Glover.

ABBREVIATIONS

MMC	Monopolies and Mergers Commission
DTI	Department of Trade and Industry
OFT	Office of Fair Trading
WHO	World Health Organization
SEC	American Securities and Exchange Commission
PLC	Public Limited Company
MD	Managing Director
AGM	Annual General Meeting
EGM	Extraordinary General Meeting
'The City'	Shorthand expression for the area of London where most banks, stockbrokers and finance houses are situated — otherwise known as 'the Square Mile'
Takeover Panel	Voluntary body run by stockbrokers and merchant banks to police takeover battles
Takeover Code	Code of practice drawn up by the Takeover Panel
'White Knight'	A Company that comes to the rescue of another during a takeover battle.
'Poison Pill'	A means of escape open to a Company threatened with a hostile bid, usually involving spending a large sum of money on an acquisition.

CAST OF CHARACTERS

Ernest Saunders: joined Guinness October 1981, from Nestlé. Shortly afterwards became managing director. Appointed chairman in September 1986. Sacked in January 1987. Accused of offences under the Companies Act, May 1987.

Thomas Ward: Partner in Washington law firm Ward, Lazarus, Grow and Cihlar. Had worked with Saunders at Nestlé, assisted Guinness in takeover of Bell's and became key confidant and adviser to Saunders in Distillers bid. Became a non-executive director in 1984. Resigned 1987. Alleged to be recipient of £5.2 million fee for services to Guinness.

Olivier Roux: Joined Guinness in 1982, aged 32, as management consultant with Bain and Co. Became director of financial strategy and development in 1984, and had key role as financial adviser to Saunders. Ceased working with Guinness in December 1986, and resigned January 1987.

Roger Seelig: Corporate finance director with Morgan Grenfell, who advised Guinness during Distillers takeover. Resigned from Morgan Grenfell in December 1986.

Anthony Salz: Partner of City Law firm Freshfields who acted for Guinness during Distillers bid. Played major role in organising the legal arrangements of the merger with Distillers.

David Mayhew: Partner with stockbrokers Cazenove who advised Guinness during Distillers bid.

Scott Dobbie: Member of stockbroking firm Wood Mackenzie who also worked for Guinness. They resigned in July 1986.

Lord Iveagh: Third Lord Iveagh who became chairman of Guinness in 1962. In July 1986, he became president to make way for Ernest Saunders as chairman.

Anthony Purssell: Managing director of Guinness between 1975 and 1982, when he became deputy chairman. Appointed Saunders, but left in 1983.

John Connell: Worked his way up through the Tanqueray gin division to become Chairman of Distillers in September 1983. He resigned in April 1986 when the company was taken over by Guinness.

David Connell: Younger brother of John Connell and managing director of John Walker and Sons. Continued as Guinness director.

Anthony Parnes: Stockbroker who advised Saunders in Distillers bid. Recipient of £3 million for services rendered

Sir Jack Lyons: 71-year-old consultant to Bain and Co, he had powerful clout in political circles. He recieved fee of £2 million.

Gerald Ronson: Boss of Heron Corporation and associate of Tony Parnes who is believed to have offered to buy up to £25 million Guinness shares. He received £5 million for his services. He later returned all money given to him by Guinness.

Ephraim Margulies: Chairman of traders S&W Berrisford whose American company bought Guinness shares. He later returned money given to him as an inducement.

Meshulam Riklis: Flamboyant American founder of Rapid-American Corporation which owns Schenley, the US distributors of Dewar's whisky. Owner of rights to the lucrative Dewar's trademark in USA. At one time owned 5% of Guinness.

Ivan Boesky: American 'arbitrageur' and financial wheeler dealer. Bought Guinness and Distillers shares during bid. Guinness put $100 million into his investment fund. Disgraced in November 1986 after admitting insider dealing.

James Gulliver: Campbeltown-born founder of Argyll group of supermarkets in 1983, having previously run Oriel Foods and Fine Fare. He bid for Distillers in December 1985, but lost in April 1986 to Guinness.

David Webster: Finance director and part of management triumvirate of Argyll group. Has worked with James Gulliver for since the early 1970s.

Alistair Grant: Marketing director of Argyll Group, who came with Gulliver from Fine Fare. The third leg of the Argyll managing triumvirate, and now managing director.

Rupert Faure Walker: Corporate finance director, Samuel Montagu, who advised Argyll Group during Distillers bid.

Sir Thomas Risk: Respected governor of the Bank of Scotland who was drafted in by Saunders to be neutral Scottish non-executive chairman of new Guinness/Distillers group. He never held the position, and was axed by Saunders in May 1986.

Charles Fraser: Edinburgh lawyer and chairman of Morgan Grenfell, Scotland. Helped Saunders in bid for Bell's and at early stages in Distillers campaign. Nominated as director of new group but was dumped with Risk.

Lord Spens of Blairsanquhar: Merchant banker who advised Raymond Miquel during Bell's bid. Resigned from Ansbacher in January 1987. It was later disclosed that Ansbacher had purchased £7.6m worth of Guinness shares.

Raymond Miquel: Chairman and chief executive of Arthur Bell, who sought vainly to defend his company in June 1985 against Guinness, led by Saunders.

Peter Tyrie: Boss of Gleneagles Hotels which was taken over by Bell's in 1984. Advised shareholders to accept the Guinness bid at a critical point in the defence.

Sir Norman Macfarlane: Scottish businessman who joined as non-executive director after the Risk affair, and when Saunders left became chairman.

Anthony Tennant: Joined Guinness from Grand Metropolitan as chief executive replacing Ernest Saunders.

CHRONOLOGY OF EVENTS

1981

October: Ernest Saunders recruited to Guinness from Nestlé.

1982

January: Saunders becomes managing director of Guinness.

1983

November: James Gulliver and associates form Argyll Group.

1984

February: Gulliver considers takeover bid for Distillers.
June: Guinness acquire Martins, the newsagents business with 500 stores, for £45 million.
November: Guinness purchase health spa group Champneys (including spas at Tring and Stobo Castle) for £3 million.

1985

January: Guinness health division boosted with acquisition of Nature's Best Health Products (vitamin producer).
February: Acquisition by Guinness of Neighbourhood Stores with UK franchise for '7-Eleven' outlets for £12 million.
14 June: Saunders launches £330 million bid for Arthur Bell.
19 June: Raymond Miquel, chairman of Bell's, returns to Britain from USA and attacks Guinness bid.
25 June: Saunders and Miquel meet in London but talks break up without any progress.

27 June: Guinness publishes formal offer document for Bell's.

12 July: Bell's respond with defence document.

23 July: Department of Trade give the go ahead to the Guinness bid.

25 July: Bill Walker MP tells the House of Commons of 'skulduggery in the City'. He attacks Morgan Grenfell switching from Bell's to Guinness.

2 August: Ladbroke's reveal they own a 3% stake in Bell's.

2 August: Guinness buy Southland-McColl of Texas, owners of the RS McColl newsagents chain, for £24 million.

5 August: Bell's release formal defence document and profits forecast only minutes before midnight deadline.

7 August: Guinness increase bid to £370 million. Bell's reject offer, but one director, Peter Tyrie, dissociates himself and advises Bell's shareholders to accept.

9 August: Bell's board meet without Tyrie.

10 August: Miquel hints that Bell's may be looking for a 'White Knight'.

14 August: Guinness acquire 5% stake in Bell's held by the Kuwaiti Investment Office, which is placed with friendly institutions.

17 August: Rumours that Bell's have asked Rothmans International to come to their rescue.

23 August: Guinness win control of Bell's, speaking for around 70% of the shares.

30 August: Raymond Miquel agrees to stay on at Bell's.

1 September: Argyll and Lazards agree with Takeover Panel that there will be no bid 'at the present time' for Distillers. A three-month embargo is agreed.

2 September: Gulliver makes statement on his intentions.

13 September: Distillers appoint Kleinwort Benson as merchant banking advisers.

19 September: Distillers AGM in Edinburgh. John Connell admits to having had talks earlier in the year with Gulliver.

October: Bill Spengler appointed deputy chief executive of Distillers.

Late October: Olivier Roux tells Distillers stockbrokers Hoare Govett that Guinness would be 'prepared to help'. Saunders later tells Gulliver he knows 'nothing about this'.

November: Guinness acquire Cranks health food restaurants.

15 November: Raymond Miquel announces resignation from Bell's.

21 November: Distillers bring forward announcement of their results.

28 November: Sir Nigel Broackes joins Distillers board.

2 December: Argyll bid £1.87 billion for Distillers.

17 December: Argyll dispatch formal offer document.

23 December: Saunders holds planning meeting at Bain's headquarters in London to discuss a move for Distillers.

30 December: Distillers send out defence document.

1986

1 January: Ernest Saunders is skiing in Switzerland. John Connell flies over for preliminary talks on a Distillers/Guinness merger.

4 January: *The Times* speculates on possibility of Guinness bidding for Distillers.

9 January: Trade Secretary Leon Brittan clears Argyll bid.

13 January: Saunders and Connell meet. Merchant bank adviser also in attendance to discuss financial details of a merger.

17 January: Sir Thomas Risk asked to be chairman of new joint board.

18 January: Saunders visits Connell at home for eleventh-hour talks.

19 January: Strong press rumours about Guinness intentions.

19/20 January: Distillers board decide after marathon meeting to recommend a bid from Guinness. Offer worth £2.2 billion.

27 January: Argyll complain to Takeover Panel over Distillers agreement to pay Guinness bid costs. Panel reject complaint.

6 February: Argyll file writ alleging costs agreement is in breach of the Companies Act.

6 February: Argyll raise offer to £2.3 billion.

13 February: Guinness bid referred to the Monopolies Commission.

19 February: Monopolies Commission agree that the original Guinness bid can be dropped.

20 February: Guinness make new £2.35 billion offer, including commitment to sell five whisky brands.

25 February: Argyll apply to courts for judicial review of the Monopolies Commission decision. They argue that new Guinness bid is not sufficiently different from the old one.

28 February: Bank of England outlaw purchases of shares by merchant banks to the value of more than a quarter of their capital base.

3 March: Guinness unveil formal offer document which includes commitment to locate head office in Scotland and the appointment of Sir Thomas Risk as chairman.

5 March: Argyll case is thrown out by the High Court.

5 March: Stock Exchange prevent future arrangements for a company to pay another's bid costs above 25% of profits.

9 March: Gulliver admits part of *Who's Who* entry is wrong. Offer to resign is rejected by fellow board members.

13 March: Peter Tyrie leaves Gleneagles Hotels.

14 March: Guinness sue Argyll and others over bid advertisements.

15 March: Argyll take costs case to the Court of Appeal, but fail again to get Monopolies Commission move overturned.

21 March: Office of Fair Trading clear second Guinness bid. Guinness agree sale of five brands to Lonrho. Argyll increase bid to £2.5 billion.

22 March: Samuel Montagu, on behalf of Argyll, attempt to buy £700 million worth of Distillers shares but can't find sellers.

13 April: Atlantic Nominees revealed as purchasers of 6 million Guinness shares.

15 April: Guinness claim to speak for almost 32% of Distillers.

17 April: Cazenove buy a 3% stake in Distillers from Warburg Investment Management for 700 pence a share. Argyll complain to Takeover Panel.

17 April (evening): Guinness announce they speak for 46% of Distillers shares.

18 April (lunchtime): Ernest Saunders declares victory. Guinness have won control of 50.7% of Distillers.

22 April: Morgan Grenfell announce plans for Guinness to 'buy in' 90 million of their own shares.

6 May: Guinness pay Henry Ansbacher £7.6 million. Just over 2 million Guinness shares are held by Ansbacher.

18 May: Sir Thomas Risk meets Ernest Saunders and Thomas Ward in Washington, their first meeting since the takeover. Risk told he is not to be appointed chairman.

28 May: Guinness invest £69 million in the Ivan Boesky fund.

26 June: Risk dines with Saunders at the Savoy Hotel in London.

10 July: Risk meets Lord Iveagh at Guinness headquarters. Saunders and Ward are also in attendance.

11 July: John Chiene and Scott Dobbie of Wood Mackenzie threaten to resign if Saunders insists on being chairman.

11 July (evening): Party at Saunders' mansion to celebrate takeover of Distillers.

13 July: *Sunday Times* argues that Saunders should be allowed to run the new group singlehanded.

14 July: Guinness confirm that Saunders will be chairman and that the board structure proposed in March will be dropped.

15 July: Risk makes public statement denying that he fell out with Saunders over Guinness banking business. Wood Mackenzie resign as brokers to Guinness.

13 August: Guinness announce appointment of outside non-executive directors after pressure from Stock Exchange and Department of Trade.

22 August: Guinness circulate shareholders with details of new board and reasons for not appointing Sir Thomas Risk.

8 September: Charles Fraser resigns as chairman of Morgan Grenfell (Scotland).

11 September: Guinness EGM at the Mount Royal Hotel in London. Saunders supported by Robert Maxwell in the *Daily Mirror*. Board changes approved by a large majority.

November: Ivan Boesky confesses to insider trading and agrees to co-operate with investigations by the American Securities and Exchange Commission. He pays a fine of $100 million to the SEC.

1 December: Department of Trade Inspectors arrive at Guinness.

11 December: Schenley admit acquiring more than 5% of Guinness in latter stages of Distillers bid without informing the Takeover Panel.

18 December: Revelation that Guinness had invested £69 million in the Ivan Boesky fund.

19 December: Freshfields replaced as lawyers to Guinness by Kingsley Napley. Olivier Roux clears his desk at Guinness.

28 December: Sunday newspaper revelation of £7.6 million payment to Henry Ansbacher.

30 December: Morgan Grenfell resign as merchant bankers to Guinness. Roger Seelig resigns from Morgan Grenfell.

1987

4 January: Ernest Saunders returns home from a skiing holiday amidst calls for his resignation.

5 January: Olivier Roux writes to Sir David Napley, Guinness solicitor, outlining his knowledge of events in the 'Roux letter'.

6 January: Guinness board meet throughout the day at Portman Square. Television news says 'Saunders will go within the hour', but Saunders stays on.

9 January: Family members of the Guinness board see the 'Roux letter'. Executive directors meet Saunders, who agrees to 'step aside' during DTI enquiry.

11 January: Sir Norman Macfarlane appointed acting chairman.

12 January: Roux resigns his directorship at Guinness.

14 January: Guinness board meet and announce that Saunders is to be sacked. Arthur Furer resigns as a director. Thomas Ward is asked to resign.

16 January: Guinness announce existence of mystery £25 million invoice list and £50 million deposit with subsidiaries of Bank Leu. Sir Norman Macfarlane outlines details in a letter to shareholders.

20 January: Christopher Reeves and Graham Walsh depart from top jobs at Morgan Grenfell, after pressure from the Chancellor and the Bank of England.

21 January: Gerald Ronson admits receiving £5.8 million for help with Distillers bid and says he's paying it back to Guinness.

22 January: Lord Spens resigns as managing director of Henry Ansbacher. S&W Berisford admit that a subsidiary received a fee from Guinness, and they offer to repay it

23 January: Argyll announce £681 million purchase of Safeway supermarkets.

23 January: Bain confirm that Sir Jack Lyons has been dropped as UK adviser.

27 January: Alexanders, Laing and Cruickshank sever connection with Tony Parnes.

28 January: Labour spokesman Robin Cook makes allegations about Cazenove in the House of Commons.

29 January: Cazenove make public statement denying illegal activities during Distillers bid.

10 February: Guinness board meeting in Edinburgh to discuss new chief executive.

18 February: Anthony Tennant appointed chief executive of Guinness, while Michael Julien becomes managing director, finance and administration.

27 February: Guinness begin legal action in Jersey to uncover the reasons for payment of £5.2 million to a local company.

11 March: Court in Jersey hears claim that Thomas Ward received £5.2 million for services during Distillers bid.

19 March: Guinness issue writs against Saunders and Ward for recovery of £5.2 million.

25 March: Allegations in the High Court that £3 million of the mystery invoice passed through a Swiss bank account in Saunders' name. Injunction granted freezing Saunders' and Ward's assets.

8 April: Sir Norman Macfarlane asked by the board of Guinness to continue as chairman for two years.

15 April: In the High Court the Vice-Chancellor rules that the £5.2 million payment could not have lawfully been made. Freeze remains on Saunders' UK assets.

5 May: Sir Norman Macfarlane writes to shareholders with annual report.

6 May: Saunders arrested at the London offices of his solicitors.

7 May: Saunders appears at Bow Street magistrates court, on three charges.

12 May: Saunders reappears in court and is granted bail of half a million pounds. Lonrho boss Tiny Rowland puts up £250,000, while the rest is guaranteed by Herbert Heinzel, a family friend.

18 May: Henry Ansbacher return £7.4 million to Guinness and confirm they've sold their Guinness shares.

19 May: Bank Leu sell 40 million Guinness shares through London stockbrokers James Capel.

19 May: Saunders granted variation of bail conditions to allow him to visit his wife in Switzerland.

26 May: Bank Leu return £50 million deposit to Guinness.

26 May: Saunders tenders resignation as a director of Guinness.

27 May: Guinness Annual General Meeting at the Connaught Rooms in central London. Sir Norman Macfarlane refuses to read out letter to shareholders from Ernest Saunders. Saunders' solicitor confirms that proceedings are being launched against Guinness, alleging unfair dismissal.

What the Companies Act (1985) says:

Section 151 — (1) Subject to the following provisions of this Chapter, where a person is acquiring or is proposing to acquire shares in a company, it is not lawful for the company or any of its subsidiaries to give financial assistance directly or indirectly for the purpose of that acquisition before or at the same time as the acquistion takes place.

(2) Subject to those provisions, where a person has acquired shares in a company and any liability has been incurred (by that or any other person), for the purpose of that acquistion, it is not lawful for the company or any of its subsidiaries to give financial assistance directly or indirectly for the purpose of reducing or discharging the liability so incurred.

(3) If a company acts in contravention of this section, it is liable to a fine, and every officer of it who is in default is liable to imprisonment or a fine, or both.

Section 153 — (1) Section 151(1) does not prohibit a company from giving financial assistance for the purpose of an acquistion of shares in it or its holding company if —
   (a) the company's principal purpose in giving that assistance is not to give it for the purpose of any such acquisition, or the giving of the assistance for that purpose is but an incidental part of some larger purpose of the company, and
   (b) the assistance is given in good faith in the interests of the company.

(2) Section 151(2) does not prohibit a company from giving financial assistance if —
   (a) the company's principal purpose in giving the assistance is not to reduce or discharge any liability incurred by a person for the purpose of the acquisition of shares in the company or its holding company, or the reduction or discharge of any such liability is but an incidental part of some larger purpose of the company, and
   (b) the assistance is given in good faith in the interests of the company.

INTRODUCTION

The working day started early at Guinness PLC's headquarters at 39 Portman Square, and 1 December was no exception. Senior members of staff were at their desks at 8 a.m. Chairman Ernest Saunders was there, discussing with colleagues what colour he should print the cover of the brochure for the half-year's results. He was in two minds whether it should be grey or silver. He opted quickly for grey and moved on to another meeting, and more decisions.

Elsewhere a stockbroker was on the phone to a director wanting to talk about the timing of the announcement of the results. As he heard the answer from the Guinness man, his eyes glanced up to the screen in front of him, and they read the announcement: DTI investigates Guinness. He asked his Guinness contact, so conveniently on the phone, 'Do you know anything about that?' 'No,' said the contact, 'and I'm in Guinness.' Talk of the results came to a halt. Alarm bells rang. Ernest Saunders was engaged, but financial director Olivier Roux was available. He said that there were two men in reception who had come in unannounced, and he was on his way down to see who they were.

Roux went down, immaculately dressed and coiffeured as ever, and politely enquired if he could help. One of the two men asked if he was an officer of the company. He said he was a director and was handed a piece of paper identifying the two men as appointees of the Department of Trade and Industry. They were shown into a waiting room at the lavish building, one picked up a copy of the annual report and the other read *Private Eye*. Ten minutes later the one reading the annual report left, and an hour later the second had gone.

For the two cold winter months after the Inspectors arrived in December, there was a media free-for-all in one of the world's leading financial centres, the like of which has never been seen before. The time was ripe. The media was gorged on tales about the grossly inflated salaries, and the rip-roaring lifestyles of the insider dealers and sharks. People at last thought they were seeing the City for what they had always known it to be, a place for the greedy, the unscrupulous, and the enviably wealthy. It was 'Dallas' all over again, but in daily instalments.

The media were not alone in enjoying and exploiting the sight of the City on the run. Politicians had to react. Government ministers were embarrassed by the transgressions of their supporters, and sought to act to root them out. The Labour party used the capitalists' illicit activities as ammunition for campaigns in the election which they all expected later in the year.

One group was less than gleeful about the discomfort of the Guinness bosses. The thousands of people in the Scotch whisky companies whose brands were being bartered away knew their very livelihoods depended on the outcome. But they could only look on helplessly as their industry was carved up in boardroom battles fought out in a few plush Mayfair offices.

When all is said and done, perhaps what happened should be the Saunders Story rather than the Guinness Affair. One man charmed, teased and bullied his way around the corridors of financial, industrial and political power. In the end his dreams and the means took him over the edge of genuine ambition and into the realms of megalomania. But the dividing line is fine, and good businessmen do not proceed by thinking small. And then there are his friends. Without the influence of some of the supporters, Saunders might still have the reputation for being a marketing genius that the men who appointed him believed him to be. But other acquaintances now rue the day they met him. These people are now badly scarred. The fear of Saunders still lives and, for fear of a writ, they have not allowed us quote them by name.

With hindsight people ask: Why wasn't anything said at the time? Why was not Saunders stopped in his tracks? Responsibility for that lies at the door of the City regulators. The great and the good who man the Takeover Panel, the Stock Exchange and the other watchdogs were shown to be men of straw when Saunders struck. Their codes of practice were torn to shreds. Without a tip-off from the American stock exchange watchdog, not a word about Guinness may have come out, and the inadequacies of City regulation would have continued. Now the London watchdogs, like the bankers and the other City financiers, are on trial.

The story that we tell is as complete as facts allow at the moment. It is based on the accounts of many of the participants, of unsuspecting bystanders, and of commentators and observers, mostly told in confidence by frightened men. Obviously more will come out when the men who arrived on Guinness' doorstep last winter report the facts as they have discovered them. But by then, the motivations and impressions of the participants, victims and bystanders will be lost. Here they are saved, and a drama recounted that changed many people's perceptions of the City and finance, once and for all.

CHAPTER ONE

GUINNESS: A FAMILY BUSINESS

While Wolfe was assaulting the Heights of Quebec, an Anglo-Irish immigrant to Dublin was quietly establishing a brewery that was to make his drink and his line of descendants famous and rich for many generations. In 1759 Arthur Guinness took over the St James's Brewery in Dublin for the production of ale. The sharp-witted entrepreneur spotted that porter — the original drink of the Covent Garden porters — was successfully being imported and taking away his markets; as a result he changed over to the distinctive heavy black liquid that later became the stout akin to the drink that we know today.

Arthur was an independent-minded and ruthless man. There's an early story told of how he waved a pickaxe around to frighten off locals who tried to divert his water supply. The patriarch won the fight to keep his patch and retain the quality of the stout. He did not flinch from taking tough commercial decisions either, boldly telling customers that they could pay twice as much for their stout as they paid for ale. The company already saw the world as its drinking glass, and because of the peculiarly heavy consistency of its beer was able to export where other brews couldn't reach. There's a nice account of a wounded soldier at the battle of Waterloo demanding a Guinness to revive him; and Guinness travelled still further afield, to Africa.

Arthur used his wealth to high purposes. He founded the Sunday School movement in Ireland, as an offshoot of the Church of Ireland. However, there was a whiff of scandal around as well in those early days. In the potato famine, the Guinness family told the starving locals that they would not get any credit out of the company. It hardly enhanced their esteem in the community. But it made commercial sense, and anyway their eyes were set on the big City of London, and not Dublin or Sligo.

The modern history of Guinness begins in the 1870s, when two brothers, Arthur and Edward, were running the company. Arthur, however, appeared to lose interest in the business. An apocryphal anecdote may suggest why. Apparently some locals threw bottles of the stout over the wall at a garden party he was giving. His wife began to think that trade was not appropriate to their station, and suggested to her husband that he sold out to his brother. He did this for a massive two-thirds of a million pounds, and took up politics.

Edward, who later became the first Lord Iveagh, took the reins in 1876. He developed a fearful reputation, being regarded by family and colleagues as a martinet. The company was in his thrall, and woe betide the managing director who tried arguing with him. Iveagh ensured that working for Guinness was no holiday. Rigid rankings leading up to the pinnacle post of brewer were introduced. Every aspiring manager climbed the ladder. In the early days of course, this meant that people knew their place and that the machine worked smoothly. Later on, in the twentieth century, it became as ossified and bureaucratic as the union closed shop.

There was a soft side to the tough aristocrat, though. He took time off to establish some charities with the family wealth. The Guinness and Iveagh Trusts, set up to look after the housing needs of the poor in London and Dublin, were his way of repaying his workers for the damage he had done to their livers. Iveagh also made the first major leap for the company out of Ireland when he floated Guinness off on the London Stock Exchange. The Irish were upset that the merchant bank, Barings, excluded them from receiving shares, but Iveagh knew that the real wealth would come out of England, not Dublin. They got rapped over the knuckles for this by the Committee of the Stock Exchange, but that would not worry the aristocrats of the world's biggest brewery, and some of Ireland's wealthiest sons.

The family members kept a third of the shares at the float, but nobody questioned this when they held on to half a dozen seats on the board. They assumed it was their business in all but paper. Said one managing director: 'They had 25% of the shares, and acted like it was 75%.' Family members found out how well the company was doing by attending tea parties held on the day before the annual results were announced. The managing director of the day addressed them, and answered questions. These tea parties went on until way into the 1960s. For the most part, the MD was seen as a necessary but not very wholesome tradesman. Ernest Saunders was later to tell of a Guinness family wedding, where he was in fact seated on the tradesmen's table.

Lord Iveagh's son Rupert had to bide his time before taking his father's mantle. He went into the domain of politics, and succeeded in doing in the political world what his family had always done in the world of trade and commerce, namely set up a patriarchy which, astonishingly, lasts to this very day. Rupert began as Conservative and Unionist MP for South East Essex from 1912 to 1918. He was elected for Southend-on-Sea in 1918 and held the seat until 1929. His wife took over between 1929 and 1935, and Henry (Chips) Channon, their son-in-law was the Member of Parliament between 1935 and 1959. His son, and later Secretary of State for Trade and Industry, Paul Channon, holds the seat today.

Rupert eventually got the call, at his father's death in 1927, and new ideas started to flow from the company. The one that he will be remembered for is the injection of advertising into the recipe. The old man may have had the idea put before him, but traditionalist and patrician that he was, saw it as vulgar and cheapening — perhaps also unnecessary. There had never been any complaints about the sales of Guinness, the family had grown very rich and, anyway, advertising might spoil the underground legend that had developed around the stout. This legend alleged medicinal qualities for Guinness. It was subtly encouraged by the gift of Guinness to hospitals, where doctors' testimonials were used to confirm its validity in the therapeutic process. Moreover, hypochondriac Chinese were thought to believe that it thickened the blood, and Africans were convinced that it added to potency. In Britain people would have a bottle of stout to pick them up after a day's work. To this day Edward Guinness, the leading brewer on the board and a survivor of recent purges, uses a bottle of the stout to revive him after a day's labour. After recent events it may well have grown to two bottles.

Guinness now wanted to add to this already positive, healthy publicity. In 1928 the first test campaigns were launched in Scotland, and the following year it came down South. The slogan was 'Guinness is good for you'. An agency executive, after three months' work on a campaign for the drink, was summoned to a board meeting and asked to outline his plans. He scribbled on the back of an envelope the famous five words, and the marketing people never looked back. It was the base for future marketers to build on, and play with. The Guinnless campaign of Allen Brady Marsh that launched recent attempts at reviving the brew shows how a message can stick.

John Gilroy, a distinguished designer, produced the famous image of the Guinness-drinking muscle-man holding up a mighty iron pillar. He introduced the family of toucans and other animals. But the novelist Dorothy L Sayers, who was working for Bensons while she wrote *Murder must Advertise*, penned this piece of nonsense verse that twisted off many drinkers' less-than-steady tongues.

If he can say as you can
Guinness is good for you,
How good to be a toucan,
Just think what two can do.

Bensons in the end held the advertising account for the company for 41 years, a remarkable length of time. Nothing they every produced irked or displeased the sensitive tastes of the family, and the advertising was very much geared to what would be seen as inoffensive. Like Benson and Hedges ads, people admired them, but nobody really felt sure that they sold more of the product. It was, as it were, an ego-trip for a product, not a seriously researched marketing exercise. In fact, one doubts if any market research was done to see who was drinking Guinness. If it had, they would have spotted sooner that Guinness had become the drink of older people, while lager was beginning to appeal to the young.

Despite this toying with advertising, the company's culture was production-oriented. The family believed that as long as they churned out the beer in good quantities, and as long as the quality was right, it would sell. Chemists were hired from the older universities to manage quality control, and even at different stages to run the business. In the late fifties, however, a new development came on the scene which was to change the product and the future of the company drastically. This was aeration. Draught beer at once became a good commercial bet, whereas previously it had suffered from a poor appearance and transportation difficulties. As draught took over, sales of the bottled beer declined. But in the ten years between 1960 and 1970, sales of draught Guinness rose from 30,000 barrels a year to a million.

The beer had not stopped flowing, and the thirst for it was far from quenched, when the elderly Rupert, or the second Lord Iveagh as he was dignified when his father died, embarked on a diversification to help out an old friend. Major A E Allnat, the retiring founder of sweetmakers Callard and Bowser, came to him and asked him to buy his business. The two men knew each other because they shared the Park Royal site at Ealing, and probably without a great degree of planning, Rupert took it on. The close location made the management task look straightforward, and Callard's were doing quite nicely selling sweets into post war, post-rationing Britain. It became the first Guinness diversification. Callard's also had a chain of newsagents, where their sweets were sold. However, Guinness were concerned that the enterprising, sales-oriented Callard and Bowser culture might upset the long-established, bureaucratic Guinness hierarchy; consequently, the two businesses were deliberately kept well apart.

In the early sixties the pressure on the big brewers started to build up. Rivals, like Bass and Mitchell and Butler, began to swallow up smaller rivals, and Guinness, which had no chain of pubs into which to sell its brew, began to see the first effects of inflation hurting discretionary spending.

A desperate policy of diversification and expansion was begun. The results of this became quite fateful for a company which had been sailing along nicely on the one product — stout — and had no experience of developing a serious strategy. First, the company made a move into lager. Second, it opened up overseas operations. Finally, it tried to make a business out of its expertise in fermentation and biochemistry.

In 1926, a change of chairman took place. Rupert had soldiered on because his only son, who should have succeeded him, died in the Second World War. At last, at the age of 88, he was able to hand over to the only natural heir, his grandson Benjamin. He went in at the age of 25, a complete tyro, without business or work experience, and without much of a liking or aptitude for management. 'They groomed him totally wrongly' is the view of Tony Purssell, managing director between 1975 and 1981 who worked closely with Benjamin. 'The family should have brought somebody else in as a caretaker chairman until he was 40 and had done a job of work. Then he should have been offered the chairmanship. In fact he's been something of a *deus ex cathedra*.' Benjamin inherited the title Lord Iveagh on his grandfather's death in 1967.

For tax reasons, Benjamin has been destined to be something of an absentee chairman. A decision to take Irish citizenship meant he had to spend large parts of the year in Ireland, and his role as an active and involved chairman of the board suffered. Regular bouts of sickness have not helped. It has certainly been an awesome task for him to fulfil the duties that are implied in the chairman's role, in which he has had to select the board of directors and to ensure that the interests of the shareholders are protected. His interests are more with the gentlemanly pursuits of horses and literature. He is also a very shy and retiring man, not given to the rough and tumble of the public arena.

For company directors working in this sort of regime, it meant there was a vacuum on the board, and the possibility of quite enormous and unchecked power. There were very few non-executives, and most of the other board members held the position primarily by virtue of their family membership, so they were able to exercise little accountability over the operational managers.

'You had the opportunity to run a private fief,' said Purssell. 'You could have told the board as much as they wanted to know, or as much as you thought you could get away with.'

Nevertheless, the diversification programme went ahead with some notable successes. Harp Lager was developed by a consortium of brewers, with Courage and Scottish and Newcastle joining forces with Guinness in the setting up of a brewery in Ireland. Growth was meteoric. Between 1961 and 1971 sales went from nothing to a million barrels annually, and five years later they had doubled again. The overseas expansion was rapid. Guinness moved into Third World countries like Malaysia and Nigeria. After the Biafran War there was a surge in sales in Nigeria and two breweries were built there.

The third prong of the expansion, the move into the products derived from the fermentation process was less successful. The company established a joint venture with the Dutch firm Philips to buy Crookes, which made Halibut Liver Pills. They also bought an international distribution business together with a chain of chemists. The roots of the interest in the health business can already be discerned.

A mass of other companies had started to cling uncontrolledly on to the Guinness hulk. Plastic moulding, for example, had sprung out of the brewing technology. In the early fifties wooden casks gave way to aluminium ones, and it looked as if a lot of coopers would be put out of a job. To avoid having to sack them, the family got the old coopers to learn the technology required to make the caps for the new shiny metal casks. Thus began quite a major, if unrelated, arm of the brewing business, which was eventually to encompass activities like making plastic fittings for supermarkets.

Fish farming was one of a motley collection of ventures that sprang out of the company's need to appease their Irish hosts. The Government of the Republic would often require a job-creating venture in return for a beer price rise. With some 90% of the Irish stout market in its pocket, the pickings of a price rise must have given many curious business decisions an appealing logic. It was probably in this way, too, that the company entered the business of selling boating holidays. What began as a small enterprise on the Shannon grew into quite a large leisure concern extending to the canals of France and the Mediterranean. Film financing was an even more curious enterprise for the company, since it is believed to have led them into unprofitable movie making. In complete contrast, the company has long had interests in orchid growing, the origins of which are lost in the Irish mists.

The recession of the late seventies, together with labour troubles and changes in the beer market, was gradually making the management of the rag-bag of a business an altogether tougher assignment. The drink that sold at a premium price to other bitters was looking very expensive with inflation. People were also turning to wine in droves, and the off-licence was growing in importance as a retailing outlet; but here Guinness did not have the distribution system to take advantage. Moreover, moves to dispose of some of the obviously unrelated businesses were stymied. Purssell, for example, had wanted to sell off Callard and Bowser, which was squeezed between the confectionery majors, and making a minimal return on capital. But the family-powers-that-be objected — 'It's a lovely product — butterscotch, super,' was their initial response. Later they yielded, and the business was on the verge of sale when Ernest Saunders entered with his wholesale divestment policy. It later irked Purssell when Saunders claimed credit for the sale of Callard and Bowser. The acquisition of the newspaper and confectioners chain of Martins was also planned before Saunders arrived, but the founder of Martins turned down the offer and the idea was dropped. Later, of course, it was accomplished and became a key plank in the Saunders strategy.

By 1980 the company had acquired a motley array of products — after over 200 years with just one — and a management which did not know whether it, or the family barons, were really at the helm. Amidst this chaos, salvation was at hand. Or so, at least, it appeared when a strong new manager came on the scene in 1981.

CHAPTER TWO

SAUNDERS THE SAVIOUR

Ernest Saunders came to prominence in the business world at a time when the City, the politicians and the wider public were looking for management heroes. The government had thrown the ball at their feet, and they were being encouraged to run with it. Saunders ran with it hard and committed a number of fouls along the way. He also scored own goals, but without the revelations of the admitted insider-dealer Ivan Boesky he may never have been tripped up, and would still be on the field alongside the other management stars of his day, Ralph Halpern, Phil Harris and Lord Hanson.

Managers do not succeed by being nice, and no one claims that Saunders is a particularly warm or engaging man. Certainly he can be charming, and he has the salesman's gift of saying to his audience exactly what it wants to hear. He advanced primarily by hard work and application. He left no one in doubt that he was aggressive. The way that he tensed up, hunched, and with his head thrust forward, when he was describing some project, testifies to that. Colleagues speak of an addiction to the whispered remark behind the hand that persuaded you that you were number one until you saw that he was exactly the same with the next person.

He was a powerful, dedicated workaholic, and what he lacked in strategic insight he compensated for with a very strong will. Colleagues maintain he was a stimulating man to work with, finding him 'very good company, full of ideas, very exciting to be with, you felt as if something was going on and you got caught up with it'. But he could also work with people like an oak tree works on its roots, sucking them dry before going on to the next one.

His inability to level with people was remarked by some. He would often use somebody else to handle awkward confrontations, and it was for this purpose that the American lawyer, Thomas Ward, turned out to be very useful. Said a close colleague, 'He wouldn't look you in the eye and say, "I'm sorry, I think you should look for pastures new." He always got somebody else to do that.' Jeremy Bullmore, chairman of advertising agency J Walter Thompson, is quite sure 'there was something incomplete about the man.'

Ernest Saunders tried from his earliest days to give the impression of being a native Englishman. That was his first myth. In fact he came to Britain with his family in 1938 at the age of two and a half, a refugee from the Nazis. His father, a prosperous medical man, could afford to set up a practice here, and to send Ernest to one of London's top schools, St Paul's. The family integrated quickly into a society which at the time was unsympathetic to the plight of the Jews in Europe. The name changed from Schleyer to Saunders, and from Ernst to Ernest.

Saunders seemed to grow apart from his family. There was an early feud with his brother when Ernest left him to carry the can for some prank that he had devised. The incident created a rift that was never healed. In later life he appeared to disown his parents when he omitted them from his *Who's Who* entry. In 1963, at the age of 28, he married Carole Stephings, who was from a solid English middle-class family (although he was later to fall out with his parents-in-law). In recent years he has been a regular supporter of the local church.

The picture that emerges is of a solitary, self-contained man who does not need many friends for support or affection. He went to football matches for relaxation — he was a keen supporter and director of Queen's Park Rangers — but even then he sat by himself, looking rather friendless, as a fellow fan observed. The bulk of Saunders' efforts went into the pursuit of worldly success. He measured these in terms of the Rolls

Royce, the house in the home counties, the accumulation of wealth, and perhaps one day the knighthood. He was to have all but the last.

It was while he was in his first year at Cambridge studying law that he heard about the subject of marketing. American companies conducting their milkround — the annual search to recruit bright young students — came to explain what this discipline involved. Saunders, still knee-deep in his legal studies, heard talks by representatives of companies like Procter and Gamble, and began to take an interest. He read avidly about the subject, and when he graduated he duly found a marketing job as a trainee at computer accessories and hardware company 3M. The job was a disappointment. 3M had him knocking on doors, selling the product cold. The young graduate of law, by now versed in some of the more theoretical marketing texts, had to get out. He moved on, in 1960, to the huge international advertising agency, J Walter Thompson, where he saw a sophisticated marketing department in action. JWT, one of the world's largest advertising agencies, researched response to their advertising using an in-house department. Saunders stayed six years, but made no particular mark. Today's chairman of the company, Jeremy Bullmore, has no recollection of Saunders' time there.

But Saunders had spotted an undeveloped sector of industry that was to develop out of all recognition. Selling, like profit, was still a dirty word for British industry, which believed that if the product was right, the customer would be banging on the door wanting to purchase it. Guinness was a perfect example of this anachronistic fallacy right up to 1981. The US was decades ahead of British industry. Since the fifties, gurus from Harvard Business School had talked about marketing, showing how marketing strategies could embrace every part of the selling process. Companies in every sector of American business had learnt this lesson, and marketing had quickly become an important competitive tool. They also created a vocabulary which every manager worth his salt had to pick up in order to hold his own in the brave new world of the market place.

It was not until the mid-seventies that Britain woke up to the importance of marketing. Then the marketers wanted recognition, and they created degrees, magazines, clubs and institutes to support their cause. Most of all, they wanted to stress that marketing was not selling. Saunders was to become one of the heroes of the marketing fraternity, fêted at meetings of the Institute of Marketing, of which he is a fellow. Magazines like *Marketing* and *Campaign* first created the Saunders myth.

Having done a longish stint at JWT, in the mundane area of product testing and market research, he sought out a middle-management opening. It came in 1966 at Beecham, the large multi-national, famous both for its drugs and for its consumer products like Lucozade and Horlicks. The transition to Beecham was effortless. He was already known to the company as their account handler for toiletries at JWT. It was a routine brand management job, organising advertising campaigns for the Third World markets, distributing product round Africa and keeping a check on sales. The work involved plenty of travel, and responsibility for a small department. Saunders did the job well, said the recently ousted Beecham chairman Sir Ronald Halstead, who was chairman of the consumer products division when Saunders joined. If he had a flaw, it was impatience which 'ruffled colleagues' feathers', but this did not unduly trouble senior management. 'A thrusting young person gets impatient, and he did push people very hard.' Saunders appears to have tried pushing around people outside his own department, and that rubbed them up the wrong way. Halstead reckoned he had the ability to make the board, perhaps even succeeding him as chief executive, but no space could be made for him.

Saunders would not wait, such was his eagerness to get on to the board of a major public company. He moved to Great Universal Stores to run their international mail order business. But two years later the break had not come, and he tried a Swiss engineering company called Eutectic. Still no luck for the international salesman, but the jobs kept coming. The next was to be important.

It was in the familiar field of brand marketing, and it provided the chance to go into a large cosmopolitan business, Nestlé, conveniently positioned in Switzerland. One of his assignments there was to lead to some controversy. The World Health Organisation had a campaign underway to boycott Nestlé, in retaliation for the company's heavy marketing of its powdered milk to the Third World. Not only is breast milk more nutritious than powdered, but there is a serious danger that, in the Third World, contaminated water will be used to mix up the powder. For Nestlé, the powdered milk was an important new product, taking them into untried markets. A campaign was managed by Saunders, using public relations and media manipulation. Nestlé contributed $25,000 to a right-wing Washington research centre which had commissioned *Fortune* magazine to write an article countering the WHO's campaign. The article was mailed to American churchmen who were seen as key 'opinion formers'. He did this in conjunction with American lawyer Thomas Ward, whom he later drafted in to Guinness.

It is questionable whether the campaign worked. If anything, the document confirmed suspicions rather than allayed them, and more bad publicity was generated. During his period at Nestlé, Saunders made some powerful friends. When he joined the international management committee, he got to know well the chief executive, Arthur Furer, who later joined the Guinness board at Saunders' request. Saunders was by now in the mould and of the status of the international globe-trotting manager, who spent large amounts of time on aeroplanes, and very little time in the UK. He was bi-lingual, knowing German because it was his parents' native tongue.

In 1981 he joined Guinness for his first general management post. It was a bold move, since the company was on its uppers and Saunders appears to have had no previous experience in general management. The brief to the headhunters was vague. Guinness seemed not to know whether they were looking for a general manager to wield an axe or for a marketing man who could sell the beer harder. It was par for the course for a management that was muddled and in severe difficulties.

Saunders' reputation was for quality marketing ability in the area of consumer branded goods. Headhunters had chased him for years on that basis, and Guinness had snared him. Saunders believes he was headhunted at the request of some major institutions who owned shares in Guinness and were seeing their investment in the business being eaten away by falling profits. When they saw the possibility of a dividend cut they went to see the Guinness chairman, Lord Iveagh, to say, in effect, 'either you change the management, or we do'. Later Saunders was to explain, 'I think they had taken the view that the company needed somebody with general management skills, and an international perspective.' Somebody, conveniently, like him.

Deputy chairman Tony Purssell tells a quite different story. He says that in 1980 he began looking for a successor who could take over from him in five years' time, when he would be sixty. The position he was seeking to fill was deputy managing director, and the brief would be to beef up operational management, strengthen the marketing of the beer and push forward some restructuring. The first choice for the job, whose identity is still not revealed, turned it down because his employers offered him promotion. However, he suffered a sad fate, dying within months. The next down the list, Ernest Saunders, was known for his marketing experience in the Third World and for his sales positions at Beecham and GUS. As far as Purssell was concerned, 'Saunders had no reputation. I imagined he had been involved with selling. It was difficult to find out more.' Purssell was not known for his energetic commitment, but still he went to Switzerland to see the possible recruit and found him 'dynamic, friendly and interested. He made the right noises.' A subsequent interview took place in Britain. The testimonials, from Sir Ronald Halstead of Beecham and Arthur Furer of Nestlé, were good.

When Saunders had been offered the job and the two men were negotiating terms Purssell got the first wind that the new man was not going to let him sit as comfortably as he had done for the last 30 years. Saunders said it would not be appropriate for him to join as mere deputy managing director, since that would appear a demotion from his Nestlé position on the top management board; he wanted to be managing director. Purssell, who himself carried the title of managing director, went to the board and relayed this view. They agreed that Purssell should become deputy chairman — a position he assumed in December 1981 — and Saunders should be managing director. The sniping between the two men was to last until January 1983, when Purssell would retire with a distinct lack of grace.

The board may not have been very happy about Purssell's 'promotion', and one suspects they were rather concerned about his management performance. It was a realisation that dawned late, and one wonders how much responsibility they themselves should bear; but many of them were shareholders whose pockets were being hit by the declining share price.

The company was in dire straits, and even if the institutions had not come in, as Saunders alleges they had, there is no doubt they must have thought hard about it. The interim figures for 1980/1, published in June 1981, were the gravest jolt. The profit fell 13.2%, as non-beer interests hit by recession haemorrhaged funds which should have been going into brewing. The profit contribution of non-brewing businesses fell 67%. Beer held up well and was seen as a 'source of fundamental strength'. The worst news from the shareholders' point of view was that a cut in dividend was threatened by the chairman. This took 12% off the share price, which fell to an all-time low of 50 pence.

Saunders came in the role of company doctor. His cure for the ailing drinks firm was in three parts. First, cutting out the non-core, largely loss-making businesses; second, rationalisation of the core business; third, building up from the new reduced base.

Cutting out a host of diverse subsidiaries was the first task of the new manager. Saunders, unbeknown to Purssell, brought in a firm of management consultants. It was probably the most far-reaching management decision Saunders took at Guinness. The firm he went to was one of the most highly regarded and secretive in an area of business noted for its secrecy and deviousness. Bain and Co is the *crème de la crème* of the consulting profession. They are the second largest after McKinsey and have around 1000 consultants.

Reports vary as to why Bain was chosen, but the divergence gives an interesting example of the Saunders infallibility myth. He has said that he went to three management consultants and asked each one whom they regarded as their biggest competitor, in the event that they themselves did not get the contract. The unanimous reply was Bain, an offshoot of the American Boston Consulting Group. Purssell's simpler, and convincing, account is that Saunders' first choice was McKinsey, but they had another drinks client, and saw a clash of interest, so he turned to Bain and Co.

Whether Sir Jack Lyons, the company's representative in the UK, played a part in their selection has yet to be discovered. The company with which he was associated, J Lyons Chamberlayne Co, was later to feature on a list of invoices paid by Guinness for

£300,000. He personally has admitted receiving £2 million as advisory fees from Guinness.

The importance of the Bain role in developing a strategy for Guinness, and conducting product and financial research cannot be over-emphasised. The measure of this importance is perhaps the great lengths to which Saunders went to keep the Bain connection quiet. He was not a man to share credit for triumphs with which he was associated, but Bain also spoilt the myth of the manager single-handedly righting the wrongs of previous generations of Guinness incompetents. When John Plender asked him on Channel Four's 'Business Programme' in 1986 about the role of Bain, he denied any knowledge. In the Bell's bid Raymond Miquel threw at him the allegation that the company was run by management consultants and Saunders, instead of tackling it head on, brushed it aside as a diversion. Bain played a vital role in Saunders' takeover strategy; they even dedicated one room in their West End Connaught Place office purely to matters relating to Guinness. It was said to be so secret that even the founder, Bill Bain himself, would not be able to have access. But Saunders and his public relations and other advisers would regularly troop round from the Guinness HQ in Portman Square to check and write documents in this takeover bunker.

Some fifteen Bainies (or Baineries, as they are less affectionately called) definitely entered the company in October 1981, the month when Saunders joined. This grew to as many as 70 towards the end of the Saunders era. Bain were the most constant of the myriad of advisers who hovered round him like flies around a light.

Saunders, in conjunction with Bain, managed the sell-off of the diverse businesses. Much is often made of the size of the operation, and indeed in terms of numbers of individual businesses it was large, but they fell into roughly three categories. These three categories are general trading, plastics and materials handling and leisure, and the businesses themselves were mostly small.

In the year to February 1983, 40 businesses had been sold, and in the following year another 56 were divested. By the end, Saunders was to claim 149 companies had either been shut or sold. Saunders described in a radio interview his method for dispatching the Guinness businesses. For financial analysts, read Bain: 'I worked with specialists in financial analysis who looked rapidly at the 140 situations. I developed a formula. Every Friday afternoon, between four and six o'clock, the financial group brought me a series of brief synopses of a number of companies. We examined simply the question, "did these companies have prospects for growth". If they didn't, "did they need instant surgery, or could they be fixed". Over six months we reviewed the whole lot. We decided the majority should be sold. One or two had some future, and they were all in the retail group.'

The conflict with Purssell grew as the divestment gathered pace. Both men were agreed parts of the business needed selling off; the question was, which bits. Purssell's fondness for technology and his chemistry training indicated to him that the engineering and plastic moulding parts of the business should stay. For Saunders that was complete anathema. He wanted to prune it back to a strictly brands and retailing based concern, cutting out all the oddments that had accrued along the way. When the crunch came, there was no argument. It all had to go. In the words of a stock market analyst, 'Guinness effectively got rid of the rubbish and loss-making subsidiaries, and restructured mainstream businesses to lower the cost-base.'

The involvement with Bain did not end with the chopping of the 149 businesses, as it might have done with a more conventional consultancy. Bain liked to have long-term involvement in a company's affairs. They are keen to advise on restructuring of businesses, suggesting which parts to sell off and what to acquire. They also assist with financial and personnel planning, and the management of technology change. They claim, in fact, that they act 'almost as strategic partners with a company'.

It is a point which is seen to add value to a service which in the early seventies when Bain was established had lost credibility because managers saw consultants walking away from difficult situations, leaving them with little more than a nicely packaged set of papers offering advice.

In the case of Guinness, the scale of involvement, so much trumpeted by Bain as a selling point, reached unprecedented proportions. The Bain secondee, Olivier Roux, is at the core of the quake which has erupted around the company that employed him.

Although Roux worked for Guinness solidly for five years, his employers were Bain, and not Guinness. Roux, a hand-some, Gallic 36 year old, joined the consultants in 1980, and moved over to Guinness in 1981. He joined the board on 31 July 1984 as director of financial strategy and administration. This caused ructions at Bain, where the rules state consultants should not join the board of client companies. Roux needed special dispensation at the highest Bain level, namely from founder Bill Bain himself. By becoming a director, a consultant is taking on legal obligations that might conflict with the consultant's duties to his own firm.

It will not happen again, says Bain's Guy Cogan. 'We regret that we made that one.' According to Cogan, 'At the first instance Olivier went on the board as a non-executive director, and it was at the request of the client that he became an executive director. There was some discussion about it.' It is not clear whether Saunders made Bain's continued employment with the company dependent on having Roux on the board as a full-time executive director. Indeed, taking the managing consultant on to the board is contrary to the rules of the British Management Consultancies Association.

Roux, however, was a boon to Saunders. His logical mind acted as a brake on some of the chief executive's more grandiose aspirations. He was very astute financially, and addressed issues with great precision, whereas Saunders could seem highfalutin' and vague. Moreover, he was not burdened with traditional British reluctance to innovate.

The cost to Guinness of Bain grew steadily as more consultants became involved. But they were probably worth the money to shareholders, who were appreciative of their divestment skills. It has been argued that Bain received in its last year £17.2 million from Guinness. According to Guinness, £8 million is a more realistic figure.

Bain took on another role at Guinness that was just as important as their conventional management consultancy services, and far more controversial. At the time that they were assisting in selling off bits of the company, they were also in-structed to divide the loyalties of the staff and thus undermine the authority of the deputy chairman, Tony Purssell. To those familiar with the means adopted by headhunters to unseat, or replace management, it will not come as a surprise. But it does open up the vista of rival teams of management consultants operating within a business, each seeking to unseat board members and win lucrative consultancy contracts.

To Purssell, it definitely did come as a surprise. His own management style was one of consultation; there was a team of managers backing him up and he expected support. Now he not only found a rival who was exceedingly ambitious for himself and who subscribed to management philosophies which were quite alien to him, but he also discovered that that rival was supported by a host of agents working inside the firm. 'They tried to isolate me,' Purssell said. 'The staff didn't know whether to be loyal to me or to him.' The consultants were also used as number crunchers to provide Saunders with ammunition to influence the board against Purssell. In effect, there were two camps within the company.

The contest between the two men would eventually have to be decided by Lord Iveagh and the board. Saunders' most persuasive line here was that he could retrieve City support. It was a story that the board desperately wanted to believe. The share price had fallen so low that the directors must have been wondering whether the toucan which had laid the golden eggs for two centuries was destined to go on living much longer. The fact that takeover talk, which had been in the air during Saunders' first year with the company, ceased will have helped Saunders persuade the management that he should be put in sole charge.

Deputy chairman Purssell had little to throw back at him on this score at least. He had made some ill-timed financial comments which had hit the share price, and dented the confidence of the family bosses in his financial ability. He later said he regretted not having some non-executives with financial nous to back him up.

The battle for control was partly fought in public. Using the public relations skills he had picked up at Nestlé, Saunders, said Purssell, launched a press campaign against him alleging anybody who had been in the company longer than three months was incompetent. In one article Saunders boasted that he at least was not an Oxbridge rowing blue, nor was he a brewer.

Purssell did not leave the board until January 1983, but Saunders was rationalising the business way before then. The company had a board which had been allowed to become inbred with Guinness family members, who were not experienced in modern management methods. This was to change quite dramatically over the next few years. Between 1 January 1982 and 23 January 1983, seven directors retired. Nine months later, the Saunders men started to emerge, with Dr Arthur Furer, his old boss at Nestlé, listed as a non-executive director in the 1983 company report. Lord Iveagh gave him a fulsome tribute: '[He is] a man of great distinction who is highly respected throughout the world business community.' Four years later, the same man of distinction was under a heavy cloud, as a Swiss bank, Bank Leu, where he is chairman of the supervisory board, appeared on the list of major supporters of the Guinness share price in the battle with Distillers.

With the new Saunders broom went the company's advisers. It was, according to one observer, an exercise in massive egocentricity. The company's auditors were changed in 1982, from Ernst and Whinney — who were appointed as recently as 1980 — in favour of Price Waterhouse, who were no more prestigious. Headquarters also moved from one part of the West End to another — the current office on Portman Square is a slick, US-style corporate HQ, with security systems enough to protect a military hide-out. They are large, bright offices that could not be more removed from the environment in which the beer is brewed — at Park Royal to the west of London.

The advertising agency was another casualty. J Walter Thompson handed over to the high-profile, brasher, Allen Brady Marsh. It was an important move for Saunders. But the firing of JWT took place in a typically indirect way. Saunders phoned the JWT chairman and said he would like to meet him, not at his Portman Square office, but rather at the Park Royal Guinness building. It seemed Saunders had to meet him there because the other directors did not know what he was planning, and he wanted it to stay that way. When agency Allen Brady Marsh in its turn was fired after the Guinnless campaign, one imagines sparks flew, and no love is lost today between the extrovert Peter Marsh, who runs ABM, and Saunders.

In 1984 Saunders' City relationships were thrown into turmoil after the firm of brokers, James Capel, was replaced by

Wood Mackenzie. Some insinuated it was because Wood Mackenzie wrote flattering research. Wood Mackenzie says that they simply spotted quicker than anybody else the need for the divestment policy and wrote about it. As early as 1980, when they had visited the Guinness headquarters, the Woodmac analyst had noticed the large number of name plates on the wall and asked the finance director accompanying him how many companies there were in the group. He replied there were 300, and the analyst queried how they ran the budgets for so many. The reply came quickly: oh we don't budget, we just count up the costs at the end of the year. The brokers knew then that something had to change.

When Saunders arrived, Woodmac asked him round to lunch, displaying some quite canny marketing of their own, and a few days before his bid for Martins they were appointed. Saunders' reservation, that they did not have the placing power for the major bids that he intended making, was overcome by a written assurance from Woodmac that they would use Cazenove for any major market placing work in the event of a bid. The bankers, N M Rothschild, took the high jump, and were replaced by Morgan Grenfell.

Bain's and Saunders' success in cutting out the loss-makers quickly became evident. By the middle of 1982, analysts were already seeing financial progress. Work had also begun in tightening up manning at the St James's Gate brewery in Dublin. Pre-tax profits had risen 9%, even allowing for the redundancy costs, turnover was up 21% and the non-brewing businesses were back in the black. The conclusion of brokers Panmure Gordon for the 1981/2 year end was that 'Guinness has £1 billion of sales, and only £50 million of profit, giving plenty of scope for improvement in the hands of a determined management.' The brokers were in little doubt that Ernest Saunders had the determination, though they were less certain about the long-term strategy.

The second plank of the turnaround was the rationalisation and rethinking of the core product strategy. Saunders was retrieving a situation which, he said, previous management did not have the tools or the foresight to tackle. The management he found was way out of touch, he asserted monotonously. 'The product orientation at Guinness was extreme', he said later. 'That doesn't mean they weren't making an excellent product, but the world had passed them by. The rest of the world was concerned with selling and marketing and finance. Guinness were concerned with continuing to brew a superb product.'

The sales of the black beer were falling. When Saunders joined, Guinness was selling 2.1 million barrels — no more than 4.5% of the total beer market in the UK, and it had dropped by a third in the past decade. Even in Ireland, the loyal and home market, Guinness' share had dropped from 80% to 60%. More bottled Guinness was still being bought than draught beer, but the bottled market had been declining over the years, and the more profitable draught side was falling back with it. The brew had a rather elderly image; its high-profile advertising was considered ingenious by the advertising buffs, but the ads had stopped selling the beer. Saunders set his sights on the turnaround of the draught beer. While this decision is generally seen in hindsight as sensible, even obvious, people do not usually count the cost of the advertising (£14 million in five years) that was required to make the turnaround, and set it against what could have been done with the company's lager which was also in trouble but was allowed to go unchecked. Harp steadily declined over the Saunders years from a 64% share of the British market in 1982, to 40% in 1986, even though the market was growing.

Saunders used massive advertising to restore the fortunes of the stout. The Guinnless campaign appealed to the young 18-to-35-year-old pub-goer who would normally drink ale in a pub or club. It was a new-look Guinness campaign, a long way from the subtle, contrived toucan commercials. It signalled to the world the change of agency from J Walter Thompson to Allen Brady Marsh. Some of the ads were distinctly hard-hitting and they did not appeal to the Guinness family. But they may have had some effect in stemming the decline of draught. In 1983 overall volume sales of the beer — both draught and bottled — were down on 1982, but volume sales of draught Guinness between January and September 1983 were up on the previous year. Many brokers, however, were cynical of the Saunders claims about halting the beer decline. Said one, 'They had a chance to stop the beer volumes going down, and many people thought they had succeeded at it. I don't believe they had.'

In 1985, for the first time, more than 50% of sales were accounted for by draught, and this offset the decline in the bottled Guinness. In 1986 Guinness actually grew ahead of the rest of the draught beers, by 14%. 'It was one helluva of an achievement,' reports Sandy Soames of Panmure Gordon.

But perhaps the most important point is that draught beers are a declining market, and the wisdom of the decision to sink all the expensive advertising into the sector is questionable. In fact, many fewer people today are drinking Guinness than when Saunders arrived. When he arrived the company was selling 2.1 million barrels; by 1986 this had dropped to 1.61 million. Over this period the switch of emphasis from bottled to draught beer was made, and some gave Saunders credit for spotting the decline of the bottled beer market. Saunders liked to be judged on his achievement in increasing sales of draught Guinness. He was very sensitive about allegations that total sales (i.e. draught and bottled) had declined under his stewardship. Argyll made this point during the battle for Distillers.

No one disputed Saunders' success in tackling the stout's manufacturing and pricing problem. There was wide disparity in the pricing of Guinness from one pub to another. Guinness had no tied pubs of its own, which meant that advertising featured very large in their marketing strategy. The owners of the pub chains, most of whom were brewers producing ale competing with the black stout, priced it at the top of the range, in line with expensive lagers.

Saunders' solution was to fiercely cut costs in the manufacturing process and reduce the price to the publican. The productivity at both Park Royal and Dublin was low by industrial standards, partly because of low investment in plant, but the management was also highly paternalistic and inefficient. Upwards of one thousand jobs were quickly lost, but investment in plant to the tune of £100 million was planned to stretch to the end of the decade. He had to tackle the unions in a company whose industrial relations were good, and apparently they admired his unflinching determination and toughness.

But once all the cutting and rationalisation was done, where now for the beer? About 70% of Guinness beer was drunk in the UK (30%) and Eire (40%) in 1985. Saunders' answer was to develop the international market. He may have seen Guinness becoming in time a premium world brand like Budweiser, Heineken or Fosters. But Guinness had a very long way to go before it came anywhere near that. Its overseas markets did not extend much further than Nigeria and Malaysia. These countries actually started to have problems in the eighties as currency fluctuations, devaluations, and delays in transferring profits back to the UK eroded their importance.

The boom in speciality beers in the States appeared to offer Saunders hope, and he was quoted as saying that 'he liked doing business in the States', but there is no evidence that Guinness ever made major inroads there. In 1985, it may have had 5% of the small speciality beers market, but the contribution to profit was no more than £3.9 million. Sales in Germany and the US were rising by 15% and 20% respectively but clearly from a very low base. The task of offsetting the Malaysian and Nigerian profit contribution had a long way to go. Saunders later boasted of his achievements in international brand marketing; in truth what he'd done was very small beer indeed.

The third prong of the Saunders strategy, after divestment and rationalisation, was diversification and growth. Of course, management at Guinness had tried this before and it had not worked. Effort number two was to begin, and even then people were asking whether it would be any more successful. His chosen sectors seemed as far removed from the original beerage as the businesses he'd already discarded.

Saunders' formula for diversification concentrated on retailing, and here Guinness had a head start with its Lavells and Drummonds shops already in-house. In June 1984, just after Saunders took on Morgan Grenfell, Martin the Newsagent joined the fold. Saunders said he was invited in by Martins following a bid from W.H. Smith. In fact, the links with Martin had already been forged before Saunders arrived. The old Guinness management had made a behind-the-scenes approach to Martin which was rebuffed. Smith's bid forced this previously family-owned business to think again. It was an acquisition not free of controversy. The Martin chairman was later to allege that promises given by Saunders about job losses in the post acquisition period were broken.

Martin, with its 500 shops, made the second business area of Guinness (after brewing) look more credible. The scale of the offer (for £45.2 million) pales beside the later megabids; however, it was seen as very generous by analysts. It contrasted with the offer of £36 million put in by W H Smith which paved the way for Saunders' white knight bid. But Saunders was feeling his way into a new area of expertise. He had never conducted a takeover before, and was still only learning the financial tricks.

The acquisition was beneficial because it took retailing turnover up to 20% of the total. This part of the business was to grow in the following year when he bought Lewis Meeson, R S McColl and the 7–Eleven stores. Eventually the retailing chain grew to a sizeable 1200 stores.

The other non-brewing strand was health. Saunders' health kick came in 1985, when he acquired Champneys, Cranks and Nature's Best Health. The interest in health products derived from his days with Beecham and Nestlé, both of whom conducted research into the health trend. While Guinness' later decision to stay with health suggests that they are confident there is still life in the market, analysts are divided. Some believe it may be merely a fad which will pass, rather than an enduring trend. One explanation for his entry into the health sector was that Carole Saunders went to Champneys, liked it and persuaded her husband to buy it.

The diversification and growth were certainly not going to stop at retailing and health. Saunders' plans were always grandiose. Now the aim was for an international beverage (not brewing) company. Many companies were looked at and Saunders appeared to believe that money would be no object.

The expansion was eventually to be achieved through the acquisition of Arthur Bell and Sons. Accounts of the reasons behind the choice of Bell's differ. Saunders' public view is that Bell's was the logical development of his strategy of building the drinks side of the business. 'We believe that our knowledge of the market worldwide will be more fully utilised,' he wrote in his annual report for 1985. It seemed to some that Saunders was beginning to believe his own propaganda about the power of marketing to turn round any drinks business.

Scott Dobbie of Wood Mackenzie believes tax advantages may explain the choice of Bell's. A large part of Guinness profits came from Ireland, which meant that the company was paying a very low rate of UK corporation tax. But Guinness had to pay heavy British tax on its dividends, some of which could be saved if there were British profits against which it could be offset. In short, said Dobbie, 'the shareholder would get more income if the two companies were merged, than if Guinness stayed separate.' This sort of explanation makes sense to accountants and the City and no doubt looked eminently sensible to Roux and Saunders. It completely conflicts with the usually accepted rationale for takeovers, namely that the new management can make better use of the assets and people than the old one. It was also an explanation which took no account of Bell's, and of its boss Raymond Miquel.

This was not going to worry the Guinness man. He probably relished a fight, and while a novice in the world of high finance, had aspirations to be counted in the ranks of the great financiers. He believed that the world-wide repute of Guinness could be used to support major financial deals, and put him alongside the likes of Lord Hanson and Sir James Goldsmith.

CHAPTER THREE

THE MIQUEL REGIME

Arthur Bell's was a whisky management success story. Against a background of declining demand for dark spirits, the Perth-based distiller had built up traditional markets in the UK. It had succeeded, where industry leaders Distillers had failed. Bell's secret was salesmanship, instilled with obsessive enthusiasm by the chairman, the highly individual and ferociously independent Raymond Miquel. But in the era of marketing, the bells were to toll for Miquel.

Miquel's father was a chef of French origins who worked in the Central Hotel, Glasgow. Raymond Miquel was 25 when he joined Bell's in 1956 as a works study engineer. He worked his way up quickly to become production director and then deputy managing director by 1965. Three years later he became managing director and in 1973 was appointed chairman.

The ascent to the top had not been smooth. Miquel clashed with the older-established managers and directors who had connections with the Bell family. One observer noted 'he upset people' and later was to find that 'he had no friends when he needed them'.

Miquel wanted Bell's to be the most popular whisky in Britain, and with 25% of the home market this had been achieved. The sales message was traditional — 'Afore ye Go' adorned bottles of Scotch which either hung from shelves in pubs and clubs or occupied family drinks cabinets. The Bell's logo was also familiar to *Financial Times* readers with its advertising slot on the front page. New sales opportunities, like supplying the supermarkets with cheaper blends of whisky that could be sold under the shop's own name, were obstinately rejected. Miquel thus missed sharing in the whisky market's biggest sales growth area. Miquel's forte was the on-trade — the pubs and clubs. He would insist that the Bell's bottle was always on the right hand optic at the bar for visual impact. He employed a highly effective sales force who cultivated land-lords and publicans up and down the country. They'd be dressed in a distinctive Bell's uniform and Miquel encouraged them to be very aggressive. It was out of the question for them to collaborate with the opposition. Word got back to Miquel that at a sales conference one of his staff had been seen chatting at the bar with a Whyte and Mackays man; it was enough to have the salesman promptly fired. Bell's energies went into selling in the UK. Their presence in the US was not helped by some half-hearted marketing campaigns. Miquel sent out market researchers to see how Bell's brands were doing in America; some of these were students who were expected to go around off licences and count how many bottles of Bell's were on the shelves!

The chairman would lavish time and effort on local pubs and outlets in Perth. Each year he'd personally show hundreds of publicans around his distilleries. He was highly popular with his customers . . . On one occasion he heard that the son of one of the local club owners was a keen tennis player. So the chairman of Bell's saw to it that the boy got a ticket to the Centre Court at Wimbledon. Miquel himself was a sports fanatic and ran in marathons. One army captain remembers being asked by Miquel how quickly he could run the marathon. He told Miquel it was 3 hours 25 minutes and was then informed that his time would be beaten when Miquel ran the next Glasgow marathon. The army man, out of curiosity, later on looked up the results and noted that Miquel had completed the course in 3 hours 24 minutes! The devotion to fitness did not stop with his own participation. Locals in Perth became accustomed to the annual run around the town's open space, the North Inch. All Bell's managers were expected to take part but Miquel, of course, had to run at the front. Compulsory tennis tournaments for employees were also regular events on the company calendar.

Raymond Miquel effectively ran Bell's as his own fiefdom, and this was to prove his ultimate undoing. Senior members of staff stood to attention when he entered their offices, and depending on their seniority addressed him as Mr Miquel or Sir. His secretary wrote all letters from Miquel in the third person. There was a complete prohibition on smoking throughout the office, except in the canteen, which was in a constant smog.

All in all, it was a highly individual management style. Nevertheless it proved effective and he won grudging admiration from Scottish analysts and financial institutions. The record shows that pre tax profits had risen from £4.1 million to £31.4 million between 1975 and 1983 with turnover increasing threefold to £246.7 million. It was enough to enable Miquel to pay himself very well; he was one of the highest paid executives in Scotland, and drove a Lagonda.

Dour Scots found Miquel's flashiness suspect, and his autocratic manner won him no friends or contacts in high places. As one senior Edinburgh banker put it, 'Raymond was a maverick. He offended people.' Conversations with outsiders about Bell's often turned into monologues with Miquel singing his own praises. One journalist remembers interviewing him for television. At the end of the live broadcast Miquel got straight out of his chair and left the stage still talking. The journalist pursued him but could not get a word in edgeways even as Miquel was climbing into his car and driving off. As a public relations gesture, he made a film about Bell's. But he insisted on appearing in every single shot. Scottish analysts now reshow the film for uncharitable entertainment value. Miquel had little support in the investment community because he made no effort to cultivate finance houses; and he played no part in the Scotch Whisky Association.

The unappealing style made sure that when Scottish shareholders were given an opportunity to get their own back, they sold out and backed the Guinness offer. Miquel seems to have failed even to have any informal contacts with the insurance giant General Accident, whose head office was literally fifty yards from Bell's. The General Accident stake was later to prove critical at the height of the takeover battle.

Another key Bell's shareholder was a family trust fund set up by the founding father Arthur Bell. When the old man died in 1942 his shares went to the Gannochy Trust which acted as guardian of the family interest in the company. In 1971 when Bell's was floated on the Stock Market, the Gannochy Trust held a 50% stake. After that the family shares were slowly sold off but the holding in 1985 was still 6%. The Gannochy trustees, posibly nursing a grievance, also voted against him later on.

But Miquel's biggest problem in the months before Saunders fired in his bid was inside his own boardroom. Effectively there was only one voice in opposition to the chairman, that of the hotel supremo, Peter Tyrie. The festering antagonism between these two highly capable and single-minded executives led to the now infamous split during the takeover battle which Guinness was able to exploit so effectively.

Peter Tyrie was a survivor from the takeover of Gleneagles Hotels. In 1983 British Rail began selling off their famous but crumbling Victorian relics, the British Rail hotels. It was one of the first moves in the Government privatisation programme. Gleneagles itself was sold with the Edinburgh hotels, the North British and the Caledonian. The new company which was bought by a consortium of financial institutions was optimistic about the potential for breathing life into the hotels. Tyrie, who had been headhunted for the purpose from Ramada Hotels in the Far East, set about his task with a vengeance. He began by refurbishing leisure facilities at Gleneagles. The famous golf courses were in an appalling state, so Tyrie spent £23,000 on sprucing up the greens. Soon Gleneagles was granted the coveted five-star status, and became the only hotel in that category in Scotland.

Tyrie then turned his attention to the Piccadilly Hotel in the West End of London. Gleneagles had a so called underlease on the hotel but Tyrie had ambitious expansion plans and decided they should negotiate to buy outright a 99-year lease. He decided it should be redeveloped to act as a feeder for the rest of the group. The London-based outlet was to be used to lure American tourists up to Edinburgh and Gleneagles. But £30m was needed to renegotiate the lease with a property company controlled by the Kuwait Investment Office. Tyrie demanded that the company raise the cash through a rights issue (where shareholders are given the chance to buy new shares in proportion to their own holdings). Then things began to go wrong for the new manager of the young company. The original backers of Gleneagles were divided over whether to provide the cash for Tyrie's redevelopment plans.

British Rail still held a 30% stake, but the Government refused BR Investments permission to pour more money into Gleneagles. So BR were unable to take up their rights. Tyrie then fell out with his banking advisers, the mighty Bank of Scotland; this is a name which is appear again in the story.

It is claimed by Tyrie's camp that the Bank of Scotland in a fit of pique went to Bell's, who were long-established customers, and suggested they might take an interest in Gleneagles. Bell's stepped in and bought the shares owned by British Rail. It gave them a vital strategic stake. The failure of the rights issue undermined the confidence of the larger shareholders in Tyrie, which included British Linen Bank (a subsidiary of the Bank of Scotland), Coats Patons and even Distillers. The Tyrie camp claim they were never given a fair hearing by British Rail. Some suggest that Morgan Grenfell — the advisers to BR Investments — were keen to deliver the hotel group to Bell's who were also clients. Morgan's, as we shall see later, played a key role in the change of ownership of first Bell's then Distillers.

Bell's made a full takeover offer of £27 million and won control of Gleneagles in February 1984, barely 6 months after the group was born thus dashing the high hopes that it would be an independent Scottish hotels company. Some fund managers grumbled that the Bell's price was too low for an embryo company that should have been allowed to prove itself. Scotland's grandest three hotels were to change hands three times in two years. The Gleneagles takeover ensured that Miquel crossed swords with the Scottish financial establishment and alienated more potential allies who could have come to his rescue when Guinness made their attack.

It was one of Raymond Miquel's lifelong ambitions to own Gleneagles — a rather more grand fulfilment of the dream of many Scotsmen to own a hotel. He knew the hotel well, having lived for some time on the Gleneagles estate, where he was able to indulge his passion for golf. The bond with the place was enhanced when his daughter married the professional's son,

Brian Marchbanks. Miquel began immediately to develop commercially his obsession with fitness and sport at Gleneagles. The thought of losing the hotel was possibly Miquel's worst fear when he found himself under siege from Guinness.

Peter Tyrie chose to stay on at Gleneagles, to the surprise of many. Apparently he and his family liked Edinburgh. Miquel recognised his talents and Tyrie went on the board of Bell's. In October 1984 the Piccadilly Hotel was closed for a £12 million facelift and leisure centre development as planned by Tyrie. But it was becoming clear that the two men did not get on.

Miquel tried to interfere with the running of the Gleneagles chain, say Tyrie's friends. He tried on one occasion advocating decoration plans based on his experience of staying in hotels around the world. Tyrie at one point was close to completing preparations for bringing a major new golf tournament to Gleneagles, the Dunhill Cup. Miquel 'threw a fit' according to one observer and insisted the tournament went elsewhere because Dunhill were also in the whisky business. But Tyrie was also noted for being a high spender. He spent some £3000 on the locks for the rooms at the Piccadilly Hotel to the horror of more frugal managers. The big spending mentality in the end was likely to appeal more to Saunders than to Miquel.

Tyrie felt that he was heading an army imprisoned in occupied territory. He saw the interests of the Gleneagles Group and employees steadily growing apart from Bell's, and he began to consider a separation. Miquel was close to being persuaded to allow a management buy out with Bell's keeping a residual stake. It kept Tyrie stringing along. But the uneasy truce in the boardroom at Perth and any buy out talks were blown away when Guinness sprang their bid in June 1985.

CHAPTER FOUR

BELL'S: A HEAVY TOLL

Raymond Miquel had a rude awakening in the early hours of 14 June 1985. He was in Chicago, promoting the company and visiting important customers, when at 1.30 a.m. the phone rang. An adviser from Perth was on the line to say that Guinness had made a bid for Bell's. The chairman was caught unawares. He was thousands of miles from his headquarters, and had had no reason to suspect that anyone was pursuing his company.

The situation in the Guinness camp could not be more different. Ernest Saunders, unveiling his bid for £330 million, was supremely well prepared when he told a press conference that he would use his marketing skills to develop Bell's as an international brand, the first stage in his plans to make Guinness a worldwide beverage group. Saunders credited the Bell's management with building a success in the home market, but pointed out that their market share had fallen since 1980 from 25% to 20%.

This was the culmination of a period of meticulous planning by Guinness, going back to March 1985, conducted in the utmost secrecy. Then, at the last moment, the news leaked out. This was a major upset, and they had to bring the announcement of their offer for Bell's forward by three days because of a sharp rise in the Bell's share price. On Monday 10

June it stood at 158 pence, but by Thursday evening had soared to 183, way above its previous high that year. Guinness were obliged to come up with a higher offer than originally planned and Saunders subsequently filed a complaint alleging possible insider trading.

Only a handful of people inside Guinness knew what was afoot. One small office in a separate building from Portman Square was set aside as a planning bunker, away from the main corridors of power and the day-to-day running of the business. The codename for Bell's was Whale, which appeared on all the documents. Guinness itself was known as Orion. After each of the top-secret planning meetings all the documents would be checked and counted before being filed away, and no one was allowed to remove any of the paperwork. A major panic developed on one occasion when a document went missing. But one participant remembers that it simply contained an account of how successful Guinness had been and talked about increased sales of draught Orion. Someone even addressed a document Orion plc, 39 Portman Square. Those privy to the confidential plans even felt unable to buy a shot of Bell's in the pub. One of the team was dispatched to Gleneagles on a reconnaissance mission but instead of enjoying the luxurious splendour of a five-star hotel, spent the visit worrying that he'd be recognised or mistakenly sign a register as a Guinness employee. Certainly the secretaries at Portman Square knew nothing, although most were perplexed that their bosses would often disappear for long periods of the day for unscheduled meetings. 'I think she must have thought I was some sort of loony really the way I was actually behaving because I didn't tell her what I was doing,' said one participant. After two months of seven-day weeks and obsessive secrecy the Orion/Guinness brigade were infuriated that somehow advance news of their plans seemed to have got out.

Whether there was any systematic, or orchestrated, leak of the Guinness intentions remains a mystery. There was unusual interest in Bell's shares from the Far East in the week leading up to 14 June when the bid was launched. The only player in the drama with Far Eastern connections was Peter Tyrie. As we have seen he had good reason to want a change of ownership of Bell's.

Leak or no leak, by 14 June when he announced his bid for Bell's, Saunders had information flowing out of his ears about the company and its eccentric chief executive. His own patter was also immaculately presented. He informed journalists lined up and ready to pass on his every word that he could use his marketing skills to develop Bell's as a major world brand. It was part of his overall plan to develop Guinness into an international beverage group, he told the waiting scribes.

Saunders' PR performance contrasted dramatically with the style of the Bell's boss. Any journalist who was lucky enough to get through to him at his Chicago hotel was told that it was a Scottish issue and that Guinness should not be allowed to interfere with an independent company. He said little about his own performance with the company, and failed to counter Saunders' arguments about the need for global marketing for Bell's. Moreover, Miquel was fully determined not to be bullied into changing his American plans; so he stayed in the US.

That gave Saunders yet more time to firm up the press. On Sunday 16 June he and his team held another press conference, this time in Edinburgh. They had realised the importance of winning friends among the Scottish media and made a point of putting stories the way of city journalists on a Sunday to fill Monday's pages — never the easiest to fill with really hard news. The Sunday press conference was to become a feature of the Guinness takeover campaigns. Miquel was still in the States, almost out of contact. First blood to Saunders.

When at last Miquel returned to London on the Wednesday, he fell on another banana skin. Instead of returning to Scotland and fighting the battle on home territory, he addressed the press in London. It was a disaster. He was not used to dealing with journalists and treated any unfriendly question as a personal insult. He managed to lose his temper with a television crew who interrupted him in full flow. He was flustered by persistent questioning about his overseas performance and domestic market shares, and when he was tackled about the Guinness claim that his share of the UK market had fallen by 5% between 1980 and 1985, his answers were not convincing. The apparent unfamiliarity with the details of finance and marketing, led analysts and commentators, frustrated for many years by the lack of coherent information about the company, to exploit his weakness.

Shortly afterwards, the two champions, Saunders and Miquel, met in London's Tower Hotel. The man who set the meeting up, Henry King, a solicitor, had hoped to put together a merger, and avoid the acrimony of the contested bid. But Miquel was in no mood to talk, and nothing came of it. King's position was very awkward; he was an old friend of Miquel's and served as a non-executive director on the Bell's board, but King's firm, Denton Hall and Burgin (now Denton Hall Burgin and Warren) also acted as Ernest Saunders' family solicitor.

After the meeting with Saunders there arose a more pressing problem for the chairman of Bell's. He'd discovered that his merchant bankers, Morgan Grenfell, had joined the Guinness camp, as their chief advisers. It was devastating news. Morgan's were not short of explanations, pointing out that they had severed all connection with Bell's. Miquel naturally saw it very differently, since Morgan Grenfell had been the firm's bankers for 20 years, and had developed a close understanding of how Bell's was run. Now there was the possibility that information could be passed to Guinness.

What particularly enraged Miquel was that he'd been warned at the end of 1984 that Saunders might be plotting a bid and that Morgan Grenfell would be handling it. Consequently, Miquel went to his bankers, at that time Morgan Grenfell, for reassurance. Morgan's gave it without reservation.

Now, Guinness were at the door, and Miquel was without a merchant banker to protect him. He turned to Lord Spens, known formally as Baron Spens of Blairsanquhar, a flamboyant character with a reputation for being something of a maverick in the financial world. His longer-than-average hair, rubicund face and even slightly unkempt manner are exceptions in a City world where the dark-striped suit and short-cropped haircut are passports to membership of the club. But Spens has as acute a mind as any City gent, allegedly a photographic memory, and a disarmingly impish manner.

Ironically Spens had worked for Morgan Grenfell and had met Miquel back in 1969 when Morgan's were advising Bell's about their Stock Market flotation. As with many first meetings, it was not typical of what followed. The banker innocently ventured his opinion that Bell's relied too much on one brand and this would damage its prospects on the market. For Miquel, it was like a red rag to a bull, confirming all his prejudices about City slickers. However, the two men made up their differences and worked together until 1982, when Spens quit Morgan's, saying they were becoming too big.

He surprised many colleagues by moving to a small and little known bank, Henry Ansbacher. But Spens kept in touch with Miquel. In fact, Miquel had turned to him for advice during the earlier bid speculation, and it was on Spens' suggestion that he went to Morgan Grenfell's Christopher Reeves to check it up. Now Spens was on the scene again. His first move was to call in the Bell's lawyers, Denton Hall and Burgin. He felt there were ample grounds for getting a High Court injunction stopping Morgan's acting for Guinness. By the Friday, a week after Miquel's phone call in Chicago, Spens had prepared his case and was confident of success at the hearing due for the Monday. As a temporary measure he sought to stop Morgan's sending out to shareholders the official Guinness offer document. But late on the Friday night, Denton Hall announced they were pulling out due to a conflict of interest. This mystified Spens, who now opted to take a new tack and make a complaint to the Takeover Panel, the regulator of bid activity.

The Panel acted something like a court of appeal for takeover disputes. Its rulebook was the Takeover Code. The people that sat on it were City worthies, mostly merchant bankers who could not see a great deal of career development in their own companies. The panel was a respectable body, but it hardly was likely to put the fear of God into aberrant City financiers. It had no statutory power where it found abuse, and very meagre resources to root it out in the first place. Worst of all, the Panel has difficulty ducking the accusation that it is too compromised by its City membership to make any serious criticisms.

When Ansbacher, Bell's merchant bank, found themselves making an official complaint about Morgan's, it was very much the City minnow against a major. Bell's alleged to the Panel that they were put at an unfair disadvantage by Morgan's switch to Guinness. They said they were without a key adviser at a critical point in the defence against a hostile bidder. Morgan Grenfell in turn produced a letter from Bell's, dated

November 1984, which apparently indicated their services were no longer required, and that they had stopped working for Bell's long before the approach from Guinness. The Bell's camp countered with the claim that Morgan's had been advising them on internal matters not long before June 1985. Analyst Thorold Mackie of the Edinburgh stockbrokers Bell Lawrie, who were Bell's brokers, recalls: 'I was at the announcement of results in the late spring of 1985 in the Rooftop Bar at the Hilton and it was invitation only — only Bell's two brokers were there and their merchant banking adviser and the press and PR person. The merchant banks that turned up were Morgan Grenfell and Ansbacher. To me there was absolutely no doubt at the time that Morgan Grenfell counted themselves as an adviser to Arthur Bell.' Spens meanwhile claimed that in late 1984 Morgan's had earned £20,000 of fees from a Bell's deal, and there was a further transaction in March 1985.

On the Monday, the Takeover Panel executive — the low-level administrators — issued a simple rebuke to Morgan's. It was a slap over the wrists, but required no action. Spens wanted to take it further, and asked for a full hearing of the Panel which took place on the Wednesday. The three parties, Ansbacher, Morgan's and the executive paraded before this august City assembly, chaired by Sir Jasper Hollom.

At risk for Morgan's if Spens got his way and had them ruled out of court were millions of pounds of fees. The huge underwriting operation which Morgan's had organised would also have been jeopardised. Morgan's would still have a legal obligation to meet their commitments to the other underwriters, said to run to £6.5 million. So concerned were Morgan's about the outcome of the case that they had chief executive Christopher Reeves there to represent them.

Reeves took pains to contrast the millions of pounds of business with Guinness at stake with the much smaller amount of fees ever earned from Bell's. Saunders tried to stay in the room for the evidence and the questioning of the key participants by the legal eagle Hollom in the chair, but he was ruled out of court.

The evidence over, the three parties withdrew leaving the Panel to deliberate. This took all of three minutes. They were called back in, and Saunders this time was admitted, despite

Spens' protest. The verdict: a clean bill of health for Morgan's and even a withdrawal of the earlier slap on the wrist from the executive. To many who witnessed the proceedings it looked like a whitewash, and a harbinger of some very weak-kneed decisions of the regulatory authorities in months ahead.

Miquel took the defeat badly, seeing his empire beginning to slip away from him. In contrast, Saunders was jubilant; this was his Rubicon.

The legal and regulatory questions dispensed with, Saunders now had to tackle some political hurdles. His first was the so-called ring fence which was supposed to protect Scottish companies from foreign predators. In earlier days this had been grounds for defence. The Royal Bank of Scotland had used it to escape the clutches of Hong Kong and Shanghai Bank in 1982, and four years earlier a bid for Highland Distilleries by the Canadian-owned Hiram Walker had been thwarted with a similar recourse to sentiment. So Guinness needed to find out whether the ring fence was still in place and if it was how, to clear it.

The test came at the right time, as Secretary of State for Trade and Industry Norman Tebbit had rethought policy towards company takeovers. In line with the avowed government policy of the market primacy, competition became the litmus test; if the proposed bid or merger did not lead to an excessive control of a market by one company then it would be waved through. Considerations of regional or national interests took a lower priority.

But there was still a Scottish financial community for Saunders to convince. Scottish institutions, which controlled 20% of the Bell's stock, were largely based in Edinburgh. There were few individual shareholders of any significance, except perhaps the one farmer in Perthshire and his spinster sister who lived with him and had half a million shares each. They were to do quite nicely at the 225 pence a share offer by Guinness.

Saunders had to become as well known in Charlotte Square, the financial ghetto of Edinburgh, as he was in London's Square Mile. His guide to the Scottish jungle was Charles Fraser, who had the honorary title of 'Purse Bearer' to the Church of Scotland as well as directorships of a score of public companies. Fraser was a lawyer at the Edinburgh firm of W and J Burness with an office overlooking Charlotte Square itself. He personified the dignified, even haughty, but shrewd East Coast establishment. Miquel, who was tucked away in Perth, was anathema to Fraser. It made Fraser a natural ally for Saunders.

The Guinness presence in Scotland was further boosted by the recruitment of two blue-blooded local firms to the campaign. Wood Mackenzie who acted as stockbrokers to Guinness, not only had a lot of clout in Edinburgh but also could provide years of expert analysis of the Scotch whisky industry. But the masterstroke was the hiring of Noble Grossart to support Morgan Grenfell on the merchant banking side. They were scions of the East Coast establishment and were able to open doors for Saunders.

The eventual outcome of a reference to the Office of Fair Trading appeared to Saunders to depend largely on how well he lobbied in Scottish political circles. So on top of a bevy of financial advisers and mentors, he brought in political lobbyists. Andrew Gifford, whose family had Scottish business interests and who had previously worked for David Steel, ran a 'political consultancy' firm, GJW. He took Saunders to the Scottish Development Agency, which has an important paternalistic role north of the border, and to the Scottish Office. The Scottish Office were very concerned about the bid, and they needed a lot of persuading. Guinness sought to win over the powerful number two at the Scottish office, and its chief economic adviser, Dr Gavin McCrone. One department of state did support Saunders — the vitally important Ministry of Agriculture, Fisheries and Food, which looks after the brewing and distilling sectors. Michael Jopling, the MAF minister, was especially courted.

Saunders found the investment fraternity in Edinburgh generally supportive. The analysts and institutions were especially pleased and surprised to see a top chief executive who was prepared to listen to, and even act on, suggestions. The contrast with the Miquel regime was painfully apparent. Saunders' tour of Edinburgh included a visit to the imposing Bank of Scotland building on The Mound, next to the Castle. There he was shown into the office of the Governor, Sir Thomas Risk, whom he asked to give public support to the

Guinness bid. The request was politely turned down but the meeting was an amicable one. It was the first time the two men had met; later meetings were to be less amicable.

Accompanying the high-level lobbying campaign, was a well-planned public relations effort. The dull world of City takeovers was taken by surprise. It was highly orchestrated, meticulous and energetic. The focus of the campaign was the Scottish press and Guinness were able to field three media experts, all of whom were Scottish.

The public relations supremos at Guinness had been hard at work before the Bell's bid was formally announced. Chris Davidson, bustling and loyal to the end, headed the team, and Alan Stewart was his number two. Stewart had only joined the company in May from Dunlop. When BTR took over, and Michael Edwardes left, Alan Stewart followed him. Little did the tall, soft-spoken Scot realise that he'd been thrown into a round-the-clock operation which worked non-stop for a year on two of the most bitter takeover battles the UK had ever seen.

Saunders told Stewart on the Monday morning before the Friday announcement that Bell's was to be attacked. Quickly they decided to establish a Scottish base and hire local expertise. That night Stewart got on the phone to the Glasgow office of the public relations firm Charles Barker.

The man who picked up the receiver in Glasgow was Colin Liddell. His first thought was that it was Alan Stewart MP, Government minister in Scotland. 'Good God, why's he calling me?' The conversation was low-key, with the Guinness man anxious not to give too much away. Stewart needed to know who Charles Barker's clients were and whether they were close to Bell's. They weren't, even though Colin Liddell could reel off a number of other contacts in the whisky industry. That night Liddell knocked out a summary of the business, spelling out his firm's strengths, and shot it down to Alan Stewart in London, overnight. Liddell had got wind something big was about to break and didn't want to miss out. Stewart called back to say that he was interested but would have to wait until the end of the week. On Friday Liddell phoned Guinness first thing and was told about the Bell's bid. He was given the brief of handling all Guinness corporate public relations in Scotland: that meant, in effect, selling the Guinness image to the local media.

Davidson, Stewart and Liddell were given authority to handle all the support information. They would do the groundwork for Saunders and steer him towards the right press people. Yet another public affairs expert appeared at the beginning of the bid. This was Brian Basham, the founder of a public relations company called Broad Street Associates, and a well-known practitioner of the art of takeover and City relations. He was later to rile the Guinness camp by arguing that his efforts alone were responsible for the successful victory over Bell's, and he lost the account.

The keenest PR man from the start for Guinness, however, was the managing director himself. Unlike many company bosses who might treat reporters as a lesser breed that shouldn't be allowed through the front door, Saunders realised their power and actively cultivated them. In return they loved him, flattering him in their columns and fawning on him when he entertained them.

Saunders insisted on being introduced to journalists, and would make a point of bending their ears at receptions and dinners. Ray Perman, joint editor of the monthly magazine *Scottish Business Insider*, remembers an invitation to a Guinness function. He could only spare a short time off from producing the magazine and had no time to change out of his more casual day attire. On arrival he was whisked into an office to meet the Guinness chief personally. There was Saunders, dressed impeccably as usual, rising to greet Perman with the words 'Ray, I'm so pleased to meet you.' Saunders was in his element, exuding the charm that won friends not just among journalists but also the powerful and influential. The Scottish media would get priority on the flow of information from Guinness in these early stages of the bid for Bell's. Any material released from Portman Square was immediately transmitted to the Edinburgh and Glasgow newspapers. Liddell would use couriers to make hand deliveries and disseminate the Guinness message by telex and facsimile machine. Scots journalists felt they were being treated as seriously as hacks south of the border; for once they didn't feel like second-class citizens.

As Alan Stewart has observed, 'Scottish journalists are not generally that fond of South-East of England people coming up to tell them what they're going to do with their industry. But he pulled it off as he has a very relaxed way of putting across a case and he did it very well. They were almost won over by him. He was always good copy and he was available and he talked to them.' Stewart would set up phone calls for Saunders to speak to say, the *Scotsman's* Alf Young or the *Glasgow Herald's* Ronnie Dundas, at all hours of the day or night. Saunders never refused. 'He jumped on shuttles, took private planes, and was always hopping up and down to Scotland, particularly in that early part of the campaign,' was Liddell's recollection.

The smaller regional papers also got a look-in. Alan Stewart even went to pay his respects to the *Perthshire Advertiser*, deep in the heart of Bell's home territory. He remembers it was 'really like Daniel in the lions' den because you didn't know which way they were going to react'. To his surprise he found they actually weren't very fond of Miquel. Although they approved of his contribution to the town's prosperity and his good works, there was a certain staid suspicion of Miquel's flamboyant style.

The Guinness takeover team — which was composed of PR, legal, financial and management people — came together at HQ in Portman Square at 8 o'clock every morning during the bid. To say there was a war cabinet is fanciful; rather there was a constant stream of advisers feeding information and opinion to the supremo. Stewart and Davidson, who had been in since 7.30 a.m., went through a digest of cuttings they had prepared from that day's press. They would be accompanied by Liddell, who always flew down on the Sunday night for the Monday meeting to give a summary of Scottish developments. Saunders immersed himself in a detailed appraisal of every journalist's attitude and line on Guinness.

Merchant bankers, stockbrokers, lawyers all hovered around Saunders at these sessions. The aroma of black coffee was the only reminder that such frenetic activity was being generated while the rest of London was breakfasting. The dignified figure of Tony Richmond-Watson of Morgan Grenfell gave a touch of calm to proceedings. He was happy to co-operate with the PR advisers and translate detailed financial information into press releases. Olivier Roux and Bill Young, the Bainies, supplied the nitty-gritty financial and market data when called upon. The Guinness takeover machine was well-oiled and harmonious. Stewart found working in it 'fun' as well as being stimulating. No sign then of the breakdowns and seizures that were to grip the system little more than six months later in the battle for Distillers.

Back in Perth, Miquel could only look on helplessly as Guinness forged ahead. 'Miquel didn't understand what he was up against. He didn't have a campaign team organised. He is a loner, he's perceived as a loner . . . he was friendless. When he needed friends they weren't there because of the type of personality he is,' said one observer. Miquel suffered by being rarely available for comment. He valiantly attempted to carry on running his business as well as fronting the defence effort.

Miquel also spent a lot of time just travelling around. He insisted on going by train between Perth and London. Saunders also travelled by air. Miquel was also out of contact for long periods and there was no alternative spokesman to counter the volley of claims and allegations from the Guinness camp. One exasperated employee at the Bell's headquarters at Cherrybank finally blurted out that she didn't know where Mr Miquel was, and perhaps the journalist ought to contact Guinness as she was sure they would know. Intelligence and knowledge of enemy movements were key facets of the Guinness campaign. 'We knew all the movements of the key players at any time because in a bid you try and wrong-foot them at every turn, and not be wrong-footed by them in return', observed one of the strategists.

Guinness fired in their formal offer on 27 June. The official document sent to Bell's shareholders hammered home the slogan that was to become the advertising jingle of the Guinness campaign, 'Bell's has lost its way'. The document stated: 'If Bell's continues on the present course, we believe the prospects for sales, for jobs and for profits will deteriorate.' Shareholders were told that Guinness was in a unique position internationally to give Bell's the help it needed. Saunders referred repeatedly to Miquel's inability to exploit overseas markets. But Saunders' own achievements in top-flight global marketing were never spelt out.

One factor was foremost in Saunders' mind. This was the possibility that the bid might be referred to the Monopolies Commission. And he sought to counter this threat wherever possible by stressing the Scottish angle. 'We will make Bell's a successful company once again, successful for Scottish jobs and for Scottish exports . . . Guinness guarantees no redundancies within Bell's as a consequence of Bell's joining the Guinness group.'

The document was greeted with some scepticism in the City, the consensus being that Guinness would have to offer more. The bid valued Bell's shares at around 225 pence but in the market Bell's were still at almost 240 pence. Meanwhile the Guinness share price was coming under pressure and, because the offer consisted partly of new Guinness shares in exchange for Bell's, the value of the bid was slipping. Morgan Grenfell helped Guinness by buying £1.7 million worth of Guinness shares to support the price. But for their pains their investment was now showing a loss of almost £60,000.

In the opposition camp, danger bells were ringing loud. A leading merchant banker was recruited to work alongside Patrick Spens at Henry Ansbacher. Miquel and his advisers had swallowed their pride and disappointment after the Takeover Panel's decision and opted to meet might with might. S G Warburg were chosen, but it could only be an uphill struggle since they had no time to do the groundwork. Nevertheless, at the end of June there was talk that the bid might be referred, allowing precious time to find another bidder to rescue Bell's. The favourites were Suntory of Japan or Seagrams of Canada. Even Jimmy Gulliver and his Argyll Group were suggested, though Gulliver was on the record denying any interest. At the time he was preoccupied with his own top-secret intelligence activities.

By early July the political battle had intensified. Miquel had a parliamentary spokesman in Bill Walker MP, who represented Perth and was a close friend. Walker, a teetotaller, launched a vociferous campaign for the independence of the leading whisky producer in his North Tayside constituency. He was a maverick character, and a loner in parliamentary circles. MPs on all sides of the House heard about Bell's plight ad nauseam as Walker made his own speeches, and interrupted ministerial speeches. He tabled an early day motion highlighting the alleged conflict of interest of Morgan Grenfell and claimed to have evidence suggesting a clear link between Morgan's and Bell's only 6 months earlier. He alleged that Morgan's had been plotting the downfall of Bell's for at least two years. In conjunction with fellow Scottish MPs, Walker met Alex Fletcher (now Sir Alex), the Trade Minister and Sir

Gordon Borrie, director of the Office of Fair Trading, who were urged to refer the Guinness offer to the Monopolies Commission.

Walker's efforts to defend Bell's and expose what he saw as a City cover-up were almost as dogged as Brian Sedgemore's probings on the Johnson Matthey scandal or Tam Dalyell's lone calls for an inquiry into the sinking of the *Belgrano*. But as one journalist put it cruelly: 'People took Brian and Tam seriously.'

Walker also alleged dirty tricks, claiming he'd been followed in London and had checked his suspicions by going up one escalator and down another. He believes investigations were made about his private life in New York and Washington, and friends at the Roosevelt Hotel in New York reported that questions had been asked about whether he'd had women in his room or indulged in heavy gambling. Walker also says he was leaned on by the Tory Whips Office to stop rocking the boat. He picked up hostile whisperings in the House of Commons tea room and was given a ticking off by the elders of his constituency assocation. Walker puts this down to the links between big business and the Tory party: 'It's normal in life that people will close ranks around their friends.'

While Walker waged his lone political battle, Raymond Miquel was closeted with his accountants and merchant bankers. On 12 July, Bell's were set to release their defence document, which would be the official counterblast to the Guinness offer. But Saunders outflanked Miquel by sending a letter to Bell's shareholders just hours before the release of Miquel's document. It restated his criticisms of Bell's marketing performance. Miquel's defence document drew attention to the profit margins on their premium blend which were at around 13.5% compared with an industry average of less than 10%. He promised shareholders a 50% dividend increase. The defence seemed perfectly sound and it was accepted that Warburg's had made a brave effort in the short time available to them. The City was relieved they had prevailed upon Miquel to lay off the nationalistic arguments in favour of hard financial realities.

The Guinness attacks on Bell's were fast and accurate. They drew attention in no uncertain terms to the lack of a profit forecast, and brushed off Miquel's criticism of Guinness' performance over the previous five years. What puzzled the opposition, however, was how accurately Guinness was pre-empting Bell's moves. In the light of later events, this puzzlement is easily explained.

The Bell's camp had no respite. On 14 July Morgan Grenfell announced they were to make three complaints to the Takeover Panel relating to statements made in the Bell's defence document. These mostly related to Miquel's attack on the running of Guinness, and alleged that Bell's had mis-stated the rate of growth of Guinness profits. Miquel countered by calling the action 'a smokescreen of misinformation', but he was to find that this was just the first of several instances when a public announcement by Bell's prompted a flood of complaints to the Takeover Panel.

The phoney war ended, and the battle for Bell's shares began in earnest (and for Ernest) when the Office of Fair Trading recommended that the Guinness bid for Bell's should be cleared. The Secretary of State for Trade and Industry, Norman Tebbit, then stated that there was no need for a reference to the Monopolies Commission. Not only was this yet another set-back for Miquel, it was also a watershed for industry in Scotland since it seemed to signal the end of Government regional policy. Scottish MPs were bitterly disappointed with Miquel, and accused him of not doing enough to lobby the Bell's case. They contrasted his defence with those mounted by Highland Distilleries and Royal Bank of Scotland in previous takeover battles.

Miquel's struggle to convince the OFT had been a fairly isolated one. Only one other Scotch whisky company boss spoke up for Bell's and made representations to Sir Gordon Borrie. That, ironically, was John MacPhail of Highland Distilleries, a long-standing business rival, who had built up the Famous Grouse brand so successfully that it overtook Bell's as market leader in Scotland. He and Miquel had started at Bell's as trainees together. Although they didn't get on there, when the chips were down, MacPhail came to Miquel's defence. 'At least MacPhail put in a word for him whereas nobody else did a thing, they just stood back and let him go to his fate,' said an analyst. Two English brewers, Vaux and Shepperd Neame, also backed Bell's by writing to Sir Gordon Borrie urging a Monopolies Commission Reference. They argued a takeover would harm regional interests and that the bid was a purely defensive move by Guinness to protect profitability. But their representations failed to sway the authorities.

So too did allegations made by Bill Walker in a speech in the House of Commons on 25 July, where he questioned the involvement of the Kuwait Investment Office, a secretive organisation who were emerging with key stakes in British companies. They were originally shareholders in the Gleneagles Hotel group and had subsequently taken a holding in Bell's. Walker claimed that the Kuwaitis had sold their stake to Guinness at a substantial loss on the understanding they'd be in a strong position to buy the Gleneagles Hotel if the Guinness bid succeeded. There is another explanation for the Kuwaitis' action, however. The Government of Kuwait had found out that their investment office had taken a stake in a purveyor of alcoholic drinks. As good Muslims, they ordered them to sell it off quickly.

Miquel now had to tackle Guinness head on. He questioned its management style, drawing attention to the role of Bain, the management consultants. He also pointed out that in the last four years there'd been three different main board directors overseeing financial management or strategy and he wanted to have clarified the status of Olivier Roux as a partner of Bain and a Guinness director. Saunders retorted: 'It is sad to see Mr Miquel's defence strategy sinking to the level of a daily diet of petty titbits masquerading as significant revelations.'

Other companies and financial institutions started to muscle in on the bid. On 2 August the Ladbroke Group revealed it had bought £9 million worth of Bell's shares, a 3.25% stake in the company. They paid above the prevailing market price in what was seen as a spoiling move. With their extensive hotel interests, Ladbroke were concerned about any change of ownership of Gleneagles. The chairman of Ladbroke Hotels, John Jarvis, made it clear that his company was not interested in a full-scale bid for Bell's but only wanted to create trading opportunities with the eventual victor of the takeover battle. At the present price he and his colleagues indicated that they would not accept the Guinness offer. Miquel remarked that he was very pleased to have the Ladbroke stake, apparently believing they would back him at the crucial count. But, like so many things, that was to slip away from him.

Miquel had one more chance to put his case, included in which would be the important profits forecast enabling shareholders to know how well the business, and therefore their shares, were going to perform in the coming year. His defence document had under stock exchange rules to be out by Monday 5 August, 39 days after the original offer document was dispatched.

The day dawned, progressed, and nothing had been heard from Bell's. Journalists were getting itchy by the afternoon when their stories needed to be written and they had no word from Perth. Eventually they gave up hope of writing anything, except the remarkable fact that nothing had appeared. Had Miquel given up the ghost, they wondered. Minutes before midnight the defence document was finally lodged with the Stock Exchange, the Takeover Panel and with the Guinness advisers.

An explanation needed to be found, and rumours began to circulate of a boardroom rift at Cherrybank. Guinness believed it was further evidence that Bell's had lost its way. Miquel claimed he had engineered the cliffhanger to outflank the opposition. If this was the case, it succeeded. Guinness had invested in half-page advertisements which were splashed across the Tuesday morning papers, rubbishing a defence document, news of which had not yet been reported. Miquel said the tactical ploy had been suggested by his advisers, Warburgs, who had produced a similar cliffhanger for Debenham's, facing a hostile bid from Burton's.

But Miquel also admitted that 'there was a lot of detail that had to be checked' which had delayed the release of the document. The need to check this detail arose because Bell's had suffered another *volte-face* by a key adviser. The company had brought in a market research agency specialising in the brewing industry to investigate Saunders' much-vaunted claim to have turned round the Guinness brand. The material was to be used as the heart of the Bell's defence document. But on the Saturday, as the finishing touches were being put to the paper, the agency withdrew their consent for their research to be used.

The Bell's defence document stated that profits of the company were likely to increase by only 6.5% to £37.5 million. Miquel acknowledged that this was less than some people had expected and he put it down to the fact that the refurbishment

of the Piccadilly Hotel had gone above budget. But he pointed
out that the New Piccadilly had reopened that week and that this
would be a platform for continuing growth.

The real carrot for his shareholders came in the form of a
bumper dividend payout. Shareholders were promised an
increase of 66% in the income on their shares. Guinness worked
hard to match these claims after the disappointment of the
mistimed advertising. They concentrated their fire on the profits
forecast and argued that earnings per share were actually set to
be unchanged for the third year running. In a press release
drummed up on the Tuesday morning, Guinness argued that
'the unsustainable increase in dividends highlights the board's
willingness to continue to milk the whisky brands at a time when
re-investment and re-focusing is desperately needed'.

Bell's dividend promise put Saunders under more pressure to
produce an increased offer. It had to come quickly to stay within
the Takeover Panel timetable. It duly came on Wednesday, 7
August. The new bid valued Bell's at more than £340 million
with each share worth a princely 258 pence. Saunders had
dipped deep into the Guinness coffers and was now offering to
pay almost twice Bell's market value of two months earlier.
Ladbroke who days before had explained their interest in Bell's
as a strategic investment in the hotel business quickly and
expediently succumbed, selling out their entire holding to
Morgan Grenfell in a profitable arbitraging operation.

If Saunders had any lingering doubts about his chances of
victory they were quickly to be dispelled by another astonishing
development behind the enemy lines — a defection of a key
director.

It came in an extraordinary way. Miquel rebuffed the revised
Guinness offer with his own statement, headlined 'Bell continues to reject Guinness'. It came from the Bell's board and was
drafted in exactly the same way as previous documents.had
been, purporting to speak for the whole board. This statement,
however provoked a quite unexpected reaction, not from
Guinness, whom it was meant to attack, but from his colleague
on the Bell's board and long-time adversary, Peter Tyrie.

Tyrie, who'd remained quiet since hostilities began in June,
released his own statement the same evening disowning the
original announcement from Miquel. He said it expressed a view
to which he didn't subscribe and that he'd be urging his

colleagues to recommend that shareholders accept the new offer. He concluded that 'until my colleagues come round to my view I shall be writing to Bell's shareholders giving the reasons for my decision in the course of the next few days'.

To already sceptical observers in the City and Fleet Street the Tyrie revelation rammed home the point that Bell's days as an independent company were numbered. While Miquel expressed shock and bewilderment at the open display of mutiny on board the Bell's ship, Guinness allies were jubilant as brokers quietly topped up their store of Bell's shares, taking their holding to more than 12%. Miquel described Tyrie's move as unilateral and certainly none of his five other boardroom colleagues appeared to be behind the insurrection.

The impression at the time was that Tyrie had been forced to take action because he hadn't been consulted about the statement 'Bell continues to reject Guinness', and because there had been no boardroom discussion about the new and increased bid. Tyrie, it was felt, was merely reacting to events and attempting to put the record straight. It's not clear, though, whether his decision to speak out in opposition to his own chairman was a spur of the moment reaction or the result of weeks of careful planning. What has emerged is that he engaged the services of an Edinburgh firm of financial advisers, Quayle Munro, to act on his behalf in negotiations with Guinness and their own advisers.

Quayle Munro had a close interest in the Bell's battle as they'd been instrumental in forming the company which first bought the three Scottish hotels from British Rail. Ian Quayle Jones, a director, acted for Gleneagles during the negotiations over the Piccadilly Hotel and was a friend and confidant of Peter Tyrie during his brief reign at Gleneagles. Jones shared Tyrie's opposition to the takeover by Bell's and his consequent dislike of Miquel. The two men kept in close contact and Jones advised Peter Tyrie on his position and himself consulted lawyers.

Jones argued that Tyrie was quite within his rights as a director to recommend what he believed was in the best interests of shareholders. And he felt that Tyrie's legal position was rock solid by the time that Guinness made their second, £340 million offer which Jones believed was 'way over the top' and irresistible.

It's now clear that Jones had several conversations with Noble Grossart, the chief merchant banking advisers to Guinness in Scotland. The main topic for discussion was the payment of fees incurred by Peter Tyrie in the course of his independent stand. An invoice for £50,979.61 (inc. VAT) was dispatched by Quayle Munro, but it was not sent to Tyrie himself but was addressed to the Bell headquarters at Cherry-bank in Perth. Of this total, £2,104 was listed as the cost of postage in sending out Tyrie's letter to shareholders which explained why he was breaking ranks and recommending them to accept the Guinness offer. The fees were broken down later to show that 133 hours' work had been done by one director (presumably Ian Jones) and 45 hours by another employee of the firm. It is hard to understand why all this work took place, unless it's assumed that Quayle Munro were acting for Tyrie for some time before mid-August.

The invoice was sent to Bell's in October, some weeks after Guinness had won control. This meant that it could be argued that Tyrie was simply getting his own employers to pay legitimate expenses incurred through his job as a director. In reality Guinness were picking up the tabs, as they now owned the Perth-based company. Tyrie knew that he could hardly submit the bill to Miquel so he must have been sure that Guinness would pay up. One insider described the contacts between Quayle Munro and Noble Grossart as simply 'discreet conversations'. Guinness director Shaun Dowling was later to query the £51,000 bill, remarking that 'it seemed a hell of a lot', and he asked for a full breakdown. Ian Jones eventually had to ring Olivier Roux to demand payment.

Tyrie's defection owed much to Ernest Saunders. The two met more than once before Tyrie finally broke cover, and it seems that Saunders provided Tyrie with every incentive to escape from captivity. The manager of Gleneagles was reassured that the future of his hotels would be safe under the new management. Saunders told him he would build up Gleneagles. Employment prospects were assured, and there was the likelihood of an increase in staff numbers. For Tyrie it was a wonderful opportunity to rid himself of the tutelage of Miquel, and Saunders seemed to be the right man to lead Gleneagles.

Opinions are divided on whether Tyrie acted properly as a director and in the best interests of shareholders. The Takeover

Code states that 'unless otherwise agreed with the Panel, there must be included in every offer document a statement as to whether or not any agreement . . . or understanding . . . exists between the offeror and any persons acting in concert with it and any of the directors . . . of the offeree company having any connection with or dependence on the offer.' Ian Jones maintains that he checked the drafts of Tyrie's circular with the Takeover Panel and they were cleared. He says there was no prior 'arrangement' as to fee and costs. But others feel Tyrie was delivering a stab in the back to Bell's and that his plan to support Guinness was carefully timed. The speed with which Saunders reacted to moves made by Miquel and his advisers led some observers to suspect that he had inside information.

After the Tyrie defection it was downhill all the way for Bell's. Clanger followed clanger. On 9 August the Bell's board met behind closed doors with the exception of Peter Tyrie who was barred from attending. After a five-hour meeting Miquel and his colleagues pronounced a unanimous rejection of the Guinness bid. But for the first time the door was left ajar for a possible White Knight to enter with an alternative offer; the board stated that they would only accept an offer 'which is compatible with the protection of Bell's business and employees'. Over the weekend speculation raged about a possible alternative bidder, with most commentators noting that any candidate would have a herculean task persuading the Office of Fair Trading to allow another bid to proceed. But on the Monday Miquel confused journalists by saying he still felt the company should remain independent, claiming that the board had been misunderstood after their meeting three days earlier. Shareholders would soon receive a letter indicating that Bell's would double profits within the next five years. The statement simply increased scepticism about Miquel's battle for independence; once again he'd shown himself out of his depth in mastering the details of his case. He lashed out at Scottish journalists for toeing the Guinness line; 'Wining and dining journalists is all part of the game,' was Miquel's conclusion.

Apart from arousing the wrath of the journalists who had no loyalties to Miquel anyway, his public pronouncements also earned him the rebuke of his old enemies, the Takeover Panel. Morgan Grenfell had picked up on Miquel's casual remark about profits doubling in five years and reported him. Bell's were forced to withdraw the statement and Miquel confirmed that he was indeed looking for another bidder. The final twist to the confusion over Bell's defence came with the extraordinary news that Rothmans International were being canvassed as the possible White Knights and saviours of Bell's. With Rothmans' South African connections this took Miquel into some very hot political water, and he disclaimed all knowledge of it. He failed to finally squash the rumours, until the eleventh hour when Rothmans chairman Sir Robert Crichton-Brown said there was no intention of making a bid.

Liberal leader David Steel also put in his two ha'p'orth for Guinness towards the end of the takeover; Guinness had bought Stobo Castle, which was in his constituency, for use as a health farm. It seemed to symbolise the defection of the last of any residual Scottish support for the Perth-based distiller. Closing date for the Guinness offer was Friday 23 August and the financial pages of almost all the newspapers were predicting a clear victory for Saunders and his team. Only the faithful Bill Walker, in a radio interview that morning, professed himself confident of Bell's chances. By 3 o'clock that afternoon Guinness declared victory, having won 70% of Bell's shares. This was no mean feat given the initial hostility to the bid.

At 5 o'clock Miquel held what was described as a dignified meeting with staff at Cherrybank. One employee remembers it. 'After he told us what happened he asked if there were any questions. There was only one: "Who has sold out?".' The answer appeared to be General Accident who had accepted the Guinness offer only minutes before the deadline. They were at pains to emphasise that they would decide the issue purely on financial grounds. It's understood the General Accident board allowed chief general manager Buchan Marshall to make the final decision. Bill Walker took a different view and accused General Accident of selling Bell's down the river. Walker claims to have copies of correspondence between Guinness and Sir Norman Macfarlane, who was on the board of General Accident. He says he's made these available to the Department of Trade Inspectors. Walker also alleges that Saunders offered Macfarlane the chairmanship of Bell's but he turned it down because Distillers were the biggest customer of his own company.

Another shareholder suspected of having accepted the Guinness offer at the last minute was the Gannochy Trust. But while many other institutions also backed Guinness, the Bank of Scotland pension fund did not. In the last stages of the battle, Saunders had contacted Sir Thomas Risk and asked him to instruct the fund trustees to accept the offer and exert similar influence over another shareholder, MSI, in which the Bank had an interest. Risk refused.

With the battle over and the start of an uneasy truce, speculation mounted about the future of the vanquished Raymond Miquel. To the surprise of the war correspondents now resting after the end of hostilities, Miquel chose to stay on. He did not stay long, and by December was gone. Tyrie was to last only until March the following year, departing without fulfilling his dreams of building up a worldwide hotel chain centred at Gleneagles. Contrary to his earlier assurances and promises, Saunders allowed the press to speculate about the future of not just the Piccadilly but also the North British and Caledonian Hotels. The Saunders star was at its highest and brightest. Few people looked hard at the huge price which Guinness had paid for Bell's. Rather they chose to believe the publicity and image portrayed by the chief executive.

CHAPTER FIVE

THE DECLINE OF DISTILLERS

The Scotch whisky industry could not be the same again once Guinness had taken over Arthur Bell. With a new large company entering the fray, attention was bound to turn to the industry leader, Distillers. The *Financial Times* Lex column commented on it the day after the Bell's takeover: 'If Raymond Miquel had taken over at Distillers, rather than Arthur Bell a decade ago, the Scotch whisky industry might now be in a healthier state.' The same column also observed that 'bid speculation was back in fashion, and even such mighty names as Allied Lyons, Boots and Distillers succumbed to the rumours'. How little did they know!

Distillers was a pillar of the Scottish establishment, and had allowed itself to think that its prestige put it out of reach of predators. Its long tradition, its wealth and its extensive list of top-quality brands conspired to persuade the management that it was impregnable. The men at the top in the 1980s saw themselves as the aristocrats of Scottish industry but, like the feudal lords of the middle ages, they had lost the ability to adapt. As one director admitted, the company had become a dinosaur in an age of fast-moving reptiles. But even in 1985, it was contributing 2% of British exports. Its product list was the envy of the industry. It read like the gathering of the brands — Dewars, Johnnie Walker, Haig, Buchanans, to name but four out of 30. There were also famous gins like Booth's and Gordon's, cognacs like Hine, the Cossack vodka, and Pimms. A gentleman's drinks cabinet could be amply stocked with Distillers brands alone.

The early days of Distillers could not have been more different. Two marketing pioneers, the Buchanan brothers, set up a business in the 1870s which was later to merge into Distillers. One brother made the whisky in Leith, near Edinburgh, while the other sold it where he could. Around 1880, he set his sights on London, but there the socially acceptable drink was brandy and soda. Buchanan had to do something different to show the socialites of the day that whisky was not merely the tipple of Scotland's crofters. He hired twelve young toffs to go into the bar of the Ritz hotel, and when everybody else was ordering their brandy and sodas, they demanded a Buchanans. The barman's jaw dropped, and he said, 'A what?'; 'A Buchanans, of course,' replied the toffs. 'I haven't got it,' replied the dumbfounded barman, at which the young toffs burst into laughter and proclaimed loudly: 'The Ritz hasn't got Buchanans.' From the Ritz they moved on to the Savoy and other London hotels. People began to mutter, 'What the hell is this new drink?', and the taste caught on. In a few years, the Buchanans realised that the neat malt whisky was a bit rough for refined palates, and they started blending it. A few years later, they began exporting. James Buchanan is still a major subsidiary company of Distillers.

Distillers like to date their beginning to the establishment of Buchanans, but the company in its pre-Guinness form is really 50 years younger than that. In 1926, the major whisky makers of the day, mostly private, family-owned businesses like Haig, Johnnie Walker and Dewars, merged into Distillers Company Limited. A couple of gin makers, Booth's and Tanqueray (makers of Gordon's) also joined.

But this was no ordinary merger, because what came out was a grouping of proud independent businesses who were linking merely to share some overheads. None had any intention of yielding autonomy to the umbrella Distillers company, and that was the way it continued for 60 years. Basic functions like the production of the neat spirit, the bottling and the buying of grain were shared, but marketing and selling remained quite separate. Distillers people administered the grouping but they were not expected to treat the company as an integrated whole over which they had strategic direction. This is explicitly stated by the last-but-one Distillers chairman, Robin Cater, who told a group of City analysts, to their dismay, 'Don't look to me for leadership, I'm only chairman of the trade co-operative.'

It was a curious arrangement which could only work while Distillers had a near world monopoly in the British, and indeed world, markets. Before the War it is no exaggeration to say that three-quarters of British whisky bought was Distillers, and they had probably an equal percentage of the world market. The latter was not very large at the time since whisky had mostly travelled with the flag and was little known outside the British Empire.

The Second World War put a different complexion on things. American GIs, for example, may have got their first taste of the stuff when they came over to Britain. They found they preferred it to their native Bourbon and Rye, took the news back home and Dewars took off in the States. The world market seemed to have an insatiable thirst for the drink. In the sixties the Japanese found a liking for White Horse, and in the seventies Europe and Africa took to Johnnie Walker. Distillers seemed to be able to do nothing wrong as each bottle of Johnnie Walker Black Label effortlessly brought £4 into the group coffers. Some 35% of the price of a bottle of Dewars was clear profit.

The success of Johnnie Walker, in fact, became quite a legend within the company. The story is told of a visit by the Distillers manager for West Africa to his agent in Benin. To his amazement, the manager saw that the sales of Johnnie Walker had shot up five times on the previous year. He asked the agent what his secret was, since Benin had a mere two million population and he claimed to be selling 100,000 cases of the stuff. The agent tried to duck the question, the Distillers man did not want to press, but he asked if he needed any additional marketing or sales support. The agent said: 'Well yes, I could do with some motor boats. You see at the moment I am having to take the bottles across the river to Nigeria by canoe, and motor boats would make it quicker and easier.' It appeared that wealthy Nigerians regarded Johnnie Walker as a more secure investment than their currency, and were laying the drink down in bulk.

In the sixties, Distillers suffered a public relations disaster from which, arguably, it never fully recovered. In an attempt to diversify out of its strictly drinks base, it bought the marketing rights to the Thalidomide drug — a tranquilliser which was given to pregnant women. The disastrous side-effects are well-recorded. The management at the time, who were typically retiring Scots gents, were completely out of their depth. 'It absolutely destroyed the men and the board,' said one recent director. Distillers swapped its drugs interest for BP shares, which they have sold off over the years, making a tidy gain in the process.

The first sign of looming decline for the company and for whisky in general appeared in the seventies, when wine and white spirits like Bacardi, vodka, gin became increasingly popular, tempting drinkers away from their favourite blend. It seemed to some, in retrospect, that the 100-year cycle of whisky might be coming to an end. The seventies were also a time of major problems in world trading conditions, the oil-price hike, currency fluctuations and the like, and these all hurt the great whisky maker. It was bad for the company when South American currencies were devalued; some of their best customers were the élite in the military dictatorships. South Africa was another good market, but that, too, was under political pressure. Most detrimental of all was the ruling of the EEC that a company could not charge one price for a product in its home market, and another price elsewhere in the community — so-called parallel pricing. Distillers for years had kept the price of its Johnnie Walker whisky higher overseas. At home it had to compete with the likes of Bell's and Famous Grouse, and was priced accordingly. With the EEC ruling, Distillers decided to withdraw Johnnie Walker from the UK. 'We couldn't afford to sell it on the Continent at UK prices, and we would not have sold any at home at the prices we sold it abroad.' The company had no alternative to its eventual plan of action, although it lobbied very hard inside the EEC. Annual reports record the anger and frustration of the board, especially as some EEC countries applied discriminatory taxes to Scotch whiskies to protect their own drinks industries.

The absence of Johnnie Walker hit Distillers' share in the UK, which fell between 1974 and 1984 from 54% to 20%.

World market share was also under attack, especially from the Japanese, and this by the mid-eighties was down to below 40%.

Distillers needed a brand in the UK with which to replace Johnnie Walker, but in a disappointing, but typical piece of strategic lethargy, none was forthcoming. So other whiskies marched in. There came Bell's, unknown in the sixties, managed with a vengeance by the aggressive Raymond Miquel. Highland Distilleries' Famous Grouse flew in. This was a new, slightly up-market brand, specially developed, which shortly overtook Bell's as the market leader in Scotland. Distillers was nowhere, and it did nothing to correct the situation except take a look at its marketing operations which had not changed for 50 years. Some rationalisations were sought for the overlapping brand sales departments. Each brand had its own expensive building in central London to impress its own agents who looked to Distillers as representatives of an earlier Imperial glory.

Sadly, the managers of the company had hardly noticed that Imperial glory was not enough to sell the brand, and they stuck with their buildings. But the rot had gone deeper; change company-wide had become near impossible. There simply were not the existing mechanisms to effect it, nor the will to introduce new ones. The way board meetings were administered gives some idea of the company style. According to a regular attender at the meetings, no papers were ever circulated before because, at some time in the 1920s or '30s, a member of the board had left his papers in a taxi. 'This was so traumatic that secrecy became the motto. Board meetings became rather absurd because you didn't have an agenda until you got there.' The full board would always look back at the previous month's trading performance, but never at planning for the next one. It was intensely frustrating for some of the slightly more dynamic directors, who made noises about it, but the inertia was too great for action to be implemented.

The executive running of the company was also anachronistic. Management by committee was deeply ingrained, and just as Tony Purssell had his ineffectual management committee at Guinness, so Distillers had theirs. In both cases, it was a recipe for disaster.

But the Distillers directors were a caricature of the gentleman businessman. They were 'very nice and polite', often accomplished at golf — membership of the Scottish Muirfield club was *de rigueur* — and they were, as one observer put it, 'slightly snooty and snobby'. Most had come up through whisky production. Two exceptions were the non-executives Sir Wiliam Pile (61 years old), who had a distinguished Civil Service career, and The Lord Maclean (69). Pile actually rises to the defence of his executive colleagues: 'They ran a business on the old-fashioned principles of knowing people. They had built whisky to a point where it was selling to 140 countries and it was an enormous overseas earner for Britain. All in all, it was a remarkable achievement of these rather gentlemanly chaps in their tweeds.'

By the eighties, they were despised by the Scottish community where the company had its official base, and by the City and financial establishment who had lost all faith in their management ability. The local community rarely saw the managers outside the board meetings, which alternated between Edinburgh and London. The top men played no part in local community interests, the management of hospitals or schools, for example. In fact, only four out of the sixteen board members lived in Scotland at all. The rest lived in the home counties around London, in elegant, comfortable houses alongside most other executives of Southern-based businesses.

The City treated the company with kid gloves. Everybody knew it had major problems and that nobody was tackling them, but it had an awesome reputation; according to John MacLachlan, chairman of the National Association of Pension Funds investment committee, 'They were a Scottish pillar of the establishment, and a vital earner for UK Ltd.' The institutional investors who followed the company at no time felt confident enough about planning a coup to topple the management, much though they might have wished it. Instead, they took their dividends, which were good, and waited for someone to come along and sort it out. They now realise they have to bear some of the responsibility for the subsequent mess; earlier action might have set the company on a better business footing.

In fact, on the surface profits looked substantial, and had risen satisfactorily. In 1976 they stood at £103 million on turnover of £700 million and by 1985 they were £233 million on £1.3 billion. But in view of the massive assets, in terms of stocks and property, the City believe they could have been double that with the right sort of strategic thinking at the helm.

In September 1983, there arrived at the top a man who may have given the City some hope that things would at last change at Distillers. John Connell certainly looked the very model of an old-fashioned Distillers director; he smoked a pipe, would be photographed in tweeds and was unassuming and polite. One colleague described him as 'an intelligent and good man with a great deal of knowledge about drinks around the world'. But he was also somewhat tougher than the bosses the company had been used to, perhaps because he had grown up in the less pampered gin business rather than in whisky. He was educated at Stowe School and Christ Church, Oxford, before following in his father's footsteps through the ranks of Tanqueray. But while his father had only run the gin business, Connell had gone one better and been given the chair of the whole company, the first 'gin man' to reach the top.

Now he could wrestle the company out of the grip of the old-style Distillers directors. It was not to be. An early act was the introduction for the first time of a public relations agency, Streets Financial. They wanted to do some research to see how Distillers was viewed in the financial sector. The board balked at the idea, perhaps fearing what they might discover. But Connell did tackle the problem of overstocking and excess capacity by closing down bottling halls long redundant following the market downturn of the seventies. That marked a significant change from the old style of paternalistic management which preferred inefficiency to unpopularity with the workforce. The timing was not good for Connell, as it happened, because an announcement of redundancies coincided with a hike in the dividend and a doubling of his own salary to £116,000. 'He lost Scotland with that,' believes one observer.

Connell also saw the risk to the company of its dependence on spirits and created an acquisition committee. He began to look around for a diversification. Little booklets appeared at directors' places at board meetings, summarising possible takeover candidates. One such takeover candidate that provoked some interest was Scottish and Newcastle Brewery. Another was the Bank of Scotland. Victoria Wines was considered because of the obvious advantage to the company of having control over its major outlets. Lemonade companies, health food companies, even health clubs, were mooted. But the discussion never progressed beyond the point where somebody would wonder out loud whether diversification wasn't too risky, and the subject was dropped.

David Connell, the chairman's brother, had more grasp than most of his colleagues, even those who had responsibility for planning, of the strategic need to buy out of whisky, but his expertise was in whisky and he did not carry enough clout. One major acquisition was made at this time. Somerset Importers, the American distributor of Johnnie Walker, was bought in 1984 for a relatively cheap $250 million. It was partially a defensive move in answer to the acquisition by Bell's of their American distributor, but it also helped Distillers get a handle on the lucrative but unruly US market, where Mafia influences, dating back to Prohibition days, were once evident. Distillers' Dewars brand was distributed by the Meshulam Riklis' Schenley company, a key player in future events. Matters at Distillers were not helped by the low level of advice the board received. They were not over-endowed with financial talent internally, and the 'wet' (as one observer put it) merchant bank seemed the last straw.

In 1985 there appeared on the horizon a solution to Distillers' diversification problems. It was in the form of a merger with the major food concern Allied Lyons, which had just escaped the clutches of Elders. For the three months of June, July and August, John Connell was deep in discussion with Allied chairman Sir Derrick Holden-Brown. The subject never reached either board before the talks were called off, following a mutual agreement that each business was too bitty for any use to come of the link. But there is no doubt the talks were extremely serious and indicate that Connell was well aware of Distillers' vulnerability to a hostile predator. He kept word of the talks very close to his chest, telling just a few of his fellow directors. He may have felt that the forces of reaction on the board would seek to squash such an apparently drastic move. However, these were the vital three months before Gulliver pounced, and the fact that it took so long to realise that nothing was going to come of it again throws into some doubt the value of the finacial advice available to Connell, as well as his own strategic grasp. These discussions were, in effect,

Distillers' last gasp. It now had to move very fast to stay out of the grasp of predators, and like every dinosaur, it stumbled on the way.

CHAPTER SIX

GULLIVER'S TRAVELS

For James Gulliver, the control of Distillers was the fulfilment of a lifetime's dream, as well as a massive management and financial challenge. The dream had its origins in his Scottish childhood, as Gulliver describes: 'I'd known something of Distillers from my boyhood because I grew up in a Scottish town called Campbeltown in the West Highlands, which is a distilling town. I was conscious, therefore, of Distillers and I knew in my teens some of the whisky brands because they were important to the area. As my career progressed, I began to realise how badly Distillers was run.'

A gap of 40 years separates Gulliver's youthful interest in the company from his bid to assume of overall control. In the early part of his career, while Distillers were foundering, Gulliver was establishing himself as a formidable food retailer. Most potted accounts of his life and travels begin by saying that he was 'a grocer's son from Campbeltown' who went on to run his own grocery chain. This does not give him credit for a high-flying education and some early management experience. He was later to show that he could run successfully several different kinds of business.

Gulliver feels he owes much to his Scottish roots, and he has made no effort to disguise his soft west-coast brogue. People on the west coast of Scotland, in return, regard him as the neighbourhood boy made good. The tousle-haired, thick-set and soft-spoken entrepreneur is talked about with affection in the bars of Argyllshire, with some wonder, and perhaps not a little envy. His employees may not hold him in such fond regard, as he has always had the reputation for being a hard taskmaster. But to his peers in business he is a strategist par excellence, who builds and dreams the future of businesses.

Gulliver went from Campbeltown Grammar School to Glasgow University where he gained a first-class honours degree in engineering in 1953. Then he won a prestigious Fulbright scholarship to the Georgia Institute of Technology in Atlanta, where he took a Master of Science Degree. A four week course in marketing for managers at Harvard was later misrepresented as a degree in Gulliver's *Who's Who* entry, getting him into hot water at the time of the Distillers bid. But even without Harvard initials after his name, by the age of 24 Gulliver had more academic credentials than most managers, certainly more than Ernest Saunders, who took a dull second at Cambridge.

After a short service commission in the Navy, Gulliver joined management consultants Urwick Orr for his first commercial experience. His clients there included Jaguar and Helena Rubenstein. But the precocious Gulliver was in a hurry to get into a senior management role. 'By the time I was 33 I felt ready to take a job as a chief executive,' he says. Others agreed, and he was offered and took the job of managing director at Headway Construction, a subsidiary of grocery company Fine Fare. A year later Gary Weston, who ran the parent company Associated British Foods, put him in charge of the whole of Fine Fare. In 1964, when Gulliver moved in, the supermarket chain was losing £300,000 a year. By 1972, Fine Fare was making profits of £5 million. The *Guardian* newspaper recognised his achievement by making him their Young Businessman of the Year.

Gulliver now began to look around for his own organisation. He had never had any interest in working for others; like the classic entrepreneur he was no conformist. He also wanted to own a business, and not be indebted to others. It looked as if this might be possible when Gary Weston proposed floating off Fine Fare on the market, but this plan was shelved and Gulliver went in search of a new company. He discovered Oriel

Foods, a company which had just come out of some financial problems, borrowed £1 million, and bought a 30% stake. He also persuaded his old colleague, Alistair Grant, who had been Fine Fare's marketing director, to join him. Grant, the retailer, extrovert and personable, complemented well the deep-thinking Gulliver. The last figure in the triumvirate which later aspired to overturn Distillers came on the scene when Gulliver set about arranging the loan to buy into Oriel. Helping him put the deal together was David Webster, at that time working at the merchant bank, William Brandt. Within a year he had joined Gulliver and Grant at Oriel. Webster, a Scot like Gulliver and Grant, was the financial brain. He is shrewd, diffident, and bookish, reading military history for relaxation.

In 1974 Oriel sold out to the American corporation RCA for £11 million but the three men stayed on to build up a European arm. Three years later they left in search of new ventures. Gulliver had to find a different area of business because RCA had required him to sign a document in which they agreed not to return to the food sector for three years. In April 1977 they went into double glazing with the acquisition of Alpine Holdings. This was done through a new company, James Gulliver Associates which, over the next six years, evolved into the Argyll Group.

Alpine was a considerable success for the three men, who were already very rich through their Oriel deal. Its value on the market was £1.9 million when they bought it, but six years later, when they sold out to the Hawley Group, Alpine was worth £16 million. In that time only 10% more shares had been issued, so the stake owned by Gulliver, Grant and Webster had barely been diluted and they had made another mint. In 1979, the three men went to the rescue of the meat business Louis C Edwards, and that gave them a foothold in the food business again. It also took Gulliver on to another board — Manchester United Football Club, which Louis Edwards owned. Gulliver became a regular supporter.

In the course of the Louis Edwards deal, Gulliver and the team met up with merchant bank Samuel Montagu who were later to play a key role in putting together the bid for Distillers. Montagu's Rupert Faure Walker was impressed by the three men whom he found 'hard-working, sincere, and thoroughly capable'. Walker approved of the way Gulliver had built and retained a management team. 'He creates a demanding and a very stimulating atmosphere to work in. He is a brilliant manager of people.'

There followed two daring takeovers which showed the City that Gulliver was a tycoon to be watched. In early 1981 he bought back Oriel Foods from RCA for just under £20 million in cash. And in 1982 he confidently took over a company far bigger than his own when he arranged the purchase of Allied Suppliers from Sir James Goldsmith for £104 million. It was a low price for a disparate collection of grocery shops ranging from superstore Prestos, to more mundane corner shops like Liptons. Gulliver concentrated on the development of large Presto stores, cutting back on the hundreds of smaller shops. The fast-growing Presto chain was to be the centrepiece of the Argyll Group, formed in November 1983.

Like Sir James Goldsmith, Gulliver was later to be deemed a fair target for *Private Eye*. The satirical magazine observed 'that the Gulliver publicity machine has taken Fleet Street by storm and that few City hacks have bothered to examine the details of his rapid ascent'. They chronicled allegations about share dealings while he was a director of Alpine and saucy anecdotes about his private life.

Gulliver had acquired another business along the way which was to take on greater prominence in 1985. In 1981 he negotiated control of Amalgamated Distilled Products whose brands later included George Morton whisky and OVD rum. Originally ADP was run separately from the food companies, but in 1983 it was brought into the newly established Argyll Group. In the light of this, accusations made during the Distillers bid that Gulliver was a mere retailer were inaccurate. Distillers deputy chairman, Bill Spengler, was to sneer: 'Gulliver deals in potatoes and cans of beans. We are not selling brown water in cheap bottles. We are selling Scotch.'

As we have seen, drinks businesses had interested Gulliver since his youth, and now that his own business was of a certain size he could begin to contemplate an assault on one of the industry majors. He saw many poor managements in the area, but the worst of the lot, and therefore the biggest attraction, was Distillers. 'A number of the drinks companies in Britain were not very well managed, but Distillers was particularly inefficient, and had failed to provide leadership to the rest of the industry,' Gulliver later observed.

Webster confirms the importance to Argyll of the drinks business, 'We recognised that in the long term our drinks business needed to get much bigger. We felt that we had substantially achieved that on our food side. But in our drinks business we knew we needed to make a major move.'

The Argyll trio had their first serious discussion with their advisers about an assault on Distillers in early 1984. The City men were keen but felt that, after four years of frenetic growth, they should stay off the acquisition trail and prove they had the existing businesses under control. So the Gulliver team waited another year. In that time their profits grew, the share price strengthened, and the Argyll reputation increased.

Argyll was getting most of its advice at this time from long-standing merchant bank Montagu's, and from Charterhouse. Webster was friendly with Charterhouse managing director, Victor Blank, and his advice was sought early on about a bid for Distillers. Blank also recruited to Argyll the Royal Bank of Scotland.

By April 1985 the Distillers file was being dusted down and an in-house acquisition team of eight was set up. Gulliver, Webster and Grant set aside almost half their management time for planning an assault on the whisky giant, which was almost three times the size of the Argyll group: 'What we were contemplating was like climbing Everest,' opined one insider.

Ernest Saunders may have considered Distillers himself, even at this time, but he told journalists and stock market analysts that the company was too big for Guinness to contemplate, and he would be sticking to Bell's in the foothills in Perth.

The Argyll intelligence operation was top secret. Distillers were code named Ascot because of the old joke that the directors lived there rather than in Scotland, and Argyll were named Angus. A photographer was sent round all the main Distillers plants and sales outlets and 300 colour slides were assembled. The Argyll team were able to draw upon stockbrokers' circulars on Distillers dating back to 1970. They picked their way through annual reports and made searches for further information at Companies' House, where all firms are compelled by law to lodge details of their annual reports and results. That in itself was a mammoth task, since Distillers had 80 subsidiary companies. They were helped in their research by the firm of Scottish-based brokers Wood Mackenzie.

They did not have to look too far to see the company's problem. Said Webster, 'We discovered that it was a manufacturing- and production-oriented business without sales or marketing skills. Traditionally they didn't have to sell in the home market, they just supplied it. The overseas markets were mostly run on an agency basis, and that bred arrogance and complacency.'

The research completed, the team put their findings into a shape that could be presented to City analysts and backers. There were three styles of presentation. There was the so-called 'maxi' lasting five hours which consisted of a sweeping analysis of the world Scotch and gin markets. It included a history of Distillers, a look at the company's performance, an analysis of consumer research on Distillers brands, and a detailed five-year financial projection with balance sheet and cash flows. The presentation was lightened by the use of illustrations — diagrams on slides, and photographs of the numerous Distillers buildings.

For those who didn't have the stamina to sit out five hours, there was a shorter 'midi' and even more condensed 'mini' version. The Argyll team, said Webster, 'sweated blood on the presentations', and it paid off. Drinks analysts were impressed. Said one: 'Gulliver had gone through this company with a fine toothcomb, and he had all the figures. He went through all the duplications of the various operating companies and the waste of resources there, the fact that they all had their central head offices in London. It was very, very professional.'

Gulliver happened to meet John Connell socially in the spring of 1985, in the bar at the Savoy Hotel in London. The two got on to the subject of whisky and Connell seemed interested in discussing the sale of Distillers brands through Argyll supermarkets. They arranged a lunchtime meeting, which also took place in the Savoy. Connell was so keen on the idea that he invited Gulliver to Distillers House to discuss commercial links between the two companies. Gulliver, Grant, and Webster met their Distillers counterparts but failed to reach agreement. One insider feels that even if Connell hadn't gained much from the contacts, Gulliver would not have missed this opportunity to learn more about Distillers' market share.

Gulliver was also strengthening his position with some of the leading figures of the Scottish business world around this time. He did the rounds of the great and the good, carrying more conviction because he was a member of the Scottish Economic Council. His leading Edinburgh merchant bank, Noble Grossart, put him in touch with the top Scottish financiers long before Saunders began his own lobbying over Bell's. One place where he had a good reception was the Scottish Office, which loathed Distillers because of their aloof attitude to the Scottish community. He paid particular attention to Dr Gavin McCrone, the permanent secretary and the chief economic adviser to the industry department for Scotland. Thirty or more Conservative MPs were entertained and contact was made with Liberal MPs Jo Grimond and Clement Freud. Some of Distillers' food manufacturing subsidiaries were in Freud's Ely constituency, and he wrote to Gulliver offering support.

The Argyll team watched with interest from the sidelines as Saunders and Miquel fought over Bell's. Webster was surprised, and at first concerned, by the Guinness bid, 'but quite quickly one saw that if Saunders got Bell's what he had done was knock himself out of the ring for Distillers'. In the latter stages of the battle for Bell's, Gulliver was asked by Warburg's to meet to discuss a possible rescue move. He and Webster met Raymond Miquel and Michael Smith of Warburg's at the Sheraton Park Tower hotel in London. When they were asked whether they were interested in coming in as a White Knight, the Argyll duo pretended that they did not know enough about the whisky business to take over a whisky company, but they also said that the price required to top Saunders' terms would be far too high. 'My own view,' says Gulliver, 'was that Saunders made a fatal error in the sense that he was buying a brand which was already successful and paying a top price for it.' Press speculation about a possible move by Argyll led Gulliver eventually to write to Saunders reassuring him that Argyll were not interested in Bell's.

By the time Saunders was celebrating victory on the night of 23 August 1985, Gulliver and Webster had other more pressing matters to worry about than the fate of Arthur Bell. They were waiting for a phone call giving them the green light for the unveiling of the Distillers bid. The man at the other end of the line was to be Arnold Weinstock, boss of the engineering giant GEC, who was expected to play a key role in the financing of the operation. Weinstock was a very powerful force in the City, and his company also had an enormous mountain of cash of its own.

The chief role planned for GEC was as underwriter of some of the £800 million of new shares which would have to be issued, if Argyll were going to be able to reach the £1.5 billion tag they were placing on the company. This still meant they would have to borrow a vast £600 million — the size of Argyll's market capitalisation — but without the underwriting of GEC, Distillers was out of reach. Weinstock was in effect saying that if investors did not want to stump up the money for the shares Argyll would have to issue to make the bid, he would buy them up himself. Weinstock was accepting a lot of risk, but he would receive in return generous fees, based on a percentage of the amount he underwrote. It was the traditional banker's role, but the industrialist appeared ready to be a pioneer.

The Argyll advice on having a major backer looks unnecessary in the light of later, equally highly geared bids. At the time they were bidding, however, the 'leveraged bid' where the company has to borrow a very large amount in comparison to its size, had not entered the UK, although Australians like Elders and Bond were already experimenting. With GEC behind him, Gulliver felt his own highly experimental arrangement would carry more weight.

The way GEC entered the fray at all was curious. It came through the City's most blue-blooded bank, Lazards. Ian MacGregor, the hammer of Arthur Scargill and a Lazards man by profession, appeared to have heard of Gulliver's interest in Distillers, and phoned him with a proposition. As a fellow-Scot he wondered whether Gulliver was concerned by the performance of Distillers and whether he'd had a closer look at the company. Gulliver was puzzled that MacGregor seemed to know of his intentions. But he assumed it was purely coincidental and that MacGregor was merely concerned about a Scottish business that was being badly run. Gulliver was told that Lazards might be able to help out through what they claimed was a close connection with the mighty GEC.

Now Argyll already enjoyed close relationships with merchant banks Samuel Montagu and Charterhouse, but when

Lazards intervened, he put them on the back burner, and waited to hear the GEC story. On the surface it looked good. For a start, GEC actually owned 4% of the Distillers shares.

Weinstock had bought these in the belief that he could influence the sleepy management to change its ways. He had taken some criticism for his massive cash mountain, and he felt turning round inefficient businesses might be a way of deflecting this. In fact, he had already approached the Distillers management to see if they were interested in some sort of joint venture, but they had flatly turned him down. He then went to Grand Metropolitan to see if its management would be interested in taking over Distillers. But they declined. He now saw an Argyll takeover as one possible solution to the Distillers problem. As the master of takeover strategy in the early sixties, when he completely reshaped the British electrical industry, Weinstock knew every trick of the trade.

Through friends of Gulliver's and Webster's at GEC — Malcolm Bates and Philip Ralph — meetings were arranged with Weinstock at GEC's Mayfair headquarters, just around the corner from Argyll's Chesterfield Hill head office. Soon a daring plan started to emerge. GEC would act as major financial backers, not only committing their 4% stake to the Argyll cause but also providing almost half of the vitally important underwriting. The Weinstock name would be behind the venture, and that would give it strong credibility when it was unveiled to the City. Gulliver and associates were breaking new ground, and they hoped the GEC factor would convince the doubters and reassure Argyll's own stockbrokers, Rowe and Pitman and Panmure Gordon, who were understandably nervous of such a large undertaking.

By the beginning of July, Argyll was confident all was well. The discussion with Weinstock had been positive and he seemed to be interested. Certainly, Lazards felt GEC were serious. Gulliver started to raid the Stock Market for Distillers shares, picking them up for under £3 apiece. He stopped when he had acquired just over 1% because at that stage he believed he was acting in concert with GEC, and a combined stake of over 5% would have had to be declared under company law. The next stage was the full bid, and for this Gulliver needed the commitment of Weinstock.

By the middle of August nothing had been heard from the great man, and Gulliver was beginning to get worried. He was itching to announce the bid but was finding it impossible to get in touch with Weinstock. Malcolm Bates at GEC was sure all was well, but he was powerless until the managing director's seal of approval had been granted. Unfortunately, this had to wait because Weinstock was incommunicado. His own management, intermediaries at Lazards, and Gulliver himself, were all in the dark as to his intentions.

During the long delay, Gulliver found he had to provide more information to GEC. The company had numerous committees, each ferreting around and collecting information on which Weinstock could base his decisions. There was a suggestion later that Weinstock was unobtainable for a full three weeks in August because he had gone on his annual pilgrimage to the Salzburg festival. In fact Weinstock said he spent just one night at Salzburg and all told was out of the office six working days during the month. There was also the unfounded suggestion he had spent long hours at Deauville — the French Mecca of horseracing.

This led one colleague to advise Gulliver to watch the weather to assess his chances of getting a reply. 'If you look out of the window and it's raining, you'll almost certainly get a decision because Arnold will be in the office. If it's fine, I doubt that you will because he'll be at Deauville watching his horses.' Weinstock's interest in horses was well known and something of a laughing stock among people who had seen his teleprinter wire in his office to check the results.

By 20 August nerves were on edge at the Argyll headquarters in Mayfair. Rumours were beginning to emerge about a bid for Distillers and the share price of the spirits giant was rising. Still no word from Weinstock.

On the Bank Holiday weekend in England, when Ernest Saunders was toasting his acquisition of Bell's and resting after his long campaign, Argyll held a council of war with their advisers, Lazards, Montagu's, Charterhouse and Noble Grossart, in order to work out a plan of action. 'There were four merchant banks and a steamy weekend,' recalls Webster, 'and phonecalls all over the place.' When City dealers returned to their desks on the Tuesday morning, offices were abuzz with talk of someone building up an interest in Distillers. The

Distillers price raced upwards and that week gained 47 pence
to reach an all time high of 360 pence. One block of ten million
Distillers shares changed hands at 375 pence each. It was a
critical time for Gulliver who could see his prey slipping out of
sight as he waited for the elusive Weinstock. Gulliver was
convinced that someone had deliberately revealed Argyll's
plans: 'We were badly let down by certain people who knew of
our intentions and clearly leaked it to others for their own
benefit.'

On the Thursday of that week, the Argyll team instructed
Lazards to contact the Takeover Panel; it was clear that
something had to be done to squash the speculation and take
the heat out of the Distillers share price. The Panel thanked
Lazards and asked that some sort of clarifying statement should
be made to clear the air. The Panel indicated that they didn't
mind what was said but they insisted the statement was out by
Monday. Argyll and advisers were set for another steamy
weekend.

By now it was pretty clear to Gulliver that Weinstock was not
going to play ball. On the weekend of 31 August /1 September,
calls were put through both to his Wiltshire home and to the
London office, but they went unanswered. So Gulliver and
Webster had to decide with their advisers whether they could
make a bid without the support of GEC. By the Saturday
evening they had rejected the idea. On the Sunday, Lazards
spoke to members of the Takeover Panel to agree the text of the
statement to go out the following day. The words agreed are
now infamous: 'Argyll, does not intend to make an offer for
Distillers *at the present time*.' (Authors' italics.) The Panel
insisted that there had to be a clear understanding of 'the
present time' and Lazards, after consulting Gulliver and
Webster, agreed that a period of three to four months was
appropriate. The Argyll men felt that it would take at least
three months to 'warm up GEC'. Soon they deeply regretted
giving their consent to that interpretation of the agreement.

The statement was released by Lazards on Monday, 2
September 1985, the day when James Gulliver and associates
should have been announcing the largest and most daring
takeover bid ever seen in the UK. Most observers in the City
were shocked and confused. One banker put it thus: 'Nobody
really understood that statement and thought it might have

been done to throw the hounds off the scent.' Some took the view that Gulliver should have either denied any interest or intention or stated that he did plan to bid within a certain period. At Panmure Gordon, Argyll's brokers, one analyst apparently ran through the office with his head in his hands when he discovered what Lazards had agreed with the Panel. Another observer called it 'a stupid statement'. Later Argyll might have reflected on the cost of sticking too closely to the rules of the takeover game

Argyll say they agreed to the three- or four-month embargo because they could see no way of bidding without GEC. Webster quickly realised that a mistake had been made. 'Within 24 hours we knew that we didn't need a GEC. Market sentiment was such that the phone never stopped, calls from brokers and indeed other banks saying the money can be raised. We were moving into the era of the leveraged bid when the David could go for the Goliath and no one had fully realised that.'

That weekend was to prove critical for the futures of Argyll, Distillers and, arguably, of Guinness. It is almost certain that if Gulliver had sprung his bid on the Monday or soon afterwards he would have toppled Distillers. One broker's view is that 'if he'd have gone ahead then, and been allowed to go ahead, there is no doubt he not only would have acquired Distillers, he would also have acquired it very much more cheaply. Guinness, having just taken over Bell's, would not have been in a position to attempt, or even consider, being a participant in that bid.' A price at that time of £4 per Distillers share might have been enough. In the end, Distillers went for almost double that.

James Gulliver has been criticised for making the costly mistake of deciding to delay for three months. Arguably he was too cautious and should have taken the risk of going it alone without the support of GEC. But he was acting on advice from City professionals. Heads later rolled at Lazards in connection with the bank's role in planning the bid. Whatever, the mix-up over GEC scuppered Argyll's chances of a quick takeover of Distillers. Argyll quietly parted company with the services of Lazards, and Samuel Montagu resumed their position as leading merchant bankers.

The reasons for GEC's curious failure to commit themselves to Argyll remain a mystery. Gulliver has suggested an explanation for Weinstock's apparent change of mind: 'I think it was a slightly unusual transaction for him anyway, it wasn't a straight investment. We were also asking him to play a role as a core underwriter and that is something he had never done before. It's traditionally a City occupation, and he probably began to feel uneasy about the possible risk involved.' Another Argyll insider is more critical of the man who'd built up one of the country's biggest conglomerates and leading employers: 'I think he's lost his bottle.' Rupert Faure Walker sums up the feeling in the Argyll camp. 'We felt let down.'

But Lord Weinstock's recollection of events is very different. He indicates unease about James Gulliver's capabilities: 'Ian Macgregor introduced Gulliver to us, with a view to our helping him make a bid for Distillers. We thought, as a shareholder, something ought to be done. Although they had made a few moves in the right direction, it was really very little and we still felt they weren't going to run the company properly.

'When Gulliver wanted to do something, we thought in principle we ought to help him, but he translated this into a proposition to underwrite £350 million of Argyll stock on terms which were remarkably unattractive to us. This was turned down within ten minutes of my people putting the detailed proposition on my desk.

'All the same, we said we would help, and that he could tell other investors we were willing to join in. But we were not going to put up £350 million with the chance of being locked in with Argyll and maybe unable to get out. That would not have been a sensible use of our cash reserves.' Whoever was at fault, the ludicrous misunderstanding over who would pay was to reshape the course of the battle for Distillers.

There was time for one last appeal to the Takeover Panel to relax the conditions agreed on 1 September. Argyll claimed that the time-scale should be reduced because there was no useful purpose in making them wait three months. The Distillers share price was edging higher every day and there were rumours of a counter bid in the offing from the American drinks corporation Seagrams. But the Panel refused, emphasising the need for companies to stick to the spirit of public statements. Once again the Takeover Panel had made an important and contentious intervention and shaped the future course of a bid. Argyll were left to lick their wounds and regret the day they'd been seduced with offers of help by Ian MacGregor and Lazards. The phoney war had begun.

CHAPTER SEVEN

THE PHONEY WAR

On the fateful weekend at the end of August, John Connell was on holiday in a hotel on the South Coast. He was unaware of any threat to his company and knew no more than what he had read in the newspapers about the rise in the Distillers share price. He was shocked to find out that the potential predator was the Argyll Group, whom he'd previously considered as a possible ally. Other Distillers board members reacted with a mixture of surprise and hostility. Finance director Bob Temple was reported to have said: 'Who'd want to take us over with our problems?' Some took the view that Gulliver would have trouble raising the cash, but generally there was relief that Argyll had been put into purdah. Gulliver's reputation was well known and as one director put it, 'He was quite a different kind of person than would have been associated with Distillers'. They were all horrified at the thought of being taken over by a food retailer: 'Our business was one of selling a luxury product in 140 countries outside the UK and his was selling low-margin products in rather tatty food stores in impoverished parts of England'. The snobbery of the old company was not hard to detect.

Connell for once acted fast and on 13 September the heavyweight merchant bank Kleinwort Benson were drafted in to work alongside the existing team from Robert Fleming.

Kleinwort's gave one of their top corporate financiers, Bay Green, the task of mastering the defence. It was the beginning of a five month slog in which he would have just one day off, Christmas Day. Green also worked on another 'mega-merger' in the period — the link up between Habitat and British Home Stores.

Green began by going up to Edinburgh the following week to attend the Distillers AGM at the North British Hotel in Edinburgh (by now, of course, owned by Guinness). Connell launched his defence at the meeting, announcing that he was dispensing with the management committee. From now on, the bosses of each of the four main operating divisions would report directly to the chairman. The threat from Gulliver may have accelerated the move to a more executive style of management, but Connell must have considered it earlier in the year when some institutions said to him that they were worried about the company's tortuous decision-making process. Connell also announced that he was introducing incentive schemes for middle management which would double their pay packets if they achieved targets. He surprised shareholders and journalists by admitting that he'd had talks on trading matters with the Argyll Group over the previous few months, and many assumed that this referred to some sort of merger proposals, or even a possible bid for Argyll.

The Distillers defences were strengthened still further in early October, when the American, Bill Spengler, was appointed as Connell's number two and deputy chief executive. Connell had appointed Spengler a non-executive director almost a year before, and in fact even tentatively offered him an executive role in the January of 1985, but he had characteristically dithered, and it needed the Argyll avalanche to make him act. The 57-year-old came out of retirement, and he moved over with his wife to London, hurriedly renting a flat in London at the company's expense. Expense it was — the annual rent was £34,000! Spengler acted quickly. Having moved into an office at the grand Distillers headquarters in St James's Square, he brought in a firm of management consultants, PA Strategy Partners, who, ironically, were mostly former Bain people, to tackle Distillers' strategic problems. They set about creating a central department to handle marketing for all the different brands, replacing the separate brand operations of before. Spengler also sought to bring all production activity under one director and had won agreement from all the separate parts of the Distillers empire to do this. Events overtook most of the Spengler innovations.

Had Spengler been appointed chief executive months before, and replaced Connell, as some institutions had urged, Distillers might have got more backing at the critical times. As it was, even those investors who believed things were changing at Distillers saw it happening much too slowly to give it their support. Spengler's main role subsequently was to be the mean man, matching the flow of punches from Gulliver while his chief executive looked on helplessly.

One or two of the Distillers directors sensed the urgency of the situation. John Connell's younger brother, David, who ran the Johnnie Walker operation, and non-executives such as Sir William Pile shared Spengler's sense of urgency, and they pressed the intensely shy John Connell to adopt a higher public profile for Distillers in the City. It had some effect, because for the first time drinks analysts were invited to look at some of the company's bottling and production plants. They were taken to the Gordon's gin operation at Basildon in Essex and to the Johnnie Walker headquarters in London. Local managers gave presentations which generally impressed the visitors from the City. One analyst was even moved to write a report beginning with the words 'How wrong I've been'. Another came away convinced the Distillers share price was worth at least £6. Yet another, looking back after the event, feels that Distillers were actually 'showing up the tragedy of their situation. We saw how they worked the management lower down the line, but of course things ran ahead of them.'

While the stockbroking analysts were being whisked around the whisky and gin operations, journalists were herded round the company's head office. Alistair Campbell-Harris of Streets Financial, the public relations advisers, tried to persuade John Connell to forget his old suspicions of pressmen. A series of City Editors' lunches were arranged but they weren't a great success; Connell couldn't master the art of communication overnight and had little aptitude for it. On one occasion, late in the afternoon, journalists and analysts were summoned to a reception at Distillers. After keeping them waiting for an hour, Connell appeared and asked the by now irritated gathering: 'And what can I do for you gentlemen?'

Distillers tried putting its message across in Scotland as well, but it proved an uphill task with many observers sceptical of their motives, and the long years of neglect meant there was a great deal of good will to make up. The scepticism was ubiquitous. 'Even taxi drivers in Edinburgh were aware that Distillers was managed from England and they were also aware that it was very badly run', said one observer.

It was a humdrum campaign in Scotland, and Connell made no special effort to woo Scottish financiers or approach the key opinion formers as Saunders and Gulliver had done. Distillers brokers, Bell Lawrie, were left to fly the flag with two company managers, Tony Oscroft and Ian Ross. Shareholders and fund managers were impressed with the Distillers men, but felt they really needed to speak to directors, rather than well-intentioned managers. Said one Edinburgh financier: 'They weren't exactly the office boys, and they were extremely able individuals. But they could hardly give a hand-on-heart promise that they'd increase the dividend 40% or whatever, when they had no authority to do so.'

At the end of November Distillers hired their first public relations adviser in Scotland. Kleinworts approached the PR firm Charles Barker, and Colin Liddell again found himself at the centre of a takeover war. But by then it was too late for Liddell to do much for the Distillers cause.

It began to look increasingly unlikely that Distillers could remain independent, and speculation was now growing that they might look for a rescuer. The American company Seagrams were rumoured to be showing an interest. One tactic for a company under siege is to look for something to buy and spend so much money on it that the predator decides it is too expensive (in City jargon, the 'poison pill'). Some speculation surrounded the possibility that Distillers, which had some food interests of its own, might bid for Argyll, and see off the aggressor that way. It was to come to nothing. John Connell had several conversations with Alick Rankin, chairman of Scottish and Newcastle Breweries, but no formal proposal was put before the board. Kleinworts drew up a list of possible takeover targets for the board to consider but, again, no action was taken.

Bay Green thought Charles Fraser, a luminary of the Scottish financial establishment, might be able to advise on a rescue. Fraser was opposed to a Gulliver takeover. But he realised how close it could be after he had been to the authoritative Scottish Council for Development and Industry at Gleneagles in early November, and discovered to his surprise that the support was completely behind Argyll and that the Distillers cause was all but lost. Fraser reported his findings to John Connell and told him bluntly he should step down in favour of an outside chairman, and also appoint a dynamic new chief executive; he said he even had candidates in mind. Fraser presented this as the only way to win back the confidence of shareholders in time; but Connell rejected the plan.

Ernest Saunders was also at the meeting at Gleneagles, in the hope of making good contacts in the right places. After the takeover of Bell's, Fraser, who was still a Guinness legal adviser, discussed with his client a possible move on Distillers some time in the future, and Fraser suggested that in preparation Saunders should be seen in the right circles in the Scottish political scene. The two men realised that it was too soon after the hard slog of the Bell's takeover for Saunders to think about moving, but both were concerned about how quickly Gulliver had moved and how close Argyll had come to snatching the top prize.

Saunders began to realise that he'd been overtaken by events. Many analysts, advisers and journalists remember occasions in the summer of 1985 when they suggested to Saunders that he should go for Distillers rather than Bell's. But he always replied that Guinness was not big enough. One broker remembers: 'I said to them in July of that year, "Yes you've done the right thing in making a takeover, and I can see the sense of it. The only thing is you've gone for the wrong company." They replied, "What do you mean?" I said "You should have gone for Distillers", and they said "It's far too big."' Saunders' defenders have since argued that he had to take over Bell's to acquire the firepower to go for Distillers. But before absorbing Bell's, Guinness was capitalised on the stock market at over £500 million, which was only slightly less than

Argyll. If Gulliver could contemplate a bid for Distillers, why not Saunders? The answer probably lies in the differing talents and visions of the two tycoons. Saunders had paid a very high price for Bell's and found himself with a brand that had only limited sales potential in the British market. Gulliver's vision, on the other hand, was much wider and longer-term. He saw all along the possibilities for Distillers' worldwide brands, and took direct aim. Saunders' talk of building an international drinks empire based on Bell's looked hollow by comparison. Perhaps the truth of the matter lies in one observation on Saunders at the time: 'He just didn't want Gulliver to be a bigger player.'

Saunders knew he was hardly in a position to outflank Gulliver with an alternative bid. Bell's had only just been swallowed up and, apart from the financial considerations, there was the obvious problem of the Monopolies Commission. He would have to bide his time.

Now Saunders had to act quickly and decisively. But by instinct he was a man who liked to have every eventuality sewn up, to have gone through every operation many times to check that there were no loopholes. For Distillers, there simply wasn't time for the countless run throughs and repeats that he had done for Bell's. In short, Gulliver had caught Saunders on the hop, and instinctive reaction was not the Guinness chief's strong point.

By early October the Bain team were pulled off routine duties and all leave was cancelled. They were put to work on a comprehensive analysis of Distillers and its position in world markets. The top secret bunker at their headquarters at Connaught Place was reopened and once again a confidential planning operation swung into action. They were not starting from scratch, since the planning for Bell's had given them a useful start. The old charts and flow diagrams on market share were unfurled but there were hours of homework to get through if they were to catch up with the Argyll class over at Chesterfield Hill.

Later in October Olivier Roux, the Guinness director of financial strategy and administration, was at a lunch with the stockbrokers Hoare Govett, brokers to Distillers. Conversation got round to the state of play following Argyll's aborted bid. Roux took a keen interest and let it be known Guinness would be only too pleased to help beat off Argyll. His remarks got back to James Gulliver.

Now Saunders and Gulliver knew each other quite well, and had a friendly rapport. They'd first met at a Christmas party in 1981, just after Saunders had taken over at Guinness. Saunders joked about the huge number of subsidiaries he'd inherited and Gulliver asked for a list of anything that was up for sale, but nothing ever came of it. Later they met at football matches for drinks in the boardroom when Manchester United were playing Queen's Park Rangers: 'He seemed to me to be very keen, in fact I think he was keener than I', joked Gulliver. Gulliver had sent Saunders a friendly letter in the latter stages of the bid for Bell's assuring him that Argyll would not make a counter bid.

The two men met for lunch and Gulliver was reassured that Saunders knew nothing of Roux's conversation, and whatever Roux had said was spoken without his authority. Gulliver pressed him further: 'I was very direct about it because Ernest Saunders is a man who's quite clever with words , and he might have chosen a form of words that in retrospect could have meant almost anything. I did pin him down and I asked whether it was true what I'd heard, that you've offered to help. He said "I know nothing about this." I then said, would you be interested in a bid for Distillers, and he said we are not interested in a bid for Distillers at the present time.' Gulliver had got the answer he wanted; the next time he spoke to Saunders was to be in very different circumstances.

Meanwhile the mood at Distillers was less relaxed. Kleinworts knew that more had to be done before a bid from Gulliver could be confidently resisted, but they were hampered by not knowing when he would strike. The first time he could bid was 2 December, three months after the September fiasco, but he might choose to lie in wait till after Christmas.

Anticipating the worst, Bay Green advised Distillers to bring forward the announcement of their half-year results by a month to 21 November. In effect they'd be playing their joker — revealing healthy profits and cashing in with a rise in the share price which would convert doubting shareholders. Ideally the Argyll bid would be shot out of the water.

The plan backfired, although the Distillers share price survived almost intact. News of the move leaked out to the enemy camp; 'One of the Distillers directors at a cocktail party in Edinburgh spoke a little more liberally than he should have,' said David Webster. 'The word came back to us so we knew a week before they produced their figures when they were coming out. Such was our state of knowledge about the company that we felt we could predict what those figures were going to be almost to the million.'

When the figures were finally unveiled they showed that profits had leapt by over 40% to £124 million while the interim dividend was hiked by 22%. But the explanation for the improvement did not suggest that the performance of Distillers had changed very much.

Reading the figures was not helped as new accounting procedures had been adopted which, as one journalist put it, 'created a Scotch mist' over the results. Comparisons with the last year's performance were difficult, since a dock strike had distorted the earlier figures. Finally, the numbers had been boosted by the introduction of some orders relating to the previous year which had not been shipped until 1985 so the proceeds were booked to the latest half year. The impression given, though this may have been unintentional, was that Distillers were trying to buy support with artificially inflated figures. The exercise was badly received in the press.

Time was fast running out, and on 28 November, Distillers announced the appointment of a new non-executive director. Sir Nigel Broackes, head of Trafalgar House, the engineering, oil and publishing empire, was recruited after a discreet approach from Kleinworts. They knew Sir Nigel well because they were his advisers at Trafalgar House; he was a successful businessman who was battle-hardened after many takeover campaigns. Kleinworts had earlier presented the Distillers board with a list of suitable candidates to be non-executive directors. Three were approached but the only one to accept was Broackes. Kleinworts hoped that more boardroom changes would be made and perhaps that Broackes would ease his way into the chairman's seat. But Broackes was the last hand to board the Distillers ship before it was over-run. He was aged 51, and if nothing else the appointment reduced the average age of the Distillers board!

At this time the Distillers banker actually met Saunders. Bay Green was responding to an innocuous phone call from the

Guinness chief, during which he suggested that he might be able to advise on defence tactics. It was a strangely brief meeting — Saunders actually left it halfway through to talk to his PR director — but enough to test the mettle of the advisers with whom he would be discussing merger talks.

In late November Green met Ernest Saunders and Chris Davidson (the public relations director) again. The conversation ranged around general subjects of mutual interest; Green was interested to hear about Guinness's PR tactics in the Bell's campaign and the wooing of City institutions. There was no discussion of a merger, and in fact the possibility was never raised.

On Monday 2 December, Argyll put in their bid. 'As sure as night follows day we were there,' said Webster. 'We came with a power and a potency that I think the Distillers board never recovered from.' It caught Distillers off-balance, although they had more notice than most takeover victims of an impending bid. Argyll mailed a glossy document to Distillers shareholders entitled, 'It will come as no surprise that Distillers should be taken over.' Apart from an impressive range of graphs, there were newspaper clippings to support their case, including the following lines from the *Daily Telegraph:* 'Distillers is one of the worst-run large companies in Britain. In its way it is a classic British failure.' The tone of the document was an unpleasant surprise for the gentlemen at Distillers. As an Argyll insider put it: 'The directors wouldn't be very happy that their wives were reading that sort of thing when they opened the *Telegraph*, it was really quite tough.' But Argyll knew they had to attack Distillers head on to establish their own credibility. It also meant that they lost any chance of getting the Distillers directors to negotiate an agreed bid or merger. Gulliver gave a clear commitment to have the headquarters of the proposed new company in Edinburgh, where his management team would be based (significantly he held his press conference on the morning of 2 December in Edinburgh).

The Argyll offer valued Distillers at £1.87 billion, or 513 pence per share, more than 70% higher than the price at which they'd first been buying in the market back in July. They were now planning to buy a company three times their size, but that hadn't scared the four-year-old David from attacking the 100-year-old Goliath.

The financing of the deal was revolutionary in itself. The £1.87 billion they were offering was to be made up of £1.2 billion worth of new shares which had to be underwritten and £600 million borrowed from four banks. For the first time in City history, the underwriting was success related — if the bid failed the institutions would receive fees of just 0.125%, but if it succeeded the reward would be 2.5%. Argyll would pay less than £10 million if the whole thing fell through, but more like £74 million in fees to the bankers and institutions if Distillers was captured.

The package was a triumph for the duo at Samuel Montagu, Ian McIntosh and Rupert Faure Walker who'd worked flat-out since the Weinstock fiasco and the departure of Lazards. The enforced postponement of the bid had actually given them a useful breathing space, and a chance to avoid the pitfalls that had occurred in a bid going on at the same time.

Faure Walker had watched John Elliott's attempt to topple the mighty Allied Lyons — this had been referred to the Monopolies Commission because of worries about the financing of the bid. 'We were very conscious of getting away from an Elders' type structure, which was going to be all debt with very little equity. I remember thinking about the OFT decision and it was very important to keep the debt low for that reason. We kept the equity up so that a large group would have funds to expand and prosper.' Argyll seemed to have had few problems in assembling enough City backers. The American giant Citibank were one of the lenders; in November they'd played a key role in financing John Elliott. Even Lord Weinstock had agreed to play a small role in the underwriting.

The day of the Argyll bid, 2 December, was also the day United Biscuits agreed a £1.2 billion merger with the Imperial Group, the brewing and cigarette conglomerate. The two bids went along in parallel, and there were to be some remarkable similarities. It was to be the start of a madcap string of billion-pound deals involving some of Britain's top companies. Even so, Gulliver was awarded the accolade of 'acquisitive entrepreneur' in the same league as John Elliott, although the Lex Column in the *Financial Times* concluded that Argyll wasn't the most plausible bidder: 'Mr Gulliver is an inspired food retailer who would bring the necessary financial controls and management drive to the task in hand. But Argyll has had a chequered history in the drinks industry, has little experience of international marketing and has only recently established its credibility in the City.'

Argyll's tactics from the outset were to blast Distillers head-on. They had to prove that the shock of a change of ownership and management was the only hope for Distillers and that Argyll had the right team for the job. 'Within about three weeks, our document was in the hands of all the shareholders, all the leading brokers in London, all leading fund managers, all the Scottish MPs, and in the hands of the Office of Fair Trading. The idea was to get the whole world thinking on Day One that Distillers had to be taken over', remembers Rupert Faure Walker.

According to David Webster: 'It was almost like fighting a war in terms of intensity and deployment of resource. The entire bid was run from our Chesterfield Hill offices — down in the basement we've got a large meeting room with two smaller meeting rooms where at the outset we established a team of three girls who manned it almost seven days a week from 7.30 a.m. until 10 p.m. or even midnight. This was an operations room and it covered predominantly press calls, but it was a means by which anybody could call in. For example, we had disaffected Distillers employees calling in saying good for you, the board's a load of rubbish, we'd like to see them all go.'

There was a morning meeting at 8 a.m. — Gulliver and Webster would review operations with the bankers, McIntosh and Faure Walker and also Victor Blank of Charterhouse, and representatives from the three brokers, Panmure Gordon, Rowe and Pitman and Scrimgeour Vickers. There was a team working on the submission to the Office of Fair Trading, and another responsible for the formal bid documents. On advertising and public relations, Argyll employed Saatchi and Saatchi and the public relations firm Broad Street Associates. By another strange coincidence, both had worked with Saunders on the campaign for Bell's — according to one member of the team the depth and quality of research done by Argyll was far greater than anything seen at Guinness. Much of the publicity was concentrated in Scotland: 'In Scotland it was the biggest thing since the Battle of Culloden really for the media. We couldn't cough down here without having all their local radio stations and Scottish television on to us,' recalls Webster.

Distillers were still recovering from the first shockwave of the Argyll assault, when they discovered that their long-standing bankers, the Royal Bank of Scotland, had emerged in the enemy camp. The Royal Bank had been introduced to Argyll through their connections with Charterhouse and had provided some of the loan finance. This infuriated the Distillers board and the Royal Bank were promptly sacked. One assumes that the Royal Bank had thought carefully about their decision. The loss of business with Scotland's largest company was a major blow but presumably had been weighed up against the interest on money lent to Gulliver. Distillers appointed the Bank of Scotland as replacements. No doubt Sir Thomas Risk was delighted to win such a major account, although later he might have regretted a decision that was to rebound against him.

In response to Argyll's 28-page glossy brochure *It will come as no surprise*, Distillers put out a ten-paragraph letter to shareholders from John Connell who indicated that he intended to 'fight the bid with vigour and determination'. There was little in the letter to suggest that Distillers had made fruitful use of their three months' warning period. One of the Distillers advisers remembers Connell in the heat of battle: 'He was a gentleman to the core, an absolute gentleman, but absolutely stunned by what he saw happening around him. He just hadn't anticipated or expected the activity to be what it was, the hours that were required, the drive that was required, the innovation that was required.'

Distillers directors were by now suspicious that there could be a fifth columnist within their ranks. Although the board appeared to be united in their desire to beat off Argyll, there was a feeling that someone lower down the organisation may have been helping the enemy. According to one director, 'There were some leaks of information, we're pretty sure . . . it was information that was to do with our business, our performance, our statistics and data that just wasn't public information.' As a result directors' phones would be checked regularly for bugs. Spengler, who was doing a lot of the key talking, had his office swept every morning. For their part, Distillers employed a private detective to investigate Gulliver's background; they'd read enough in *Private Eye* about Gulliver's past history to feel there was mileage to be gained. It was the beginning of a dirty tricks campaign which was to hot up as the stakes were raised.

The war of words continued over the Christmas Holiday. A week after Gulliver's announcement of the bid Distillers, on the prompting of Kleinworts, put out a pamphlet attacking Argyll's record in the drinks business. It was the first time they'd deigned to reply to Gulliver's attacks on their own performance. Bill Spengler and David Connell were getting stuck into the close-quarter fighting backed up by their man in Scotland, Ian Ross, while their chairman seemed to be on the sidelines. As one adviser put it, 'David Connell and Spengler — these were the people who understood the need to communicate much more openly and aggressively. John was a much quieter personality behind the scenes.'

Over Christmas few of the main players in the campaign had much time off. On 17 December, Argyll's formal offer document was dispatched. This was felt to be a crafty move because it represented the official Day One under the Takeover Code and came just as most offices were winding down for Christmas — the Code's timetable is not halted for Yuletide holidays. Distillers and their advisers were left having to put the finishing touches to their defence document when they should have been enjoying the turkey. But Argyll's war cabinet could not afford to relax either. They reassembled at Chesterfield Hill on Boxing Day and waited anxiously for their opponents' next move. Even though their campaign had worked like clockwork, they were all nervous about what surprises Distillers might spring. Montagu's and Charterhouse even produced a dummy defence document so they could rehearse a response.

Finally, on 30 December, after what seemed like weeks of waiting, Distillers produced an official defence document to explain to shareholders why their money was best left under the care of the old management and why Argyll was bad news. There was even a video to back up the message. This document was pushed through letter boxes on 31 December, Hogmanay in Scotland where most shareholders would have been more concerned with drinking their Johnnie Walker or Haig than worrying about the company that produced them (although by this stage only about 6% of the shares were accounted for by Scots). The timing of the whole exercise seemed to epitomise the lumbering style of the Distillers organisation.

At Chesterfield Hill Argyll received an unexpected guest early in the New Year. Meshulam Riklis had taken a keen interest in proceedings from the other side of the Atlantic. He controlled the Rapid-American Corporation which owned Schenley, distributors of Dewar's in the United States. The president of Rapid American had talked to the head of Argyll's US operation after Riklis had purchased a 1.5% stake in Distillers. It was suggested that further contact should be established so Riklis flew into London on his way home from Israel. He was greeted at Chesterfield Hill by James Gulliver and David Webster. Riklis informed them that his wife was the Hollywood star Pia Zadora, and they'd flown in to London in their 'His' and 'Hers' Lear jets. This cut little ice for the simple reason that Webster hadn't heard of Pia Zadora. Riklis then got down to business and asked what the future of Schenley and the Dewar's brand would be if Argyll won control of Distillers. Gulliver ventured the opinion that the distributors had been run on a very loose rein and many had grown fat with little effort; he indicated that he planned to review the situation if he succeeded. Riklis said in reply that if Argyll wanted to talk at any time he'd be very happy to do so, and bade his farewells.

Gulliver had also been approached by a representative of the Ivan Boesky operation. Boesky was a so called 'arb' — short for *arbitrageur* — who made his money by taking key stakes in companies which were identified as takeover targets. These stakes could be used as a bargaining lever when negotiating for the best price with either party. At the end of 1985, Boesky was much admired in New York and London and was still a year away from humiliation and exposure as an insider trader. At this time American 'arbs' had never played much of a role in a British takeover battle. Gulliver was vaguely familiar with their role and had learned a little about arbitrage in conversation with Jim Slater some time before. So he was pleased to accept an invitation to find out more from Boesky's representative in London, Roger Williams.

They met for breakfast at the Savoy and Williams explained that Boesky had done a great deal of research into Distillers and believed it would eventually fall. He said they were thinking of building a shareholding and but hadn't decided whose offer they'd accept if there was a competing bid. Gulliver came away with the impression that Williams was probing to find out if

Argyll would increase their offer and what the final offer would be. He knew that arbitrageurs make most of their judgements about investments from conversations with the protagonists. Gulliver and Webster met Williams on another occasion with a broker from the American firm Seligmann Harris, but nothing was agreed and they heard no more from the Ivan Boesky organisation.

On 9 January 1986 the Argyll team could see victory in sight. That day they'd cleared their biggest hurdle by escaping a reference to the Monopolies Commission. Trade Secretary Leon Brittan made one of his last official decisions before being sacked at the height of the Westland affair. He accepted the recommendation of the Office of Fair Trading and allowed Gulliver's bid to proceed. The decision was as much of a body blow to Distillers as it was a boost to Argyll.

Since 2 December most of the Distillers directors had reassured themselves with the thought that in the last resort the bid must be referred, after all the Government could hardly allow the leaders of the Scotch whisky industry leaders to be toppled by a mere grocery outfit. They assumed that the Department of Trade would understand the real story. Distillers was the guardian of the industry with research equipment to test the quality of whisky and prevent counterfeiting. Surely the Government would not allow 'pile it high, sell it cheap' merchants to hijack the industry? But they were wrong; as one observer put it: 'They were sure the Government would refer it, and they were absolutely shocked when it was waved through. And when they realised that nothing could stop them sliding into the Argyll camp they decided they had to go to Guinness.'

CHAPTER EIGHT

GUINNESS: GREY KNIGHT TO THE RESCUE

Christmas 1985 was not a relaxing time for Ernest Saunders. Like John Connell and James Gulliver, his thoughts were on whisky — Johnnie Walker, Dewar's and the rest of the Distillers brands. But unlike Connell and Gulliver, he had to keep his thoughts to himself until the time was right.

From the beginning of December onwards the planning for a counter bid for Distillers had proceeded apace, although strict secrecy had been maintained. There were no rumours in the press and most journalists concentrated on the public joust between Distillers and Argyll. Saunders had phoned Connell at the end of November and suggested that they should talk about getting together and that he was interested in exploring possibilities with Distillers. Connell gave no commitment but discussed it with some of his fellow directors. It certainly seemed a reasonable idea but most of them took the view that any merger would be referred to the Monopolies Commission. The proposal was one of many that the hard-pressed Distillers board had heard and no one thought much of it at the time.

Saunders was not deterred by the seeming lack of interest and continued his planning. On 23 December there was a strategy meeting at the Bain headquarters. The Bain team delivered a presentation outlining their research into Distillers. Charles Fraser advised on the legal and political problems.

Saunders declared that it was time to make the big move but there was some debate on whether to make a counter-bid or whether to approach in the guise of a White Knight. One view was that 'the trouble with being a White Knight is that the damsel in distress may turn out to be a grey witch'—the logic was that the City might look more favourably on a bold hostile bid than a cobbled together merger agreement. But Saunders didn't take this advice; he decided he must get agreement from the Distillers directors even if this meant compromises. He knew that he had a huge task on his hands as he would have to persuade and cajole the Distillers board and their advisers to accept Guinness. The task was to need all his ample reserves of charm and native cunning.

Before the Christmas holiday he contacted Connell and suggested they meet. For Connell, who was beginning to realise that Distillers' chances of remaining independent were disappearing fast, it was reassuring to know there might be an escape route. Saunders seemed friendly and constructive when they spoke on the telephone. One of Connell's colleagues remembers that call from Saunders: 'He was a bit naughty, perhaps this was part of his technique, that in the middle of the worst bit with Gulliver he rang John Connell and said he was very grateful for the fact Distillers hadn't intervened when he was after Bell's, and was there anything he could do to help. Those were evil words.' Another pointed out: 'Rather than starting like Jimmy Gulliver did, a punch in the nose and saying now let's talk, he said, look these two companies go nicely together, a much better fit.'

Straight after Christmas Saunders was set to depart for his annual skiing holiday in Switzerland. Connell called him and said he was interested in talking. Saunders, eager not to let his prey lose interest, invited Connell to join the party in Switzerland. Away from the slopes, as the rest of his family enjoyed the more traditional *après-ski*, Saunders outlined his plans for a merger; there could be a holding board with the existing Guinness and Distillers boards operating as a second tier. John Connell would be chairman and Saunders said he'd work for him as the chief executive. To the hard-pressed Distillers man it seemed not only reasonable but actually very desirable. He could accept the chairmanship of a new group without any loss of dignity. Connell said he was interested but warned that he'd have to win the support of his board.

On Saturday 4 January Bay Green was trying to get in touch with Ernest Saunders. That morning *The Times* had run a speculative story suggesting that Guinness was set to enter the fray and bid for Distillers. It was the first time Green had heard the suggestion and he was anxious to find out if there was any truth in the story, which looked suspiciously like an inspired leak. After several attempts Green finally got Saunders from the ski slopes to a telephone and told him about the story in *The Times*. Saunders replied that the British newspapers hadn't yet reached his hotel; as usual he was choosing his words very carefully. When pressed further, Saunders refused to comment but agreed to meet Bay Green on his return to England. Green didn't waste any time in the next few days and began making discreet enquiries about Saunders. It was clear that Saunders had considerable stature and a strong following. He'd built Guinness into a brand-orientated company and this seemed the right approach for Distillers. The commercial sense of the merger began to look very attractive.

On 8 January, Bay Green and his Kleinworts colleague Mark Birch met Saunders for breakfast at the New Piccadilly Hotel. By this time the City columns of most newspapers were speculating about Guinness' intentions. But still Saunders was non-committal and told Green that he hadn't given a lot of thought to the idea. He did say that he'd like to meet John Connell to explore possibilities. The next day Green had a call from Roger Seelig of Morgan Grenfell, the Guinness merchant bank. The two bankers knew each other well and only two months before had been working closely together on another huge merger plan — Seelig was representing Habitat and Green was working for BHS. They discussed enthusiastically the prospect of a Guinness link up with Distillers. That weekend Saunders and Ward travelled north to see Charles Fraser. On Saturday evening they dined with Fraser at the Caledonian Hotel. They discussed their planned move and Fraser warned that the major stumbling block was the Office of Fair Trading — a combination of Distillers and Guinness (with Bell's) would control almost 40% of the British whisky market. But Thomas Ward reassured Fraser that there was no need to worry about the OFT. Fraser assumed that Ward, an American, didn't really understand how the British Department of Trade worked, so he repeated his fear that a link up between the two companies was sure to be referred to the Monopolies Commission. They met again for breakfast on Sunday morning. Ward was still adamant that there'd be no problems with the OFT; Fraser was puzzled that Ward could be so smugly confident that there'd be no opposition from official circles.

On Monday 13 January, Saunders and Ward were back in London. They met John Connell at Bay Green's flat in the West End. Connell was positive and encouraging and Saunders was not unduly persuasive. The discussion ranged around the financial details of a merger and the question of the board structure was not raised. As one of his colleagues later observed: 'John should have had some more back up, but didn't. He isn't the strongest negotiator in the world and is too much of a gentleman.' The following night Saunders was at the opera in Covent Garden. The *Financial Times* later noted that 'Saunders says that if any doubt remained in his mind about the advisability of the deal it was banished at a night at the opera when several bankers and fund managers urged him on'. With hindsight this looks suspiciously like Saunders attempting to create the impression that he was a reluctant suitor of Distillers. He could not be seen to want them badly — he had to imply that he was urged on by City financiers.

For the rest of that week there was an intensive series of meetings at the Distillers headquarters in St James's Square. The board were for the first time confronted with a proposal to sell out to a third party even though they'd been publicly proclaiming that they wished to stay independent. It was an agonising time for the gentlemen who'd run the Scotch whisky industry for generations. Connell was persuading colleagues that a merger with Guinness would be in everyone's interest, after all the Distillers board would be barely affected and would be allowed to continue running its business. The only thing that would affect them would be the new holding board but their own man, Connell, would be chairman of that and Bill Spengler would probably be there as well. Certainly the fine print hadn't been worked out but in principle, the chairman argued, it seemed a very agreeable proposition. Kleinworts were quite certain that independence was now out of the question so, reasoned Connell, the Guinness tie-up was the only way forward if they were going to escape Gulliver and his hordes. After all, shareholders would be getting a very reasonable deal and might receive 600p or more for their shares, and directors at all times had to remember their duties to shareholders.

At times during the talking and the agonising, they would ring Guinness to check details or raise queries. And it was Thomas Ward would answer the phone and handle the questions. It was virtually impossible to speak directly to Saunders. Sometimes Saunders would agree to come round to St James's Square by car but he would always bring Ward with him. One Distillers director remembers that: 'This was the first time I'd seen Mr Ward smiling away with a yellow tie, and I didn't like him one little bit.' Again and again the Distillers board pressed Ward and Saunders to confirm that they knew what they were up against; did they have the commitment to raise their offer if Argyll came up with a higher bid? Saunders assured them that he really wanted to merge with Distillers. While these meetings were in progress Bay Green and Roger Seelig were thrashing out the text of an agreement which could be put to both parties. There seemed to be no involvement of the rest of the Guinness board. Distillers found themselves dealing only with Saunders, Ward and Seelig.

On the morning of Friday 17 January, Sir Thomas Risk was due to fly down to London for a business engagement. He was on his way to Edinburgh airport when his car phone rang — the message was to call Ernest Saunders at Guinness. Saunders asked Risk if he could come round to Portman Square on his arrival to discuss an urgent matter. Risk went straight to the Guinness headquarters after touching down at Heathrow. He was shown in to Saunders' office and found Roger Seelig was also there. In the next 45 minutes Saunders described how close Guinness and Distillers were to agreeing a merger that would create a great international company and save the giant of the Scotch whisky industry. He outlined how complex the negotiations had been and how difficult it had been to agree on certain conditions. One of the only areas left to be settled was the question of a chairman acceptable to both boards. There was a short silence before Seelig said: 'And the man we've got in mind is you.' Risk's answer was 'no'; after all he had a full-time job and little time to take on a major commitment as chairman of a public company. Saunders then began to persuade Risk to think again. He pointed out that the proposal had the backing not only of both boards but also two of the City's leading merchant banks, Kleinwort Benson and Morgan Grenfell, and that it was the best solution for Distillers, and hence the Scotch whisky industry. Saunders said Risk's involvement was a vital ingredient of the merger terms. Risk had to depart to his other appointment but agreed to talk again later in the day.

When Risk returned he told Saunders that he would not dismiss the suggestion out of hand and would need 24 hours to think about it. But if the answer was to be yes, how on earth would they work together? Risk let it be known that he would want to play an active role in the running of the merged business and would need to discuss ways of apportioning jobs with Saunders. Still uncertain, Risk left Portman Square and in the car on the way to Heathrow he phoned his Bank of Scotland chief executive Bruce Pattullo. Risk explained that he'd been offered a chairmanship and that his first reaction was say no, but felt the issues were so important he couldn't turn it down out of hand. Pattullo indicated that he could see no problems and urged Risk to accept. Throughout Saturday Risk was on the phone to the rest of his boardroom colleagues; none of them had any reservations or objections. On the Saturday evening Risk, now encouraged, called Saunders and agreed in principle to accept the chairmanship of the merged companies.

The Risk factor was critical to Saunders' grand scheme. By now it was 10 p.m. but Saunders had one further important piece of business to transact. He instructed his chauffeur to drive to Walton-on-Thames, to the home of John Connell. Connell showed Saunders into the living room and offered him a drink; Saunders asked for a Johnnie Walker and suggested Connell had a Guinness so they could toast the future of the new merged company. The conversation soon got round to the structure of the board, which was a subject that seemed to have been forgotten in the hectic negotiations of the last week. Connell had assumed he was to be chairman but was unsure who from Distillers was to be on the main holding board. He had a nasty shock in store as he sipped his late-night glass of Guinness. Saunders argued that the new board must have an independent outside chairman, preferably a Scot, who could win over the doubting shareholders, especially in Edinburgh.

They must have a clean break with the past if they were to convince the City they could do better than Gulliver. And he had found the very man, Sir Thomas Risk, who had the active support of Morgan Grenfell and Kleinworts. Connell began to protest but Saunders continued to talk about the need for a chairman with standing in the financial community. Connell knew and admired Risk and in fact had consulted him after the Gulliver bid; Risk's name had already been put as a possible non-executive director of the new company. But that didn't make up for having his own hopes so cruelly dashed. Saunders had seized the initiative and Connell had been forced into a corner; he knew there was no way out as the merger was almost a *fait accompli*. That Saturday morning, Connell had read a piece in *The Times* by Kenneth Fleet — a journalist with a strong, emotional commitment to the Saunders strategy — suggesting that Guinness were all set to bid for Distillers; it seemed to be surprisingly well-informed. The chairman of Distillers mumbled his agreement and politely showed Saunders out.

That morning David Webster had picked up the newspapers as usual on the way into Chesterfield Hill. Even though it was a Saturday he was at work before 9 a.m. Gulliver was already in his office and the two men scanned through each paper for general comment on Argyll's progress. Quickly they spotted the story in *The Times*. It implied that a number of Scottish financial institutions had approached Saunders imploring him to rescue Distillers from the dreaded Argyll. Gulliver at first wasn't too alarmed — he was in close touch with many Scottish institutions and felt that most were fully in support of Argyll. But then his public relations chief Brian Basham called to warn that the story should be taken seriously. Basham, who'd worked with Guinness before, believed it had all the hallmarks of a deliberately leaked effort from Saunders.

Gulliver immediately phoned Saunders' home at Penn in Buckinghamshire. Carole Saunders answered the phone and told him Ernest was not at home and was on his way to the office. Gulliver then called Portman Square and spoke to Saunders' secretary, who said her boss hadn't arrived; Gulliver was surprised that she was at work on a Saturday morning. He called Penn again and Carole Saunders asked him if he'd like to speak to 'Mr Ward'. Gulliver knew a little about Ward because he'd played a small part in the Bell's bid. Ward denied that Guinness were planning a bid, as implied by the story in *The Times* and explained that he and other financiers were over in the UK to discuss the acquisition of an American drinks distributor. Gulliver wasn't quite satisfied and called back on several occasions. Each time he spoke to Ward, who eventually revealed that he and Saunders had wanted to meet Gulliver anyway. They fixed a meeting for the Monday and Gulliver remembers that 'I said I'll come to your offices, he said no we'd like to come to yours — so they were due at 3.30 on Monday afternoon and I still await their arrival'.

Ward promised to track Saunders down and eventually the Guinness chief called Gulliver from his car phone: 'I said, Ernest surely this cannot be true, are you interested in bidding for Distillers? And he said we are certainly not interested in bidding for Distillers. He said that story's been planted by someone else. Then I said I'm glad of your reassurance and I was about to ask some supplementaries when we were cut off and I couldn't track him down again.' Gulliver was half-reassured; he was puzzled that Saunders or Ward had spoken to him at all, as someone could easily have said they weren't available. It was the last conversation that Gulliver had with Saunders.

If there was still faint hope in the Argyll camp on Saturday evening that the whole thing was a mistake, by Sunday morning they were on full alert. The *Sunday Times* had gone harder on the story and implied that Connell was about to step aside and let Saunders in as sole chairman of a combined group. An Argyll man was dispatched to Morgan Grenfell's office in the City to see if there was any activity. His suspicions were confirmed when he discovered from an unsuspecting security man that most of the people advising Distillers had gone over to Guinness' offices. The irony of the situation was that Guinness, Distillers and Argyll all had their head offices in Mayfair, within a short distance of one another. It was no trouble for Argyll to send someone to see if there were any chauffeurs sitting in Jaguars outside Portman Square. By lunchtime Gulliver knew something big was happening. He'd had reports that John Connell's car had arrived at St James's Square, and for that to happen on a Sunday afternoon was most unusual.

The meeting of the board of directors of the Distillers Company Limited on Sunday 19 January 1986 was the most important in their distinguished 60-year history, and also probably the longest. The sixteen directors began their meeting at 3.30 in the afternoon. They knew that the press were speculating that the deal with Guinness was effectively tied up. So the pressure was on to reach a decision that day, a situation quite alien to the usual style of Distillers board meetings. The previous week they had agreed the principle of a merger, so that wasn't the issue. What they were being asked to do was to accept an independent chairman and pay all Guinness' costs of the bid. On the first point John Connell was unhappy but could see that he could jeopardise the whole venture if he dug his heels in. Ultimately he felt his duty was to act in the best interests of his shareholders, and if this meant sacrificing his own personal ambitions then so be it.

The most heated debate at the meeting came once the question of the underwriting costs was raised. Saunders had demanded that Distillers should agree to pay the costs of the bid; he reasoned that if Guinness succeeded the costs would come from the joint group anyway. But Saunders' real worry was that the bid would fail because of a reference to the Monopolies Commission, so he was determined to ensure that any bills run up before then should be footed by the other side. He made it a condition of the merger proceeding, hoping he could bluff the Distillers directors into accepting. After some preliminary discussion a vote was taken: twelve directors were in favour but four held out against. One of the dissenters describes his thinking at the time: 'I did think that simply in terms of establishing that this was a marriage between equals, I knew of no point in which we had put anything to Saunders which he had accepted. In other words it was all one-way traffic, we were actually bending the knee left, right and centre.' The other side argued that Saunders really meant what he said and that the whole deal would fall through if they didn't agree on the costs issue. 'I don't think Distillers ever had fierce debates, but this did get that way as people were actually speaking their minds for once.' After three hours of discussion the meeting adjourned and the two sets of merchant bankers got together.

While the Distillers directors were closeted in their boardroom, Saunders was putting the finishing touches to his plan. On Sunday evening he finally got in touch with Charles Fraser, who'd arrived home late after a weekend at his Speyside retreat. Saunders announced triumphantly that he'd recruited Sir Thomas Risk to be chairman but that he'd also like Fraser to be a director. Fraser was surprised and excited at the news; it seemed to prove Saunders' determination to win Distillers. For Fraser it was to be a long night of phone calls from Saunders and Connell. The Distillers directors emerged for their break to find messages to call Thomas Ward if they wanted any more information or guidance; they were also reminded that a decision was needed that night because Saunders planned to organise a Guinness board meeting the following morning to rubber stamp the agreement. The board reconvened at 9 p.m. to be advised by the company's lawyers that a unanimous decision was required — if a merger was to be recommended to shareholders it would have to have the backing of the full board to have any legal standing. Soon another vote was taken and this time all sixteen voted in favour of their company paying Guinness underwriting bills.

It was getting late but still that board meeting could not be brought to a close. One director was holding out against the idea of a merger with Guinness. Bill Forrest was director responsible for strategic planning and group employment policy and had consistently argued against any defensive acquisition or takeover agreement by Distillers. If pushed he admitted that he preferred the idea of suing for peace with Argyll rather than falling into bed with Guinness. Forrest's refusal to back down prolonged the meeting until 3 a.m. the following morning. As one observer put it, 'the poor lad was under intense pressure'. His colleagues were almost euphoric at the thought of escaping Gulliver with a deal that seemed to make very good sense for Distillers shareholders. Forrest finally withdrew his objection and the meeting closed. The directors retired to a nearby hotel and then reassembled at 8 a.m. on Monday morning, 20 January, to sign the necessary documents and issue statements to the press.

One director later summed up the feeling of the moment: 'We still thought this was meant to be an equal merger. We were in no doubt that the initiative would lie with Saunders — he was in fact a better businessman and had a better track record — but we did think, foolishly as it now seems, that this was indisputably a benevolent meeting of two like-minded companies. We were certain that that was a better future than Gulliver.' They had seen their task as not only getting the best price for shareholders but also ensuring that shareholders' interests were properly represented in the new board structure. The same Distillers director points out that 'The essence of the merger agreement was (a) the price the shareholders were asked to sell their shares at on our recommendation, and (b) the composition of the managing board'. But, for the time being, Saunders had got what he wanted — he had conceded nothing and gained everything. As announced to the world on Monday 20 January the proposed deal was for Guinness to acquire Distillers for £2.2 billion, valuing each share at 604 pence. To finance the deal Guinness organised £1.6 billion of underwriting, double the amount for the Argyll offer. But Morgan Grenfell acting for Guinness managed to find backers in the space of just a few hours worth of calls around the City. The size of underwriting costs did not depend on the deal going through. Underwriters would receive some £15 million, either way. It was announced that Sir Thomas Risk would be chairman, Ernest Saunders chief executive, and John Connell vice-chairman. There would be four main board members from each camp, and on the Distillers side, apart from John Connell, there would be David Connell, Bill Spengler and Sir Nigel Broackes. It was made clear that the new merged conglomerate would be run from Scotland. The deal was unveiled at a press conference at the International Press Centre near Fleet Street. By coincidence, Gulliver had booked a room for a similar purpose in the same building.

As the Distillers directors were negotiating away their independence, a group of journalists were in New York being shown what a fine job the company was making of its American marketing. The Scottish public relations chief Colin Liddell was doing the job of 'selling' the company and its track record. But early on the Sunday morning he was woken in his hotel room by Peter Binns, whose firm Binns Cornwall was by this stage handling Distillers' public relations in London. He told Liddell about the press speculation of an imminent deal with Guinness. All the relevant newspaper cuttings were facsimiled out and Liddell called an impromptu press conference in the hotel bar. For the bleary-eyed Scottish journalists in the party it was a bizarre situation — stranded in New York while the big story was breaking thousands of miles away. The party flew back to London that night and touched down on the Monday morning. They were met by a driver on the Heathrow tarmac who rushed them across the runway to a private jet. On board were David Connell, Ernest Saunders and Bill Young, from Bain's. The plane took off for Edinburgh and Saunders briefed the journalists en route. Soon after touching down he held his official Scottish press conference.

While the English may have been impressed with Saunders' ambitious merger plans, in Scotland the reaction was different. One adviser remembers that among the managers who'd been footslogging Glasgow and Edinburgh selling the case for the company staying independent 'there was astonishment that the board should have just handed over the keys to Distillers House lock, stock and barrel to Guinness . . . when it was announced there was stunned silence'.

CHAPTER NINE

BATTLE ROYAL: GUINNESS BEATS THE OFT

Just as a medieval king went into battle surrounded by a host of generals, astrologers, trumpet-blowers, map-readers and money lenders, so Ernest Saunders took the field for the battle against Argyll with cohorts of advisers. The group was hastily gathered together. Some had followed him from the skirmish for Bell's, others came fresh to Guinness. They were top merchant bankers, lawyers, public relations consultants, advertising agencies, stockbrokers, lobbyists. Such an array had never been seen before in a takeover campaign.

A new face represented the merchant bankers. Anthony Richmond Watson of Morgan Grenfell, who had advised Guinness in the Bell's case, was tied up with the United Biscuits bid for Imperial, so he was replaced by his Morgan Grenfell colleague, Roger Seelig. Seelig, who was just 40, sat at Saunders' right-hand at the daily morning meetings; he had the chairman's ear, and seemed to strike up a very good rapport with Ernest Saunders. The two men were highly aggressive, they both had moved up very fast, and they had both highly developed public images. Seelig was known as a banker who pushed to the limit takeover legislation and practice.

This kind of reputation, coupled with an eager eye for publicity, had made him many enemies among his less aggressive and less publicity-conscious colleagues. Labels were attached to Seelig such as 'takeover star', 'inveterate dealmaker' and the like by the media who, in the run-up to the major City shake-up called The Big Bang, were hungry for symbols of the human face of the City.

Seelig had fingers in many pies; he was a personal friend of Sir Terence Conran, served on the Habitat Mothercare board and on the board of the chemists Underwood. He made a point of becoming known to leading industrialists, and sold his and his bank's services harder than most of his more gentlemanly City peers. Seelig could appear arrogant, 'a cold fish', impenetrable and the like. He had admirers in the profession, but to junior colleagues he was a general who had to be obeyed. Seelig was not somebody who mucked around, asked for advice or left anything to doubt. He spoke in neat, clipped and ordered phrases. To his peers he had a disarming charm, a quick intelligence, but little time for small talk. His eye, one suspects, was always at least half on the clock.

He lived with his mother at weekends in a Cotswold manor house near the Gloucestershire town of Tetbury, a gentleman in the rural setting retreating from the City mire. He enjoyed the rugged country pursuits like riding to hounds with the Beaufort Hunt. But he was always a City man at heart, and had been with Morgan Grenfell almost since leaving university. He had made himself very wealthy, the £250,000 that he got by way of salary and options from his bank being only part of his income. The rest had come from investments in clients of Morgan Grenfell, which were all properly made, though a few have attracted some unwholesome publicity.

Saunders' most trusty companion was Thomas Ward. Even allowing for the fact that American lawyers are much more commercial than the average British solicitor or even barrister, Ward took the go-for-it mentality to extreme lengths. The cautious City men around him were shocked, and perhaps amused, at some of his no-holes-barred suggestions. Ward's practice in Washington DC, Ward, Lazarus, Grow and Cihlar, specialised in protecting product trade marks, an aspect of the law which could involve sleuthing and quasi-private detective work. Saunders had first used his talent for protecting trade marks when he was at Nestlé — there is some suggestion that he helped out Saunders in the Baby Milk Scandal in the US — and he had later used Ward at the Bell's bid. Ward knew the

Saunders style, shared the chairman's determination, and fearlessly grasped the jugular.

He was also a highly ingenious questioner, and made use of his forensic training to surprise the unsuspecting. One observer of Ward in action describes the lawyer's technique. 'He was very good at asking the hypothetical question. "I know you have no intention of jumping out of that window, but if you were to jump out of the window, would you go head first, or feet first?" So you'd say, "I'd probably go head first." He'd then say, "When you jump out of that window you'll have to go feet first. Can I discuss with you whether you would wear brown shoes or white shoes." But you say, I didn't say I was going to jump . . . "No, no. I'm not worried about that." Soon, you'll find yourself quoted as saying, "I'm told by that guy he's going to wear white shoes when he jumps out of the window feet first."'

Like Saunders, Ward had a veneer of great charm, and his smile is remembered by many of his combatants, and greatly feared. Saunders was later to pay a tribute to Ward, describing him as 'the man who did more, in my opinion, than any other to bring about the success of the bid'.

Saunders had taken on the leading institutional broker, Cazenove, to buy and sell shares in the bid, and they had two City aristocrats leading their forces, David Mayhew and Anthony Forbes. They came with all the Cazenove blue-blooded cachet, where heredity as well as merit plays a part in gaining membership. Anthony Forbes in fact has the added prestige of having for a brother-in-law the governor of the bank of England, Robin Leigh-Pemberton. While the pace of the bid quickened and anxiety levels rose, the gentlemen of Caz remained laid back. Saunders wanted them not for strategy, but for their much-vaunted 'placing power'. Institutions are in thrall to Cazenove and dare not refuse to buy whatever shares Cazenove offer them. The upper crust of Cazenove sat down at the same table for the Distillers bid (as they had already done for the Bell's), with relatively lower-class men from Scots broker Wood Mackenzie. Wood Mackenzie believe they were relegated to very much second fiddle for the Distillers bid because they had done some research for Argyll prior to the Guinness interest on the state of the Scotch whisky industry, when Gulliver was testing out the ground for a bid for the Distillers group. But with the benefit of hindsight, of course, many people are trying to minimise the roles they played in the takeover.

The legal aspects were covered by a leading City law firm, Freshfields. The firm's Anthony Salz, whom one Guinness adviser describes as 'a bit of a flibbertigibbet, because you could never tie him down', had a vital role. Lawyers had never before been so much in evidence in a takeover, and they probably influenced the outcome as much as the financiers. This would be standard practice in the US, but in Britain, it was very unusual. Olivier Roux or his junior finance director, Simon Duffy, were close confederates of the Saunders/Ward axis. Duffy was the Guinness director of corporate finance and supported Roux, the man from Bain and Co, the management consultants. Press men and public relations men made up the party. There were some distinguished members of the PR fraternity and their role, perhaps more than that of anybody else's, was appreciated by Saunders. Sir Gordon Reece, the one-time public relations adviser to Margaret Thatcher, was brought in to persuade politicians and mandarins of the merits of the bid. The ground work was done by Chris Davidson and Alan Stewart, the in-house PR men. They took all the cuttings from the papers for the morning meetings, and gave a comprehensive run-down on the press coverage.

As in the case of the Bell's bid, there was a meeting every day at 8 a.m. The serried ranks of advisers turned up in order to discuss the day's developments. That was at least at the beginning of the bid, but as it progressed, the large group broke up into a series of committees, and in March it stopped meeting altogether. By this stage there may well have been more going on outside the main forum than inside. One person attending in a legal capacity found that the main group became very preoccupied with public relations matters and from his point of view increasingly less useful. One of the stockbrokers claims to have been 'excluded from meetings that were taking place. The large group would meet and then you would say good night, we're off home, and as you were going you would see some other people disappearing off into another meeting.'

Much has been made in the press of a group of advisers who met apart from the main group, and took the main decisions.

This 'inner cabinet', as it came to be dubbed, could have initiated, or at least known about, share support operations. The professionals named as participants in this group, not surprisingly, deny that it ever existed.

One adviser whose name has been linked with the 'inner cabinet' describes the concept as 'a load of gibberish'. 'People didn't have time to sit around strategising. There was no regular meeting to discuss strategy.' The concept of the inner cabinet was, he said, not correct in specifics, abnormal in generalities, and while it was theoretically possible, did not reflect what people had to do to ensure the well-managed running of the bid. This itself was complicated by the large numbers of people involved, and danger of a duplication of roles. In his view, only two people had an overview of the campaign and the strategy.

Two tasks faced this phalanx of advisers immediately the merger proposal with Distillers was agreed on the weekend of 18 and 19 January. The first was to tackle the Argyll contention that Distillers agreement to pay the cost of the Guinness bid constituted 'frustrating action'. The second was to start working on the Office of Fair Trading who would begin immediately to examine the implications of the bid for the Scotch whisky market in Britain.

While the lobbying process was cranking into action, the audacious agreement reached with Distillers over costs was becoming a thorn in the side of Guinness. First, it had made journalists whose sympathies were largely with Argyll actively anti-Guinness, when they saw how Guinness had reaped themselves an insurance policy against losing which Argyll did not have. Secondly, the major investing institutions sounded off against Guinness' aggressive techniques. The costs agreement looked a sure recipe for a mass of irresponsible takeovers, but more nitty-gritty was the fact that both Guinness and Distillers shareholders would end up paying the costs. These were very large sums, when they came directly out of profits — three weeks after the merger agreement costs were said already to have risen to around £25 million. The institutions were also opposed to the arrival of the American-style poison pill in the UK — the tactic which made a takeover target too expensive to swallow by burdening it with some unwanted costs. Representative bodies such as the Association of British Insurers vigorously denounced the costs device.

The last consequence of the costs deal was to set off a series of legal actions from Argyll that were to harass Guinness during the course of the bid. Without the agreement, Guinness would not have made the bid at all, said Olivier Roux, who cited the Guinness expectation that there would be a reference to the Monopolies and Mergers Commission.

No formal announcement about the costs agreement was made before it had leaked out to the press four days after the merger had been consummated. But one PR man knew on the day of the merger announcement Roger Seelig had whispered it in his ear during the press conference.

Argyll's bankers, Samuel Montagu, first took the issue to the Takeover Panel, the City's own regulatory body. There were a number of grounds for complaint. First, they said that Argyll was having to borrow heavily for the bid and the hole in the Distillers balance sheet caused by the costs agreement, would, if they won, damage their chances of paying off quickly their loans. Secondly, they claimed, the agreement broke the law. The argument was repeated in the later writ, that the agreement amounted to Distillers aiding someone else to buy their own shares, which was against the 1985 Companies Act, section 151. The case was not clear-cut here but worth fighting all the same, said Samuel Montagu's Rupert Faure Walker. 'We took legal advice on that. It was like some of the other things that have come out, not black and white.' The last, and strongest point made by the Argyll camp, was that they felt Distillers should have their shareholders' approval before committing themselves to such a large pay-out. This came in the same category, believed Samuel Montagu, as directors writing themselves service contracts in the course of a bid, and that was against Takeover code Rule 21. The code rules that a general meeting has to be called and shareholders' approval obtained. The Takeover Panel Executive found against Argyll, who appealed to the full Panel. It was a close decision, but the panel was persuaded that Guinness' costs, which at that time were believed to be no more than £20 million, were not material in the context of a £2 billion bid. These costs rose to some £100 million by the end, making the hole in the Distillers bank balance rather larger than at the point when the regulators ruled.

The Guinness sophistry here bears a remarkable similarity with the later argument that the UK whisky market was only a few per cent of the world market and therefore Guinness' controlling 40% of the market was 'immaterial'. The Takeover Panel ruling raised some bankers' eyebrows, and others felt more strongly that yet again the Takeover Panel had opted out of taking a tough stand.

On 6 February, Argyll took a legal tack, issuing a writ. As Distillers shareholders, they were protesting about the action of Distillers directors who, they were claiming, were breaching the Companies Act by agreeing to pay Guinness costs. The case was made against Distillers company itself, not the individual directors who had made the agreement with Saunders. Gulliver said high-mindedly that he did not want to personalise the issue. It quickly came out that the Distillers directors were indemnified by Guinness anyway, which left observers wondering if all along Guinness knew that the agreement was not as above-board as they were publicly arguing. The Argyll move was dismissed contemptuously by Saunders and Roux as a smokescreen to divert attention from the 'real issues', more aptly the subjects Saunders wanted to emphasise like his much-vaunted expertise in international drinks management. Argyll quietly dropped the writ, consoling themselves with the knowledge that if they had won Distillers they could have sued Guinness to recover the costs.

On the same day they issued their writ, Argyll launched something more material than the legal action. To the surprise of all and sundry they pushed up their bid for Distillers to £2.3 billion to put it a short head ahead of Guinness' £2.2 billion. This was actually an attempt by Argyll to appeal to the Office of Fair Trading who could then appear more even-handed to Distillers shareholders if there was a bid on the table to match the Guinness bid, when it got pushed into touch at the Monopolies and Mergers Commission(MMC). The possibility of a reference to the MMC would have stopped the bid in its tracks, and was the real and pressing concern of the Saunders camp at this time. Everything was done to lobby the regulatory authorities.

The first target was Sir Gordon Borrie, the director general of the Office of Fair Trading. He is a slightly academic, raffish lawyer, who looks with some amusement at the inflated egos and voracious ambitions of the wealthy men who court him assiduously. He makes no effort to put on the appearances of the immaculate corporate lawyer. In fact, he has aspired to be a Labour politician but is now employed as a civil servant, under the auspices of the Department of Trade and Industry. But the power he wields is tremendous, since a reference from his department to the Monopolies and Mergers Commission usually puts the kibosh on a bid. The MMC has this effect because it takes an inordinately long time, at least six months, to examine the monopolistic implications of a bid.

Borrie, like all top civil servants, must work to the guidelines of his minister. In July 1984 an important statement was made by the man in charge of his department, Norman Tebbit, where he said in effect that the only bar on mergers would be if they were anti-competitive. Other considerations, such as their implications on employment, or on regional policy, were henceforth to be excluded. Borrie's task was suddenly made simpler, he had then only to tot up the home market shares of the joint companies, and if they came to more than 25%, the figure laid down in the The Fair Trading Act, then he sent them over to the MMC for their consideration. When the Distillers/Guinness merger was announced, Borrie and his department got to work on the computations of the market shares of Bell's plus Distillers. Some of the work on Distillers had already been covered, because the OFT had examined the Argyll bid for Distillers in December and waved it through.

Even though Borrie's task is essentially to assess market shares, he still has to hear other interests' views on the merger, and for this his department has its merger panel. This grouping of civil servants sifts out the implications for each government ministry, as well as the implications for employment and for regional policy — interestingly, exactly the criteria that the Tebbit ruling has now excluded from relevance to a takeover. It produces a report for Borrie to examine. The panel met three weeks after the Guinness merger plans were announced, on 7 February. Borrie also received many letters and representations from concerned people in the country and in the industry, drinks wholesalers and retailers and the like.

The real argument and pressure went on outside the drab portals of the government corridors of the Office of Fair Trading. In restaurants round the West End of London, lobbyists and Guinness confederates sought out their friends and contacts among the decision-makers and entertained them lavishly, made small talk until the main meal and wine arrived, and then broached the subject of the little matter of the Guinness bid. Guinness and Distillers had employed some of the best-known and most influential lobbyists to put their case. Sir Gordon Reece came in to support Saunders and lend his experience of working with Mrs Thatcher and the Conservative Party. Distillers had Tim Bell of advertising agency Lowe Howard Spink, who had previously worked at Saatchis, and Andrew Gifford of the public affairs company GJW, who had worked for Guinness during the Bell's bid.

Lobbying for Guinness' merchant bank, Morgan Grenfell, at the Office of Fair Trading was Sir Peter Carey, who joined the bank in 1983. He came from the Civil Service, in fact from the Department of Industry, the department with responsibility for the OFT. He therefore knew the people and the OFT's department especially well. The lobbyists tackled Borrie and the ministers to which he reports, aggressively pushing familiar lines — that they could not fairly allow through one bid and not the other. Moreover, they said they had the superior management and were intent on building an international drinks business which would create employment and be good for Britain. Argyll's relative youth and some of its less prestigious activities were compared with the venerable and established Guinness parentage.

Links between government ministers were examined to see how best the Department of Trade and Industry could be influenced. Some leading backbench MPs of the time were also heavily lobbied, notably Alex Pollock, parliamentary private secretary to the Secretary of State for Scotland, and Hector Munro, chairman of the Conservative backbench Scottish committee. Pollock duly came out in the middle of the bid in favour of Distillers.

There was a complication in the lobbying process. In normal circumstances, most attention would be paid to the Secretary of State, who makes the ultimate decision on referral. But, since Paul Channon had connections with the Guinness family, he was disqualified from playing any part. The matter was handed over to his minister, Geoffrey Pattie. Andrew Gifford said the Channon presence in the cabinet was 'the most unhelpful part of the lobbying process'. Having to deal with junior ministers 'didn't help Guinness'. Another factor also played a part. The government might want to make it transparently clear that the presence of a Guinness in the cabinet was not influencing their decision, by over-compensating in favour of Argyll.

The services of Bain in constructing graphs and arrays of figures were used extensively during the lobbying to show how white spirits were threatening the whisky market. Bill Young of Bain often accompanied the Guinness people to meetings. It was a claim that did not impress Borrie. He is not a whisky drinker himself, but believes that 'it takes quite a lot to make a whisky drinker go to rum, because most people do have an association with one drink or another'. Borrie's abstemious drinking habits had come to the notice of Ernest Saunders some years earlier. Saunders had taken Borrie out to lunch but to Saunders' disappointment Borrie would not drink his Guinness, since he stayed off alcohol in the middle of the day. 'Ah,' said Saunders, 'you must try my new non-alcoholic lager.' Borrie was diplomatic about the taste of the drink, but found Saunders perfectly pleasant.

The drinks industry itself was not exactly Borrie's cup of tea. More to his taste were the arcane principles to which the OFT had to work, and one argument put by the Saunders camp did impress the OFT man. If Gordon Borrie was going to fly the competition, free-market flag of his political masters, it would be invidious for him rather than the shareholders to decide between the two bids. But a referral to the MMC would do exactly that, by putting Guinness out of play for six months, and giving Argyll the clear advantage.

The effect of the intensive lobbying was to sew doubts in Borrie's mind. Although he knew that Guinness was creating for itself a clear monopoly, he felt uneasy about referring the bid. He says candidly: 'I did have at the back of my mind the slight anxiety that while I felt it was right for the bid to go to the MMC, suppose the balance of the argument in the end was in favour of Guinness. In that event, I would actually be the instrument which would prevent what might be desirable in the public interest taking place, by sending this bid off to the commission and not the other one.'

On 11 February Sir Gordon Borrie's verdict went round to the Department of Trade and Industry. The message in Sir Gordon's letter was that the bid should be referred. The reasons he gave were on the grounds of competition. He had added up the combined market shares of Bell's and Distillers in the UK and found they came to 38% of the home market, comfortably past the generally accepted 25% mark. The worst of Saunders' fears had been realised; people around him saw the perpetual optimist become depressed, and that led to desperation. Saunders and his team mulled over the decision 'into the wee small hours' as one participant observed. Everyone was very dispirited. Soon afterwards, Saunders went to see Paul Channon, the Secretary of State for Trade and Industry, but he was sidelined and would not assist. The Guinness camp had also expected to be dealing with Michael Howard in the DTI, and were caught off-balance when Geoffrey Pattie was given the brief.

Then Saunders went to see Sir Godfray Le Quesne, the chairman of the Monopolies and Mergers Commission. Saunders commented on the meeting: 'We discussed it with the chairman of the MMC, a judge. It was like being put on probation, and I had been told to go and see the probation officer.' Le Quesne told Saunders that the options open to him were 'either to give up or to withdraw the bid and come up with a new one that was materially different in a competition context to the first one'.

It was now all hands to the pump, as Saunders tried to keep his team on the road, and his own morale up. For the next four days, lawyers, brokers and the whole panoply of advisers pored over past precedent and options to devise a way to satisfy the competition criteria. On the Saturday morning after the referral Saunders phoned Charles Fraser, the Scottish lawyer and an old ally, and said 'we've had it. Freshfields says there is nothing else to be done.' Fraser urged the desperate chief executive not to despair, and proposed bringing in yet more lawyers for consultation. On the following day, two of the leading experts in company law, Jeremy Lever QC and John Swift QC, appeared at Portman Square, the Guinness headquarters, accompanied by Fraser who had just flown down from Edinburgh. Using the precedent, created just a few weeks before, when United Biscuits, bidding for Imperial, offered up for sale its Golden Wonder crisps company to avoid a referral to the Monopolies and Mergers Commission, the bevy of lawyers juggled with a similar reconstruction. Saunders had to prove to his judicial warder that any new arrangements were 'materially different' from the first ones. Then he could say that he was scrapping the original bid, or in technical terms, abandoning it, and was now starting afresh.

Another adviser coming to Saunders' rescue in this hour of need was his trusted colleague Tom Ward, who according to later testimony at the Jersey litigation in March 1987 was on his way to the airport when Saunders called him back.

The new form of bid devised by the lawyers involved the sale of five whisky brands. Distillers market share at home would come down to less than 25% and all the regulators with their competition criteria would be placated. David Connell, one of the few Distillers directors for whom Guinness had any time at all, spent the following four days selecting the brands and totting up their shares. They may well have had other brands and alternative schemes up their sleeves, in case the new bid format failed, and they had not sacrificed enough market share.

The Guinness men now returned to the offices of the Monopolies aned Mergers Commission to test it out on Sir Godfray Le Quesne. While they were confident that the market share problem had now been solved, the device might still appear artificial, especially in comparison with the only precedent, the United Biscuits sell-off of Golden Wonder, where there was a separate company being put up for sale.

The Monopolies and Mergers Commission was put in a highly unusual situation. Most companies either walked away from a bid that had been referred, or they allowed it to be examined for monopolistic content. Here was one that wanted to stretch the monopolies criteria. The only place the MMC, a quasi non-governmental organisation, could turn to for guidance was the government, and they were determined to keep out of industry. Judge Le Quesne and his MMC were left very much on their own to arbitrate through a quagmire of statistics, and arguments expounded by some highly-determined leading practitioners.

There were four meetings betwen Le Quesne and the Saunders team in the three vital days 17, 18 and 19 February. At the first meeting Le Quesne has said he was unsure whether to grant abandonment of the old Guinnesss bid or not. By the end of the third meeting he was convinced. The two sides were hardly equally matched. On the one side was the judge acting by himself and without other members of his commission. On the other was the Saunders entourage of John Swift, Ward, and Seelig. Sir John Donaldson, the Master of the Rolls, was later to say that Le Quesne had acted beyond his legal powers in laying the bid aside by himself.

The meetings were heated; Sir Alex Fletcher, who had previously been a minister in the Department of Trade and Industry and now was an adviser to Argyll, believed that Le Quesne had probably never experienced such unrelenting pressure as Saunders applied during those days. His barristers were accomplished and as persuasive as their chief was insistent and hectoring. Said Fletcher, 'Guinness and Morgan's very skilfully knew their man. There's no break for coffee, or lunch, or dinner with Saunders, he's the general in the field, it's attack, attack, attack. He did it with the OFT and he did it with Le Quesne.' The judge liked the Saunders claim that by not allowing him to bid, Gulliver would walk away with Distillers and shareholders would not have a choice of managements. It appealed to his sense of fair play. The pushing and the pulling, the persuasion and the table-banging, the smiling and the threats wore down the 62-year-old judge. The announcement of the abandonment came out after one of the long and hard-fought meetings, at the extraordinarily late hour of 10 p.m. The news came to Samuel Montagu man Rupert Faure Walker just as he arrived home. The tireless City people in London had switched off for the evening, but a colleague in New York, for whom it was just 5 p.m., had seen it on his Reuters screen, and thought he ought to know. It cast Faure Walker into despondency. Now he knew that a higher Guinness bid would be presented the following morning.

The Guinness men were jubilant. The dismay of the OFT referral was behind them, legalism and lobbying had seen them right. The following day, Saunders was up and running again with an increased bid of £2.35 billion and an announcement that the brands were up for sale. The same day he began new talks with Sir Gordon Borrie who had to look at the new Saunders bid, and give it his all clear again.

Now it was Argyll's turn to fight back. They had all along favoured a litigious approach, and now they sought to use the law to halt the Saunders bandwagon. On 25 February they went to law to challenge the Monopoly and Mergers Commission's judgement permitting Guinness to abandon its first Distillers bid. They asked the High Court to allow them to challenge the findings of the MMC in what is called a 'judicial review'. They claimed that decision to allow the bid to be abandoned was wrong, because the new bid was not substantially different from the old one. They also said that Le Quesne should have called together his MMC colleagues before coming to his decision and not acted alone. On 7 March, the judicial review took place. It was acrimonious but petty. Some of the charges levelled bordered on the ridiculous. For example, Argyll produced a DTI press release which they said had gone out on Reuters. Guinness riposted that the Argyll press release was forged, claiming that Argyll had mocked it up for the hearing but had transposed two words which gave it away. Argyll said the wording had been given to them by the Department of Trade and Industry. An official from the press office of the DTI was brought in, and asked whether they had given the press release to Argyll. No, said one official, yes, said another. It was trifling stuff to have such big stakes hanging on it, and in the end the two sides accepted the Argyll point that nothing sinister had occurred. Yet Saunders was later to talk about the Argyll 'forgery' as a fact. It also came at a time when allegations and some evidence of dirty tricks were flying around, and both sides sought to latch on to dirt to blacken their opponents' name.

On 10 March, Argyll went to the Court of Appeal to question the unfavourable findings of their judicial review. But on 14 March Gulliver's hopes were finally dashed when Sir John Donaldson, the Master of the Rolls, rejected Argyll's appeal against the High Court support for Le Quesne, but the Court agreed with Argyll that Le Quesne had been wrong to deal with Saunders and his team alone without the support of his Commission colleagues. But that was not enough to rule that the abandonment should be reversed, especially as 'deals had already been made that depended on the decision.' The judge was not more specific about these deals, but he suggested that the matter of law infringed here was weighed in the scales and found to be lighter than commercial criteria, amply expounded upon, no doubt, by Saunders and the lobbyists.

Saunders had one more hurdle to jump with his new offer. It had again to pass over the table of the amiable Sir Gordon Borrie. If he was apologetic before about having to refer the bid, he now positively welcomed the chance to clear it. He said: 'I was quite — I won't say pleased, but quite intrigued — by the possibilities that then emerged at the next and most exciting stage of the events. I could now see a possible way forward.'

Borrie had still to go through his administrative procedures, in exactly the same way as he had with the first bid. Saunders told him about the five brands on offer — Claymore, Real Mackenzie, John Barr, Buchanan Blend and Haig Gold Label — and asked whether Borrie thought he was selling off enough. Borrie had his standards and would not be drawn.

'I refused to get into a negotiation thing. I wouldn't allow him to come along here with ten brands, and say to me "well now you take away as many as you think is necessary". I said to him, "I can't negotiate, I can't make a deal with you and act as an adviser in order to avoid a reference. I will deal with whatever proposal you come up with." '

He also wanted to know that there was a buyer for the brands, and that it was not a sleight of hand. Saunders was not pleased when he heard about this, and proposed to Borrie a plan to park the brands with Morgan Grenfell, but Borrie turned that idea down.

In an 'amazingly short period' (Borrie's words), the name of Whyte and Mackay, the Lonrho subsidiary, was produced, as if out of a hat. Whyte and Mackay people came along with Guinness folk to subsequent meetings of the OFT to discuss the divestment. Meetings took place between the end of February and the middle of March. A binding agreement was drawn up on 21 March. As for the price of £3.5 million, that did not concern him. Said Borrie, 'I couldn't care less what the price was. In fact Lonrho had got it at a knock-down price, but that's not too surprising because they knew as well as we did how desperate Guinness were to find a buyer. They must have known that we were insisting on a specific buyer, and there aren't many around as substantial as Whyte and Mackay.' With what one observer called 'a sleazy little deal', the due official regulatory processes concerning the creation of monopolies were completed. Some legendary brands of Scotch were being sold off and in Scotland there was much rumbling.

Broker Thorold Mackie of the Edinburgh firm Bell Lawrie decribes the deal to sell off the brands as the 'bargain of a lifetime. They didn't even have to buy the distilleries and the stock, they could do that in due course from Distillers. They were buying the brands for a ridiculous price.' Distillers themselves made some half-hearted attempts at explaining the sale. One director said the brands were going to a distinguished Scottish company. It did not take long for the press to pick on the irony in that.

Bringing in Lonrho could actually have misfired for Saunders. Tiny Rowland's old adversaries, the Al Fayeds, provoked by the arrival of Rowland, saw a chance to take an interest. They suggested to Samuel Montagu that they use some of their legendary, if disputed, wealth to support Argyll. But the approach appears never to have advanced.

The bid was now clear of all regulatory and judicial obstacles, bar a late and desperate attempt by Argyll to have the faculty of advocates in Scotland rule that the merger was monopolistic under article 86 of the Treaty of Rome. That did not wash with the Scots who, Gulliver believes, had let him down yet again.

Saunders was later to brag that his entrepreneurial approach to the takeover authorities in the UK had created a precedent. He even said that he had taught Lord Hanson a thing or two. Tiny Rowland, who visited Saunders much later in Switzerland, spoke admiringly of the Guinness chief's successful dealings with the Office of Fair Trading. The role of one Saunders adviser in discussions with the regulators has come in for especial comment. Thomas Ward, the American lawyer, appeared at almost every stage. He claims to have helped persuade Distillers to come to a unanimous agreement on the Guinness merger, to have arranged for them to pay the costs, to have been instrumental in negotiating with the OFT and MMC, and in courting American shareholders. For these services he was paid fees of £5.2 million. This is a very large sum for any sort of corporate service, but doubts now arise about the exact nature of Ward's contribution. For example, Olivier Roux later threw doubt on the importance of Ward in constructing the costs deal, claiming in his affidavit to the High Court in April 1987 that Salz the lawyer was more influential. Ward also had a very minor role in the OFT negotiations. According to Sir Gordon Borrie, he appeared just once.

But Ward had one role which Saunders found invaluable. He was the man who carried out the unpleasant tasks; his role in the bid has been described as negotiating with the Distillers directors. In fact Ward was the man who told them that they were no longer wanted. To one or two he delivered promises which he did not keep. One was told not only that he could stay on, but that he would be promoted; it turned out otherwise.

The effectiveness of the regulatory and judicial authorities to lay down guidelines and ensure observance of certain standards of practice during a bid was sorely tested. The decisions of the Monopolies and Mergers Commission would certainly seem to favour the conglomerate bidder who can ditch a few brands if it means pushing through a bid. This is arguably producing a result quite the reverse of the control of monopolies for which the MMC is intended. It also does not ensure that managers who know anything about the business eventually run them. Financial nous would seem to be prized above industrial expertise. The long timetable of the MMC is also an anachronism when financial operators are moving as fast as Saunders. But perhaps the biggest problem of all is the absence of a political lead for the regulators. Acting in the vacuum of a completely free takeover market, they had one basis for letting through a takeover: the simplistic assessment of market share. It left the regulators naked. They were left vulnerable to the questionable statistical analysis at which Bain excelled, the judicial sleight of hand for which lawyers were equipped and the clever arguments dreamt up by Saunders.

CHAPTER TEN

THE DIRTY TRICKS

While the judicial game was being played in the public forum upfront, bands of mercenaries employed by both sides were sniping in a guerrilla war. While the tactics used may have seemed shocking to the outsider, the men at the front knew this was the way takeover battles were being fought and few hands stayed clean by the end.

On Sunday 9 March, James Gulliver made the front page lead story in *The Observer*. But it was not the sort of free publicity that might help the Argyll cause. Labelled 'Exclusive', the headline screamed 'Argyll's Gulliver may resign'. The story revealed that Gulliver's entry in *Who's Who* was incorrect: it stated that he had been educated at the universities of Glasgow and Harvard. The reality was that he had spent a short three-week course in marketing at Harvard. There was no mention of his genuine Master of Science Degree from the Georgia Institute.

On the Sunday morning there was a crisis meeting at the offices of Samuel Montagu. Gulliver explained to his fellow directors and bankers that a mistake had been made and he had never got round to changing the entry in *Who's Who*. He then left the room in order to allow the Argyll board to discuss the matter privately. They needed very little time to reach a unanimous verdict of support for their chairman. On Sunday afternoon Gulliver issued a statement to the press: 'One entry in the record of my academic and business career, relating to a degree achieved in 1954, has been incorrectly stated. I regret this error has not been previously corrected.' Quickly he was back on the offensive and accused Distillers of waging a dirty tricks campaign.

Gulliver may have been lucky that the episode did not have more serious repercussions. In Sweden earlier in the year there were similar revelations about the academic background of the leading business tycoon Refaat el-Sayed, who controlled the biotechnology concern Fermenta. It was alledged that his academic records had been misleading and shares in the company plummeted. The automobile giant Volvo abruptly pulled out of a planned co-operative venture with Fermenta.

The first reaction from Distillers was that the Gulliver story was nothing to do with them. But soon it was discovered that Peter Binns of Binns Cornwall, who were advising Distillers, had obtained letters from Harvard confirming there was no record of Gulliver enrolling there. Photocopies of these letters were given to the *Wall Street Journal* and the *Sunday Times*. Binns revealed that he'd received the letters from the Distillers director David Connell.

The 'Harvard' leak failed to tarnish Argyll's image in the publicity battle. As one journalist remembered: 'It should have been a devastating blow but the press handled it sympathetically.' There was a danger, even, of it backfiring on Distillers. One director later admitted that it was 'something that I wouldn't have put out — it was a sloppy leak'. But the same director believes it was justified to publicise the information because it put some of Gulliver's other claims in perspective, for example about his overseas marketing: 'It was an indication of the kind of person he was and how much you could trust the other statements he was making about how wonderful Barton Brands was, for example.' There was also some suggestion that the incident may have succeeded in sowing seeds of doubt in a few institutional people's minds.

The leak illustrates how important the media were for each of the three parties. Financial and business stories were breaking out of their ghetto on the City pages. And day after day the puzzled reader of *The Times*, the *Guardian* or the *Daily Telegraph* would find whole-page advertisements, usually with copy knocking the record of a company. Most people had heard of Guinness, because of the fame of the drink, but few knew what Distillers was or or why Argyll was so interested. One of the few rulings of the Takeover Panel during the battle for Distillers was to curtail the use of advertising by companies. The ruling barred the use of material designed to discredit another party in a takeover battle. But it was designed to come into force on 1 May, well after the end of the battle for Distillers.

The advertising battle reached such a frenzy that writs began to fly. On 14 March Guinness began proceedings for injurious falsehood and defamation against Argyll and, specifically, Gulliver, Webster, Samuel Montagu, Charterhouse, Noble Grossart, Saatchi and Saatchi, Broad Street Associates and Brian Basham. A statement from Guinness outlined the reasons: 'Guinness regret that this course of action has become necessary but considers that it has been forced upon them by reason of a regular flow of misleading and inaccurate statements which have been made in support of Argyll's bid for Distillers'. The writ cited a number of advertisements in newspapers between 31 January and 12 March. The Guinness solicitor was Sir David Napley, a leading criminal lawyer rather than a libel expert. The injunction was sought in a bid to prevent Argyll using the advertisements pending full trial. Argyll replied by saying they'd go on using them because the ads had been cleared with the Takeover Panel and their own lawyers. Nothing more was heard of the case.

Guinness tried a legal attack on another front. Wellington Importers, an American susidiary of Bell's, filed for $200 million worth of damages against Argyll and Saatchi and Saatchi in a District of Columbia court. The action was in connection with the use of the Bell's trademark in Argyll advertisements. These advertisements were in British newspapers circulated in the United States. The timing of this legal move was fortuitous in view of the bid battle that was in progress. Thomas Ward's firm Ward, Lazarus, Grow and Cihlar, were pursuing the action on behalf of Guinness. It wasn't the first or the last time that Ward would threaten legal action. Nothing more was heard of the case after the initial wave of publicity.

Saunders was acutely sensitive to what the papers were saying; he knew that the fight for Distillers was being played out in the public arena and that shareholders would be swayed as much by newspaper columns as by the cold financial arguments. He had wooed journalists in his reign at Guinness, and was particularly friendly with Ivan Fallon on the *Sunday Times* and Kenneth Fleet on *The Times*. But he became almost obsessed with what he believed was bias by certain nationals: The *Sunday Telegraph* and *Daily Telegraph* were high on his list, along with the *Observer*. He knew that the Guinness advertising budget was a powerful weapon. The takeover climate had brought a flood of new advertising revenue into most quality papers, but Guinness had always spent heavily on brand promotion, particularly in the colour supplements.

Saunders picked first on the *Telegraph* group. He called Andrew Knight, the chief executive, and arranged a lunchtime meeting. David Brewerton, who wrote the *Daily Telegraph* 'Questor' column on the City pages, was asked along. But the City Editor of the *Sunday Telegraph*, Ian Watson, decided it would be unwise to join them; he felt his position of responsibility could be compromised. Saunders reported that 'my shareholders have expressed alarm at unfair and biased reporting by newspapers, notably the two *Telegraphs*'. He noted that they had supported Gulliver from the day he launched his bid in December. Saunders was persuasive and courteous, but the unspoken implication was that they would lose Guinness advertising. After the meeting Knight rang Watson to express concern and to ask why Saunders had come to see him. Knight had been unaware of the dirty tricks and less savoury aspects of the bid timetable. Watson's response was that he'd supported Saunders during the bid for Bell's, and felt that over the years he'd given the company perfectly balanced coverage.

Watson, in fact, had known Ernest Saunders for some time. He'd first met him before he became chief executive of Guinness; early on he decided Saunders was a businessman to be watched. At the end of December 1984 he tipped Guinness as a share of the year for 1985. Watson was impressed with Saunders' approach to the media: 'He was faultless in his dealings with me.' But he'd noted that something seemed to change after the bid for Distillers was launched: 'He started prevaricating — I sensed something was going wrong.' On one occasion Saunders rang from the airport and said he objected to a piece in the *Sunday Telegraph*. He came round to Watson's office with Thomas Ward. Ward began taking notes of the conversation but Watson objected. The meeting ended abruptly.

Saunders also contacted Lord Stevens, who'd recently acquired United Newspapers, owners of the *Daily Express* and the *Sunday Express*. He made it clear to Stevens that he wasn't happy with the stance taken on the *Express* City pages and pointed out how much Guinness advertising revenue was received by United Newspapers.

One of the most bizarre aspects of the takeover war was the involvement of private investigators. Like flies gorging on fresh fruit, they spotted ways of making a fast buck out of the main protagonists. The investigators who were freelance operators, without attachment to either side, believed they could make large sums of money out of selling information. One such operator was Nicholas Vafiadis, a former SAS man. His calling card declared that he worked for 'Tempest Consultants', described as international investigators. The address on the card was in Malvern, Worcestershire. Vafiadis decided to get in on the Argyll-Distillers act in January 1986. He tracked down a former employee of the Alpine double glazing operation, Charles Walford in New York. Vafiadis offered Walford $11,000 for 'dirt' on Gulliver but discovered to his chagrin that Walford was full of praises for Gulliver's performance at Alpine. Walford discreetly recorded the meeting to protect himself. He later gave the tape to Alastair Grant. Argyll's lawyers then took a transcript and got an affidavit supporting the document from Walford. There was much speculation that Vafiadis was employed by Distillers, who denied the allegations. In years gone by he may have worked for them, checking counterfeit brands.

Unsolicited approaches were also made to Argyll with offers of information about Guinness. There were many allegations made about Saunders' career at Nestlé and the baby milk scandal. At one stage a solicitor contacted Argyll on behalf of a client who had a grievance against Saunders. The solicitor suggested that certain information be publicised, and no payment was asked for. The offer was politely refused by Argyll.

Mysterious burglaries started to occur, notably at the homes of David Connell and James Gulliver. There were also break-ins at the homes of lesser figures in the drama; Colin Liddell's house outside Edinburgh was burgled. Nothing was taken from the houses except papers, making it appear, at least on the surface, that these were not ordinary break-ins. But no one had enough evidence to make substantial allegations. Certainly all the main players had their offices swept for bugs. It was considered almost par for the course that there would be bugging, bribery and leaking and there were no complaints, however excited the press got about the stories.

But Argyll's David Webster is doubtful whether the bugging happened at all: 'Whenever we took a major initiative in the bid, it caught Guinness completely off-guard and similarly there were a couple of times when they took an initiative and caught us completely off-balance.' Another participant pours scorn on the supposedly sinister burglaries: 'The fact is that in a bid there are probably one hundred key people, a lot of whom live in London and, regrettably, because of the environment they're in, a number of them are going to get their flats broken into'.

The focus of the battle until 21 March was on the Office of Fair Trading. Before that date there was a chance the new style Guinness bid would fail to pass the scrutiny of the trading watchdog. But once it got the thumbs up on 21 March, the fight for Distillers became a straight shoot out between Gulliver and Saunders. The aim now was a 50% majority of Distillers' shares, so the argument became strictly financial. Each side had the option of officially increasing its offers. But given that both were offering their own shares in exchange for Distillers stock, the value of the bids rose as the Guinness and Argyll share price increased. So the two combatants were out to force their own shares higher as well as purchasing Distillers shares. The winning army would be the one with the greater firepower. Morgan Grenfell, on behalf of Guinness, and Samuel Montagu, for Argyll, toured institutions in the City urging them to buy shares in the companies as a 'good investment for the future'.

Overseas investors were taking a keener interest in the future of Distillers. Foreign drinks distributors continued to make approaches, offering their services. Rupert Faure Walker, of Montagu's, remembers a series of meetings with a 'thoroughly reputable international group involved in the drinks industry who wanted distribution rights to certain of Distillers brands; they wanted an understanding that in return for supporting the Argyll cause and lending Argyll a few hundred million pounds they would get certain of the brands in due course'. Faure Walker had to explain that such an agreement would be in breach of normal City practice, specifically the Takeover Code. But this surprised the foreign company who had 'been advised by their lawyers that there was nothing illegal with it and so couldn't accept that if it was against a voluntary code it couldn't be done'. Presumably some of the overseas institutions who had a connection with Guinness took the same approach.

Gulliver and his advisers were shocked and disappointed by the Office of Fair Trading's decision. They were expecting the decision to be made that week but hoped it would be different. As one put it, 'We thought that because Guinness owned Bell's it would be just inconceivable that they'd be able to buy Distillers because of the huge market shares.' But the Argyll camp moved fast, forgetting their sorrows, and smacked a higher bid on the table just an hour after Geoffrey Pattie, the Industry Minister, made his announcement. The new offer was worth £2.5 billion with total underwriting increased to more than £1.7 billion. Distillers shareholders who didn't want Argyll shares in exchange could take a cash alternative worth 660 pence. Some newspapers suggested that Argyll had found enough takers for the increased underwriting because they assumed the new bid would fail. Another commented that 'if Argyll had made this bid three months ago, a shocked market would have instantly accepted it, but today it looks a little forlorn'.

Privately many Argyll camp followers were fearing the worst. David Webster, cautious and prudent, was 'Certain Guinness would move quickly to top our offer, in which case I personally did not see that we could win.' Webster knew they were hopelessly outnumbered. Until January, Argyll and advisers had been in a one-to-one fight with Distillers and followers. But when Guinness galloped in as the White Knights they brought their own heavy artillery, Morgan Grenfell and the stockbrokers Cazenoves and Wood Mackenzie. These were all big names with plenty of clout in the City. There was also the credibility problem, described by one Argyll man:

'Guinness basically was a much better name than Argyll — Guinness was in drink in a big way, Argyll was not'.

Samuel Montagu decided on a head-on counter attack despite the opposition's larger forces. Rupert Faure Walker had a plan ready to put into action: 'The idea was that as soon as Guinness announced they'd been cleared, we'd instantly come up with Argyll's final shot and try and buy control in the Stock Market in order to get the required 50%.' In 36 hours they raised £700 million from willing lenders, including Midland Bank, Citibank and Royal Bank of Scotland. Then a call to the brokers: 'Please buy 115 million Distillers shares at a price of 660 pence — total cost of £700 million — not an order I put in every day of the week.'

When that instruction was given Distillers shares were trading at around 630 pence on the Stock Market, so Montagu's were confident of finding sellers prepared to pay 660 pence. But Faure Walker could only watch helplessly as opposition money poured into the market: 'It was from that morning onwards that suddenly this massive buying of Guinness shares started. The Guinness share price really took off with massive buying from every direction. That pulled the Distillers price up and it went beyond the level at which we could buy them so we couldn't get them. I think we only got a million or so.' The rise in the Guinness share price had increased the value of their bid to above the 660 pence per share offered by Montagu's and so deterred the sellers. Montagu's could offer no more: under Takeover Panel rules a bidder is not allowed to offer a higher price than the cash alternative listed in the official bid documents. Faure Walker was powerless: 'From this moment onwards we saw this massive buying of Guinness shares and we found it very hard to accept that it was traditional investment buying.'

The upward climb of the Guinness share price marked the start of an unprecedented campaign of manipulation. Shares in the companies involved fluctuated wildly. The big money behind each combatant swamped the Stock Market, and created a market in the shares which did not reflect their true value.

Montagu's and Charterhouse were openly purchasing Argyll shares on their own account. Montagu's bought 6.25 million Argyll shares at various stages of the bid and at each point were countered by a volley of protests by Morgan Grenfell to the Takeover Panel. According to one Morgan's man: 'Charterhouse and Montagu's bought an awful lot of Argyll stock on which they showed losses. These were substantially recompensed through fees and profits they made on the purchase of Distillers stock which they were then allowed to keep. Now, really any financial recompense is a breach of Section 151 of the Companies Act.' Faure Walker denies the allegation: 'When we bought the Argyll shares it was 100% for our own risk with zero indemnity one way or another. On the Distillers shares, we could have made money, we could have lost money and frankly we made money, about £8 million. By the end of the bid we knew we were going to make a lot of money on Distillers shares and that was why we could be so bold buying Argyll shares. We were prepared to do our damnedest to help our client win and in those circumstances we were quite prepared to buy a few Argyll shares.'

Watching the pattern of the massive amounts of purchases of Guinness shares, Montagu's could see that there was always a wave of buying in the afternoon just as the American market was opening. So the Argyll brokers would take charts of the Guinness share price performance around the City fund managers and point out the trends. They would argue that the Guinness share price was being artificially massaged upwards and that it would be best to sell Guinness shares late in the day: 'We had a campaign with our brokers to encourage UK institutions who held Guinness shares to sell those shares late in the afternoon. One or two did, but a great majority could not accept that there was any massaging of the Guinness price going on.'

Persuading others to sell Guinness shares was one way to depress their price. Another tactic was 'shorting', an old trick and the hallmark of the 'bear' in market jargon. The dealer sells shares before buying them. He hopes to pick up the shares for a lower price before the delivery date. 'Shorting' can be dangerous and lead to badly burnt fingers if the price rises quickly. There is nothing illegal about the practice. But any undisclosed 'shorting' operation involving associates of a bidding company is in breach of the Takeover Code.

The strong downward pressure on the Guinness share price in late afternoon was almost certainly due in part to 'shorting'. The American *arbitrageur*, Sandy Lewis, was believed to be responsible. It was rumoured certain Scottish financial institutions hostile to Saunders were also playing a part. Sandy

Lewis was a contact of Angus Grossart, whose merchant bank, Noble Grossart, was working with Argyll. Grossart was an important figure in the close-knit financial community in Edinburgh. But James Gulliver denies any formal link with Lewis: 'I've spoken to him once briefly on the phone. He's friendly with Angus Grossart. But he never discussed with us any form of assistance in the bid.' David Webster uses an anecdote as a denial of the charge of 'shorting': 'If I give you an instance: the Argyll pension fund bought 200 thousand Guinness shares for good investment reasons in the summer of 1985. When the bid ended in April 1986 those 200 thousand shares were still in our pension fund.

On the other side of the wire, the Guinness frontliners believed, rightly or wrongly, that the opposition were forcing down the Guinness price. Saunders, in particular, was very anxious about the situation, as one of the team from Wood Mackenzie remembers: 'There was a trauma one time when there was a bear raid one evening on the Guinness stock and the price collapsed because they were selling shares like crazy. Ernest was very unhappy after that, and we detected that there was no discussion after that about what was happening on the market and who did what. There was much less pressure on us to discuss what was going on in the market, suggesting they had a very good source elsewhere.'

This source may have been Anthony Parnes, a stockbroker, whose very existence was unknown at the time of the bid for Distillers even to the closest advisers to the company. Even now it is impossible to establish his exact role, particularly in the light of the payment of a fee, reported to be £3 million. Given that Guinness were paying handsomely for the services of two of the top ranking stockbroking names from the City, Wood Mackenzie and Cazenove, it seems extraordinary that a mere 'half commission man' like Parnes should receive such a huge sum for 'services connected with the bid'. Olivier Roux later suggested why Parnes was paid such a large fee: 'He was in a position to give the company a view of the market which its official brokers couldn't. The bid was happening pre Big Bang with the old-fashioned system of jobbers and there was no way of knowing what was going on except through access by people like Mr Parnes who have an extremely good understanding of the jobbers' positions.' Parnes' role reflects the importance of wheeler dealing on the Stock Market in the battle for control of Distillers.

Parnes was an old-style Stock Market operator who had made a lot of money fast. He'd risen from the bottom after starting as a 'blue button' on the market floor. Constantly on the phone to contacts in boardrooms, banks and brokers, Parnes was a fountain of gossip and rumour. He was known throughout the bars and talking shops of the City and revelled in the nickname of 'The Animal'. He worked out of the offices of Alexanders, Laing and Cruickshank and took half commission on business he introduced to the company. At the height of his fame and affluence, Parnes was to spend £5 million on a luxurious mansion in the up-market residential area of Frognal in London's sought-after Hampstead. This house has recently been transferred into his wife's name. As soon as he moved in Parnes installed the latest in security technology and elaborate remote-control gates. His clients included some of the wealthiest and most powerful businessmen in the country.

Parnes' role in the battle for Distillers was little known at the time. One of the 'official' team looks back on one incident now with the benefit of hindsight: 'I was going out of the Guinness offices and Olivier Roux was just ahead of me and he waited outside the door, like he was waiting for somebody to pick him up. I was curious so I waited and a very large car, an Aston Martin, came round the corner, stopped and he ran across the pavement and jumped in and it went away whoosh. And I thought no more about it until later when the whole story unfolded and one of my colleagues said, you always know Tony Parnes, he drives a very large Aston Martin.'

Another of the 'backroom boys', manoeuvring discreetly behind the public players in the bid, was Sir Jack Lyons, who had introduced Parnes to Saunders. Sir Jack was UK adviser to Bain and had known Saunders ever since Bain had been recruited at Guinness. He'd had a successful business career with United Drapery Stores, which took in John Collier and Richard Shops. The business had been built up by Lyons' father and Sir Jack ran it with his brother. In March 1980 he'd resigned under a cloud after allegations of insider trading. But he'd continued to mix with people that mattered in the world of high finance and politics. His contacts in the Conservative Party were impeccable, gleaned largely through membership of the true blue Carlton Club. Lyons entertained Margaret Thatcher and Home Secretary Douglas Hurd at the offices of Bain.

No one knew of Lyons' links with Saunders and there was probably nothing to know until the latter stages of the battle for Distillers. But Sir Jack later admitted receiving a fee of more than £2 million for services rendered in connection with the takeover. It is hard to imagine what he did to earn the money if it was solely in an advisory capacity, though it is known that Lyons had connections in high places, and may have been useful in working behind the scenes in lobbying the Office of Fair Trading to strengthen the Guinness campaign against a referral of the second bid. One Guinness insider realised how sensitive Saunders was about Lyons' involvement: 'I became aware of Sir Jack Lyons' presence in the most bizarre way. I took a call from Tony Lyons, a City PR man. The secretary had put Tony Lyons through to Ernest by mistake, thinking that it was Sir Jack Lyons. Saunders' secretary was all upset because Ernest must have given her a bollocking. I often wondered what the connection was there; I thought perhaps Ernest saw Sir Jack as something of a mentor.'

Apart from their main fees of several million pounds, Lyons and Parnes received a joint payment through a company in which they both had an interest. A sum of £300,000 was paid to an investment shell company, J. Lyons Chamberlayne. Like the other payments, it is hardly clear what this money was supposed to be for or what services were rendered to Guinness by the company.

One of Parnes' most valuable services was to introduce Saunders to an important client of his. This was Gerald Ronson, one of Britain's wealthiest and most powerful businessmen, and boss of the UK's second largest private company, the Heron corporation. Ronson, a forthright, outspoken Londoner, is the nearest Britain gets to having a mega-tycoon. He built up a £1 billion business out of property and international trading and now epitomises one of Mrs Thatcher's self-made men. In fact Mrs Thatcher has shown her admiration for Ronson by supporting his charitable efforts.

Ronson was paid even more than Lyons and Parnes put together for his services to Guinness. A total of £5.8 million went Ronson's way in return for buying Guinness shares, it is believed to the value of £25 million. £5 million would be a 'success fee' while the rest was later described as a sum to compensate Ronson for any losses incurred in holding the stock. The money was all paid back to Guinness a year later when news of the deal was revealed. How many shares Ronson actually bought isn't clear. It is known he purchased 725,000 Guinness shares in the middle of April. Ronson told others later that he had no idea of the scale of the operation, but that he saw himself as 'one of a few friends helping out'. Its also known that Alexanders, Laing and Cruickshank were heavy buyers in late March, possibly on the instigation of Tony Parnes.

Another alleged supporter of Guinness was Ephraim Margulies, chairman of the commodities house S&W Berisford, owners of British Sugar. An American subsidiary of his company received a fee of £1.5 million and bought more than two million Guinness shares both during and after the bid for Distillers. Margulies was later, like Ronson, to repay the money. He said that the fee related to a commercial transaction between the American subsidiary, Erlanger, and Guinness which had nothing to do with the ownership of Guinness shares. This was apparently arranged by the local boss after a meeting with Thomas Ward.

Parnes, Lyons and Ronson were instrumental in arranging wide ranging purchases of Guinness shares in order to boost the price and make the terms of the bid seem more attractive. So, wittingly or unwittingly, was Ephraim Margulies. Their involvement was unsuspected at the time.

Another purchaser of Guinness shares in the latter stages of the bid was the merchant bank Henry Ansbacher. Their managing director Lord Spens was an old friend and former colleague of Roger Seelig. So Ansbacher was naturally one of the institutions visited by Seelig in his efforts to find willing supporters of Guinness shares. Ansbacher bought £7.6 million worth of Guinness shares for a client account Down Nominees. Another contact of Seelig who was helpful to the cause was Jacob Rothschild. He had left the famous family bank N.M. Rothschild to go it alone. Jacob was an entrepreneur and classic wheeler dealer as well as being patron of the arts (he is a trustee of the National Gallery). Through his vehicle, Jacob Rothschild Investments, he bought Guinness shares, but

according to one insider was 'very supportive but in a totally
normal way.' It has been reported that Robert Maxwell also
bought two million Guinness shares.

The buying of Guinness shares by British businessmen and
financial institutions has been the centre of attention and
speculation ever since the beginning of 1987. After all, Section
151 of the Companies Act 1985 declares it unlawful for a
company to assist in the purchase of its own shares. But any
such activities organised in the UK are dwarfed by the scale of
share buying from overseas, and from just two sources.
Between them Schenley Industries of the US and Bank Leu of
Switzerland purchased almost £200 million worth of Guinness
shares. A fifth of the company's entire share capital changed
hands in a matter of weeks, ending up in the ownership of two
foreign institutions. No wonder Faure Walker was baffled at
the steady rise in the Guinness share price.

Meshulam Riklis of Schenley did not give up when he failed
to make headway with Gulliver and Webster back in December
1985. He and the ever-faithful Pia Zadora later visited the
Distillers headquarters. He told them he'd acquired a sizeable
stake in the company and wanted to help them in some way.
First he boasted wildly that he was thinking of bidding for the
whole company outright to foil Gulliver. This failed to wash
even with the hard-pressed Distillers board. So Riklis
proceeded to outline a share buy back plan whereby he would
acquire a larger stake and then sell it to the company. One
Distillers board member remembers the schemes proposed by
Riklis: 'They were all things which were either permissible in
the States or only just on the borderline of being acceptable
there but highly unusual on this side of the water. We had a
meeting on our own, not with him present, and concluded that
he was altogether too dangerous a chap to enter into any form
of dealings with and we told him so. My belief is that he then
simply took a taxi and went to see Saunders.'

Whether Riklis made any financial arrangement with
Saunders is not clear. In November 1986 his Schenley
Industries were given, for nothing, the rights to the prized
Dewar's whisky brand trademark. Throughout the manoeuv-
rings for control of Distillers, Riklis had been desperate to
secure his highly lucrative distribution contracts for the leading
Scotch whisky brands. That, rather than money, was what he

was after as he did the rounds of the relevant British companies. Schenley invested £60 million in Guinness shares and later in the year secured the distribution contract. By the last day of the bid timetable Schenley actually owned more than 5% of Guinness. This, under British company law, should have been declared but it never was. Schenley later claimed ignorance of the requirements of something obviously so complex as the Companies Act. Evidently they were also unaware of the requirements of the Takeover Code which dictate that any organisation with a commercial interest in the outcome of a takeover bid should declare it if they buy shares in the affected companies.

Schenley's 5% stake in Guinness was never spotted during the last days of the bid for Distillers. This was because they were dealing through an entity named Atlantic Nominees. Samuel Montagu's noticed the name on the Guinness share register on 11 and 12 April and had vague suspicions it might be Schenley, but were unable to prove it. The Guinness brokers Wood Mackenzie actually carried out some of the orders for Schenley. Scott Dobbie claims they had no idea who was behind Atlantic Nominees: 'They got a third party, a US domestic broker to buy for them — a respectable name who we'd dealt with for years — and we said to them now is your man in any way connected with the bid and we got categoric assurances there was no connection.' This seems at best naïve; several newspapers had picked up on the name of Atlantic Nominees and there was open speculation that it might be Schenley.

This argument sits uneasily beside admissions made later by Wood Mackenzie's co-brokers Cazenove. In an unprecedented step, given their usually secretive and aloof attitude, Cazenove made a press statement on 29 January 1987. This followed an internal inquiry by their solicitors Simmons and Simmons. The conclusion seems to be that Cazenove knew all along that they were dealing for Schenley but had no idea of the connection with Guinness. This astonishing claim received a rebuke even from Simmons and Simmons: 'It would have been better if Cazenove had not relied on the assurances it received that there was no association between Guinness and Schenley Industries, a US distributor of Distillers whisky, for whom Cazenove bought shares in Guinness and Distillers, but had made its own enquiries of Schenley.' It's interesting to speculate just what assurances were good enough for the most powerful and reputable stockbrokers in the land.

Cazenove also admitted dealing on behalf of the Wall Street financier Ivan Boesky. They did not buy shares in Guinness or Distillers for Boesky but sold Guinness shares for his companies after the bid. The scale of Boesky's involvement can only be guessed; he is thought to have invested £70 million in Guinness and Distillers shares. At the time of the Distillers bid, Boesky's star was shining brightest and his disgrace as a confessed insider trader was months off. He was admired and envied in the world's financial capitals as a brilliant player of Stock Markets. In May Guinness were to invest the huge sum of £69 million in a venture fund run by Boesky. They weren't the only British contributors — the Imperial Group Pension Fund for example put up £3.5 million — but Guinness were by far the largest. It was a surprising use of shareholders' money by a British company, although Guinness were to claim that the Boesky partnership was chosen as a useful stepping stone to a major acquisition in the United States. Others have suggested that the £69 million figure was linked to Boesky's share-buying during the Distillers bid.

There were other overseas purchasers, some of whom were paid fees. An Austrian bank, Zentralsparkasse und Kommerzialbank, spent almost £2 million on Guinness shares and received a sum of £250,000 as compensation for losses. How this obscure central European institution became embroiled in a British takeover battle is hard to understand; it has been pointed out that Saunders was born in Vienna and may have had contacts in Austria. The Wall Street investment firm, LF Rothschild Unterberg, Towbin, purchased almost 6 million Guinness shares and sold them to Morgan Grenfell shortly after the end of the takeover battle. It was these that Morgan's were hoping to place on the market in May when Ansbacher emerged wanting to sell their stake.

But by far the largest source of funds for Guinness shares, dwarfing even Schenley, was from Bank Leu of Zurich. The chairman of the bank's supervisory board was Dr Arthur Furer, former boss of Nestlé and a non-executive director of Guinness. He introduced Saunders and Ward to the management at Bank Leu and the result was orders for £130 million worth of stock. Some was purchased before and some after the bid. An arrangement was made for the shares to be repurchased and Bank Leu to be guaranteed against loss; allegedly the deal was signed on the part of Guinness by Thomas Ward. In January 1987 Guinness told shareholders that this agreement was one which the company 'could not lawfully have fulfilled'.

Bank Leu's biggest single purchase came on 17 April, the penultimate day of the bid battle. It was enough to tip the balance at a critical stage. The previous day Guinness had announced they spoke for around 32% of the Distillers shares while Argyll could muster just over 17%. At this juncture there were many leading institutional shareholders who were undecided; what they feared was a stalemate and they were prepared to wait until the last possible moment to see which bandwagon was rolling towards the finishing line in front. On Thursday morning (the 17th), Rupert Faure Walker was delighted to be told that Warburg Investment Management were offering to sell a 10 million block of Distillers shares (3% of the whole company). Montagu's 660 pence per share offer for up to £700 million still stood and it seemed that Warburg Investment Management were at last prepared to take the bait. But within a matter of minutes the stake had been snatched by Cazenove, paying 700p per share. The Argyll camp were horrified; they knew that the Guinness official cash alternative was only 630 and no one connected with Guinness was allowed to buy shares in the market above that price. Yet here were Cazenove doing just that. Faure Walker immediately filed a complaint to the Takeover Panel. The Panel made extensive enquiries but were assured that the purchaser was not acting 'in concert' with the Guinness team. It only emerged a year later in an affidavit that the mystery buyer was none other than Bank Leu.

At noon Faure Walker relayed the news to Gulliver, who was shocked and disappointed. The Argyll chief immediately remarked 'that's it, it's all over now'. It had been their fourth complaint to the Takeover Panel in four weeks during which the Guinness share price had jumped up from 280 pence to around 350 pence. The Panel had dutifully quizzed Guinness but had received polite denials. It was pointed out that in the official offer document the Guinness board had guaranteed that, save as disclosed, there was no agreement or understanding between Guinness and other parties. The normally sanguine Gulliver thought the evidence was so blatant that the Panel should have made even more effort: 'We couldn't believe that anyone would buy 10 million shares for cash at 700 pence — we couldn't believe there would be anyone that mad at that stage in the bid.'

At 7 p.m. on Thursday, Guinness announced that they spoke for 46% of the shares in Distillers. Argyll had not much more than 20% in the bag, although they had the satisfaction of having won the 4% stake held by the mighty Prudential. Gulliver and his colleagues were left to wonder what the figures might have been if that Warburg block had swung the way of Montagu's rather than Cazenove. Argyll might have won over enough floating voters to take them nearer the magic 50%. As Rupert Faure Walker concluded bitterly, 'all the traders in the market weren't quite sure which way the bid was going to go, but as soon as they heard Guinness had got the the 3% block the bandwagon rolled. If Argyll had bought these shares rather than Guinness, it would have been very, very close indeed.'

Just before 1 p.m. on Friday, 18 April 1986 Ernest Saunders announced to the City that he had won control of 50.7% of the shares in Distillers. A campaign to fell the giant of the whisky industry which had started in February 1984 had finally ended, but with control passing to one plush Mayfair office rather than another — Portman Square rather than Chesterfield Hill. The new ownership of the company had been decided by the wheelings and dealings of a handful of unknown financiers.

Gulliver was gracious in defeat and wrote letters to Ernest Saunders and John Connell that afternoon congratulating them and wishing them all the best. He received replies by return; the rancour of the previous weeks seemed to be quickly forgotten. For Gulliver it was a bitter disappointment, but he would survive to fight again. The costs of the bid were put at around £55 million but Argyll would make £20 million through selling their shares in Distillers, so there was not to be too damaging a dent on profits. The Guinness costs were around £120 million, footed, of course, by the new joint group. It was a battle Saunders had to win at any cost.

The Guinness and Argyll share prices fell back sharply on the Friday afternoon, hung over after weeks of upward pressure from City share dealers. One newspaper concluded that 'the party, as they say, is over'. For Ernest Saunders, now at the head of a company valued at £3.7 billion, a mighty hangover was in store.

CHAPTER ELEVEN

THE GATHERING STORM CLOUDS

When Ernest Saunders arrived at work on Monday, 21 April as the new boss, he was in no mood for back slapping or cheerful reminiscence. The Distillers people may have been expecting the new chief to rally the troops with a rousing call to the colour. But from the very start of his new regime, Saunders made it clear how much he despised the old guard and their ways.

In the listing particulars with the official Guinness offer document it was stated that 'the Board of Distillers will remain the same, with . . . Mr John Connell as executive chairman of Distillers'. Within two weeks of Guinness winning control, both these pledges were broken. The first casualty was John Connell, who was fired from his executive position at Distillers on the Monday morning. Connell agreed to resign from the job on the condition that he remained vice chairman of the combined group and titular head of the Distillers organisation within the combined group. But it was a sad demise for the former chairman who at one time expected to head the new merged company.

One old Distillers colleague remembers Connell's humiliation: 'They never put any papers to him, he was never given any business to do and he just sat in his room stewing — this was harsh, brutal treatment.' Connell quickly escaped for a holiday on the Costa Brava at the end of April. But he was allowed no respite from the nightmare of the previous three months; quite by coincidence James Gulliver had checked into the same hotel in Marbella.

Soon afterwards it was announced that six Distillers directors were to resign, including Bill Forrest, the man who'd held out against the 'merger' until 3 a.m. back in January. Saunders became chairman of the Distillers board and installed Thomas Ward along with Victor Steel and Shaun Dowling, the top Guinness executives. One newspaper noted politely that 'Guinness is thought to be going further with restructuring than Distillers had envisaged when it recommended the bid to shareholders'. There were no other voices raised in protest. There was also a boardroom departure at Guinness. Viscount Boyd, the deputy chairman and a member of the Guinness family, resigned 'to concentrate on his substantial private interests'. The company line was that the move had nothing to do with the Distillers takeover, but it was strange that it happened so soon afterwards.

Saunders then turned to the senior managers. One observer remembers that 'he was so awful; instead of saying we're all members of a new team and basically going forward together, he said "you're now members of the Guinness company and I will be sending out instructions to you on how you will conduct yourselves."' Further down the line, Distillers staff soon got a taste of things to come, as one observer recalls: 'He was unnecessarily abusive about Distillers. Soon after the takeover he walked into the head office and told the receptionist in a very aggressive manner how many people there were around the place doing nothing. It was interesting that the Distillers House telephonist used to answer the phone "Distillers" and then started answering "Guinness". She's now gone back to answering the phone "Distillers Company".'

The listing particulars of the offer document had also noted that 'on implementation of the merger Guinness will change its name'. But Saunders seemed unhappy about the famous name not being part of the new group title; he was more determined to remove the official designation Distillers. He told journalists he didn't like the idea of names that weren't promoting brands. Back in December, Distillers had become sponsors of the Commonwealth Games, providing £2 million of funds. But

Saunders changed that to make Guinness the official sponsors. All athletes were to carry the Guinness logo on their kit, although this was later to anger the champion decathlete Daley Thompson who appeared on the track with the logo blocked out.

Quickly it was obvious that this was no cosy, 'friendly' merger. The Distillers board had recommended the Guinness bid to their shareholders back in January in preference to the hostile, unwanted approach from Argyll. Now they found themselves facing hostility again, this time from the people they'd joined up with for an agreed bid; it was as if they had been taken over by an enemy corporate raider. Distillers whisky operations were being brought under the team running Bell's, headed by Vic Steel, rather than left to continue as separate businesses. It made commercial sense but perplexed the old Distillers directors who found themselves left out in the cold. 'You couldn't just have two parallel telephone lines, one going to Bell's and one going to Distillers,' noted one insider.

As the broom was swept through the upper echelons of the Distillers organisation, the Bain people were swarming all over the bloated body of the company. One member of staff remembers the impact of Saunders' henchmen: 'Everyone hated Bain coming in and asking all these questions — it was questions, questions, questions. They were number crunchers, they were fact finders, they were developing strategies. There was always a feeling that Bain's were so close to the top they were invincible.' They probed and investigated looking at where cash was going before imposing their copybook control systems. Questions were asked about the old perks and expenses: 'Do you need to travel first class everywhere? Do you need to stay at the Ritz? Do we really need a company plane running up and down when there's good shuttle service from London to Edinburgh?'

While the stables were being cleaned out the new lord of the manor was not often seen in public; he had more pressing problems to worry about. Saunders, Ward, Roux knew what the thousands of employees, advisers and consultants didn't: that the new company could face financial disaster before it had any chance to sell more whisky around the world. In the heat of the takeover battle supporters of the Guinness share price had been offered guarantees against losses incurred through holding the Guinness shares. With the price sliding after 18 April the enormity of these commitments was beginning to sink in. The supporters would want to sell their shares and would do so at a loss, which would have to be underwritten by Guinness.

A nightmare vision began to dawn on Seelig, the master tactician. Institutions who'd bought millions of Guinness shares were likely to scramble to sell all at once. The market could be flooded with as much as 20% of the company's entire share capital and the price would hit the floor. He had to ensure an orderly queue of sellers to keep the price at a respectable level and avoid a panic drop. Equally important was to keep tabs on the outstanding Distillers shares, which would be converted into Guinness stock once the takeover was formally completed. Argyll, for example, held a £360 million stake which was about to be put up for sale. And Morgan Grenfell and associates owned just under 15% of the Distillers shares.

Seelig and David Mayhew of Cazenove's quickly devised a solution to the problem of the Distillers shares. On 22 April it was announced that Guinness would 'buy in' the Morgan Grenfell stake and effectively 'cancel' the shares. This block of Distillers shares would have made up 9% of the newly merged group and it had been expected that Morgan's would 'place' these with City institutions. But under the deal this 9% was simply 'vanishing' rather than being sold on the market. Eyebrows were raised by some observers who noted that Guinness' gearing levels had shot up from 75% to 120% (gearing is the technical expression for the ratio of debt to the company's share base and is used as a yardstick to judge the financial prudence of borrowing). Olivier Roux remarked wryly to a financial journalist that the aim had been 'to gear the company up so that Ernest couldn't buy anything more. I've got the handcuffs on him'.

Seelig was soon approached by institutions wanting to unload their Guinness shares. He knew that they had to be kept off the market if the Guinness share price was to keep steady. With Saunders and Roux, he planned a scheme for all the pools of shares to be disposed of in the autumn. The owners would be persuaded to hold on until the announcement of the first set of results of the merged company. Then the financial world

would see how marvellously the Guinness/Distillers conglomerate was performing and the share price would take off.
But on no account must any shares trickle onto the market
before. The first ally to knock on the door was Lord Spens,
warning that clients of Henry Ansbacher wanted to bale out
and sell just over 2 million Guinness shares.

There are two theories about what happened next. One is
that Guinness agreed to buy back the shares from the clients of
Ansbacher and simply handed them a cheque for £7.6 million.
This represented the amount spent on the shares during the bid
at a price of 355 pence each; but in early May the market price
had slumped to just over 300 pence, valuing the stake at more
like £6.6 million. This version of events is supported by the
fact that there was a very precise sum of money involved,
which presumably included stamp duty and other dealing costs
— £7,614,682.10. The remittance went direct from Guinness
to Ansbacher on 6 May. If this was the case it was clearly in
breach of the Companies Act provision which bars companies
from buying their own shares, except in special circumstances.

The second explanation is the one argued by Seelig and
Roux. This is that the £7.6 million was a deposit at Ansbacher
designed to dissuade Lord Spens from selling the holding.
Seelig denies that it was an indemnity or a payment for stock.
'He was screaming that he wanted liquidity and wanted to sell
his shares. The company didn't want him to and asked if he'd
hold on if they made a deposit to give the same liquidity, and
that he did', was the chain of events according to one Morgan
Grenfell insider's recollection. As far as Morgan's were
concerned, the money had come from Guinness, but only as a
deposit.

Another view of the transactions is provided by an insider at
Ansbacher: 'We thought Morgan's were buying the shares and
then we washed our hands of it. A sloppy letter was dictated on
the basis of the money coming from Morgan Grenfell when the
money came from Guinness. Morgan's phoned up and said
change "us" to "Guinness". We thought we were holding the
shares in a nominee company for Morgan Grenfell. Morgan's
acted as though they owned the shares. There was confusion
between Morgan's and Guinness and the money should have
come from Morgan Grenfell. We would have held the money
for the Morgan Grenfell account. When the shares were sold

the deposit would have been repaid because the money came from Guinness and not Morgan Grenfell.' Morgan Grenfell's behaviour certainly suggested that they owned the stake — they paid stamp duty on the purchase, which they considered to be on behalf of Guinness, and Roger Seelig even voted at the Guinness Emergency Meeting in September.

The Ansbacher share controversy has never been fully resolved. The different explanations are confusing, if not contradictory. It might have been a sideshow in the drama, but the question of ownership became critically important after the arrival of Department of Trade Inspectors in December. Then a furious game of pass the parcel developed, as Guinness, Morgan Grenfell and Henry Ansbacher all sought to disown the 2 million shares.

Roger Seelig seemed able to keep the British supporters' cause at bay, but the foreign financiers who'd been cajoled into backing the Guinness share price also needed to be dealt with. There was Ivan Boesky and Meshulam Riklis to keep happy, as well as LF Rothschild and the American subsidiary of S and W Berisford. Olivier Roux, the young consultant who'd rapidly become caretaker finance director under Saunders, found himself confronted by huge commitments, most made without his knowledge during the bid. It was strange that the finance director of a major public company was a non-executive on attachment from a management consultancy. It was extraordinary that millions of pounds' worth of shareholders' funds should have been put at risk without the approval of the finance director. If the Stock Market fell Guinness could have been ruined. A solution had to be found. Management consultants are trained to find solutions and Roux got down to it.

What emerged was a large-scale cleaning up operation with Bank Leu being used as a mop. All the parcels of shares were to be purchased by the Swiss bank at prices that would ensure the 'fan club' made no losses, in other words at prices considerably above those prevailing on the London Stock Market. Bank Leu was to perform this valuable service in return for a £50 million 'deposit' made by Guinness. The shares were, in effect, to be 'warehoused' in Zurich until it was safe to free them. The Swiss bankers knew they were protected if the worst happened and the shares collapsed in value. By the end of May Bank Leu had absorbed around 15 million shares, to add to the 26 million already acquired during the bid.

The question of who was responsible for the Swiss plan is the subject of continuing court action and investigation. Was it Saunders or Roux? Roux's answer is as follows: 'Let's say it's a solution that I developed and that he instructed me to carry out. What we wanted to achieve with Bank Leu was their commitment to work with us to a successful international placement to happen later in the year, after we'd been able to show good results for Distillers which would power the price up to where it should rightfully be.'

The use of the good offices of Bank Leu was the largest part of the campaign to underpin the Guinness share price in its darkest days in May. But it wasn't just mysterious foreign money that was steered in the appropriate direction. Money saved by the 13,000 Distillers employees was also being covertly press-ganged into service. The Distillers pension fund had more than £500 million in its coffers and was a powerful investment force on the British Stock Market. It was run in-house by two fund managers, Norman MacNair and the former Scottish rugby star Colin Telfer, who two years earlier had helped coach Scotland to the coveted 'Grand Slam'. The policy of the trustees had always been to dissuade the managers from investing in Distillers; the idea was to avoid any accusations of manipulation of a fund which was supposed to be for the benefit of the workers. It wasn't impossible for the managers to buy the company's own shares if they wished, but there was an elaborate procedure which involved notifying the board and carrying out the transaction only at certain times of the year. In practice MacNair and Telfer thought the rigmarole was not worth the effort and kept all the money in other investments.

Soon after the takeover, MacNair and Telfer were approached by the chairman of the pension fund trustees, the Distillers finance director Bob Temple. He asked them to buy 5 million Guinness shares. They wanted to know why and were told there had been pressure from Olivier Roux who wanted to see the Guinness share price supported. It was a most unusual request for the two fund managers who were used to the excessive probity of the old Distillers regime. But they were not in a position to argue with the chairman of the Trustees and reluctantly obliged.

MacNair and Telfer were unhappy about being told what to do with their money and sent a memo to their new boardroom superiors expressing concern and hoping it wouldn't happen again. There was no reply so another memo was dispatched. But, like scores of others in the company, they found it was impossible to make any contact with Saunders, Ward or Roux. The story didn't end there for the one-time rugby hero and his boss. They were sacked in October, ostensibly because the new management wanted to put the pension fund into the hands of an independent investment company. But there was a lingering suspicion that they were viewed as troublemakers who had to be got rid of. Later when the press began to take a closer interest in the affairs of Guinness and Distillers, MacNair and Telfer found themselves being implicated alongside Saunders and Boesky. They asked Guinness to clear their names; a press release was prepared but never sent out. Telfer quickly found another job with an Edinburgh stockbroker but MacNair was still unemployed six months later.

It's not clear whether the managers of the Guinness pension fund were put under similar pressure. A note in the company's 1986 Report and Accounts (which covers a fifteen-month period ending in December of that year) records that during the period 'various pension schemes associated with the Guinness group acquired 7.3 million Ordinary Stock Units in the Company'. No date is given for these purchases — one can only guess whether they were made before or after the takeover bid.

Ernest Saunders was also waging his campaign to support the Guinness share price in the public arena. He was using all his renowned powers of persuasion to 'sell' Guinness as a company of the future and a dynamic investment. He knew how to woo the Stock Market analysts whose circulars were influential with clients and the financial press. He would always listen to their views and suggestions on how Guinness should be run. Sometimes he even adopted their ideas. By the middle of May most of the leading brewery analysts were recommending Guinness as a 'buy', including two of the highest-rated experts, John Spicer of Kleinwort Grieveson and John Dunsmore of Wood Mackenzie. Both firms had close connections with Guinness — Kleinworts' merchant banking team had been advising Distillers and Wood Mackenzie, of course, were brokers to Guinness.

Kleinwort Grieveson were also helping Saunders sell the Guinness message abroad. The firm organised an 'investment roadshow' for the USA and two seminars were held, in Boston on 13 May and New York on 14 May. Saunders was keynote speaker and came out with his familiar themes about Guinness becoming one of the leading beverage companies in the world. The American audiences were provided with a research briefing by Kleinwort Grieveson arguing that the shares were undervalued. There was talk of Guinness getting a quotation on the New York market. Saunders was also doing the political rounds in Washington. He and Ward were worried about the mounting trade tensions between the United States and Europe and the possibility of punitive tariffs on gin and whisky imports. There was later a rumour that they saw President Reagan but, in reality the furthest they got was an audience with a senior civil servant.

While Ernest Saunders was flying the flag for Guinness in the United States, several of his 'colleagues' back at home were getting worried. One of them was Sir Thomas Risk in Edinburgh, who hadn't seen Saunders since 18 April. He had kept a low profile during the heat of the takeover battle although he dropped into the Guinness offices from time to time to see what was happening. Saunders had been very busy and there was no time for any formal meetings, but Risk did have a few chats with Ward. Once Guinness had won control he felt it was important to have a meeting of the new board as soon as possible. He tried to phone Saunders but was repeatedly told he was in the United States.

Risk wasn't the only new board member to be wondering what was going on. One Distillers man remembers getting edgy soon after 18 April: 'I can remember ringing John Connell and saying what's happening, why no meeting, and he said he didn't know because nobody could get hold of Saunders. After a few weeks the board hadn't met and by now I think the alarm bells really were ringing — the bride is left at the altar and there's no bridegroom.'

By the middle of May the resolute Sir Thomas managed to contact Saunders just as he was leaving for the States again. Saunders said he was too busy but Risk replied it was absolutely vital that they should meet to plan a board meeting, even if it had to be in the USA. The meeting was scheduled for Saturday 17 May and Risk made the relevant travel arrangements. But at the last minute the venue and time was changed to the following day. They finally met, for the first time since the takeover, in the Ritz Carlton Hotel in Washington. As usual Thomas Ward was with Saunders as they sat down for lunch. Like so many episodes in the story, there are two versions of what happened over that lunch table in Washington.

Sir Thomas Risk remembers being told by Saunders that a full-time executive chairman was required and that he, Saunders, must occupy that position in order to get to grips with the problems of Distillers. Saunders also claimed that he'd been having great difficulty in persuading the rest of the Guinness directors to agree to installing the new joint board. Risk was astonished and told Saunders he was 'daft'. He warned that the Guinness chief could not just walk away from the commitment. Moreover, he pointed out to Saunders that there were difficult decisions to be made about some of the Scottish operations, and that a non-executive chairman could help shoulder the burden. Ward, in his usual deceptive manner, gave the impression of agreeing with Risk and the lunch broke up. Another version of that meeting was later put out by Saunders and Ward. They claimed that Risk had 'thumped the table' and demanded a dominating executive role.

Risk flew back home a worried man, but determined the new board should be appointed without delay. Still there was no inkling that a major corporate crisis could be looming. He felt that Saunders might yet be talked out of his determination to be sole chief. After all, it was not up to Saunders to dispense with Risk; the Distillers shareholders had voted Risk into the chairmanship by accepting the terms of the Guinness offer. Offer documents had given clear undertakings on the composition of the board.

Risk discussed his Washington encounter with Fraser, who had also heard nothing from Saunders. Sir Nigel Broackes was also concerned about what was happening. Like Fraser and Risk he had been listed at the time of the Guinness offer as a prospective non-executive director of the new group board.

And, like the two Scots, he had not been approached by Guinness nor heard any mention of a board meeting since 18 April. Other City names were also asking questions. Lord Rockley, the aristocratic chairman of Kleinworts, who'd been advising Distillers took a very dim view of how his client was being treated. Saunders was later to accuse Rockley and Kleinworts of interfering. Discreet calls were made to the Governor of the Bank of England, Robin Leigh Pemberton; he was warned there could be something of a squall on the horizon. More significantly, hints were dropped to the Department of Trade and Industry. If pledges in offer documents had been made in 'bad faith', there was a very real case for an inquiry into possible breaches of the Companies Act.

There were others who might have felt somewhat neglected by Ernest Saunders in the weeks immediately after the takeover. During the bid campaign, Saunders, Roux and Ward had been the public proponents of the Guinness cause. Nothing was seen or heard of Lord Iveagh or his family colleagues on the board, for example Edward Guinness and the Hon. Jonathan Guinness. Lord Iveagh had even bought Guinness shares three days before the merger was announced in January. Few investors buy shares in a company they suspect is going to make a bid, let alone directors. To put it another way, the chairman of a public company had no idea that his company was going to launch the UK's largest ever takeover bid within the next 72 hours. Saunders had long had a reputation of running Guinness single-handed with the help of Ward and Roux. Later, in a legal submission, it was claimed that 'Mr Saunders managed the affairs of Guinness in a form which was autocratic, and did so with the approval of his fellow directors, particularly the Chairman, Lord Iveagh'. Having succeeded in winning Distillers, he had good reason to feel even more untouchable.

In May and June there was little evidence of effective board control of Guinness PLC. Decisions were taken on an ad hoc basis by the executive committee and presented to the full board as *faits accomplis* on the rare occasions when it assembled. One of the Guinness stockbroking team remembers huddles of people at planning meetings at Portman Square.

Sometimes the lawyers would decide that certain decisions needed 'board' approval: 'They might say now that's an issue we need a board meeting on and have we got a quorum? Yes we have. Right gentlemen, can we agree? There'd be Saunders, Roux and Ward and perhaps four board members there. They'd disappear and then come back after five minutes, having had their meeting.'

In late April and May, these gatherings would have discussed several important items of business. Apart from the future of Sir Thomas Risk there was the matter of a pay rise for Ernest Saunders. At some stage after 3 March, Saunders' salary was increased from £196,000 to £275,000. Two service contracts dated 1 May provided Saunders with further income from the company. He was to receive a salary of $75,000 from Arthur Bell and Sons (Bermuda) Limited and also $37,500 from Guinness America Inc. (whose chairman was Thomas Ward). These two overseas arrangements were only revealed in the fine print of a document circulated at an Emergency General Meeting in September. There was no explanation why Saunders was getting the money and no one asked.

But perhaps the most important decision made by Guinness directors was the investment on 28 May of £69 million in the Ivan Boesky fund in the USA. When this transaction was revealed in December it was said that Guinness were hoping to develop contacts in the United States with a view to making an acquisition, as Roux put it, 'following the advice of Thomas Ward that Ivan Boesky would be a good person to have on the side of Guinness'. It was remarked in the press that other investors in the Boesky fund included such familiar names as Meshulam Riklis; but his Rapid-American Corporation put up a mere $5 million, small change to a man who'd once bragged about a possible bid for Distillers. Gerald Ronson also put up $5 million through an American subsidiary of his Heron group.

Saunders' pursuers were soon catching up with him. He had to steel himself for confrontations but always had the trusted Thomas Ward at his side. Sir Thomas Risk managed to arrange another meeting at the Savoy Hotel in London on 26 June. They met for dinner and Risk again urged Saunders to see sense and to appoint the board which had been promised back in March. To bring about boardroom changes all the Guinness directors would need to resign and then appoint a new board. Saunders said he'd try to persuade Lord Iveagh to make the appointments. But one Distillers director was already fearing the worst: 'I think from that point onwards it suddenly dawned on us that we were dealing with somebody who was not going to honour an undertaking. I called it a breach of faith. We then knew that the fundamentals of the merger agreement were as dead as a doornail.'

Morgan Grenfell were now trying to persuade Saunders to honour the commitments. They asked Lord Iveagh to meet Risk. Sir Thomas went to Portman Square on Thursday 10 July, fully expecting to see Iveagh alone for a 'chairman to chairman' discussion. To his surprise he found that Saunders and Ward were also present. Risk told them he wasn't prepared to discuss anything unless he could see Iveagh alone. The Guinness chairman looked nervously at his fellow directors and mumbled agreement. Saunders and Ward sauntered out of the room into an adjoining office. Nervously Iveagh steeled himself for a thoroughly unpleasant task. He told Risk that it would be unsuitable to have him as chairman. But he'd barely had time to launch into his carefully prepared preamble when Ward strolled back into the room. Iveagh and Risk had been no more than five minutes on their own. Risk decided that enough was enough and took his leave.

Now all the Guinness advisers could see what was at stake. The men from Morgan Grenfell, Cazenove's and Wood Mackenzie were huddled in informal meetings around the City and at headquarters in Portman Square. Risk told them that he was prepared to stand down reluctantly as long as another independent chairman was appointed; he could see that it was going to be difficult to work with the Guinness people and he'd hardly been enthusiastic about taking the job in the first place. All the advisers agreed that some check was required on Saunders and Morgan Grenfell drew up a list of possible candidates.

Woodmac, with a good name in Scotland to think of, was appalled at the likely fallout in the City if Risk was dumped. John Chiene, the man who'd built up Wood Mackenzie from a small Edinburgh firm to a big-time international stockbroking empire, decided to take the bull by the horns. With Scott Dobbie he confronted Ward. It was a heated meeting. Ward claimed that Ernest had been grossly misrepresented and that all he wanted was to ensure the best for Guinness. Risk, moreover, was useless and interfering and had demanded banking business for the Bank of Scotland. Chiene, an old friend of Risk, was incensed and accused Ward of impugning the honesty of Sir Thomas. Soon afterwards they were granted an audience by Saunders, accompanied by Ward. Dobbie and Chiene appealed to Saunders to think again: 'Look, as a chum, Ernest, for God's sake listen to what we're saying to you. You may well get away with it this time. But make one mistake after that and the City will be on you like a ton of bricks. You'll be eating up all the goodwill.' Finally, on the Friday afternoon, 11 July, the two men from Woodmac had a final attempt to make their clients see reason. They told Saunders and Ward they would resign if the new board was not installed. Lord Iveagh was also present but said nothing.

It was an awkward day for Chiene and Dobbie to be kicking up a fuss. That Friday evening was the official party to celebrate the 'merger' between Guinness and Distillers. Saunders had erected a huge marquee on the lawn in the 30 acres of grounds at his Buckinghamshire mansion. The marquee would get quite a pounding that weekend. Saunders' daughter was to hold her 21st birthday party under canvas on Saturday night, and on the Sunday Saunders had organised a fête to raise money to repair the roof of the local church. He was a regular in the congregation at church in the village of Penn, and locals were impressed with his generosity. The verger was employed by Carole Saunders to tend the garden.

But on the Friday it was the Distillers managers and their wives who were being fêted. They were flown from Scotland or bussed from other parts of the country and put up in local hotels. The-300-year-old Knoll House would impress them; but inside they would discover the atmosphere and décor felt more like an office than a home, slightly drab pastel shades, unspectacular prints of rural scenes on the wall, bright-coloured sofas and glass-topped tables. It didn't feel lived in, which was hardly surprising, given Saunders' jetsetting life style.

The Wood Mackenzie team, who'd played an important role in winning Distillers for Guinness, were invited as honoured guests to the knees-up. But Scott Dobbie was embarrassed about his behind the scenes dust-up with Saunders and Ward. Before leaving for the afternoon showdown at Portman Square he'd wondered whether it was right to go on to the party: 'I said to my wife, don't bother to wash your hair, we may not be able to go. However I rang her at 4 o'clock and said we're still here at the moment, we may not be much longer but we'd better go, so we went.'

At Knoll House that night it was all smiles and black ties as the band played into the early hours and the Distillers employees met their new masters. 'Ward was there, terribly smart, terribly charming.' He urged the Dobbies to visit him at his river-side house in Washington and take a trip on his boat. Saunders was hovering around, charming as always. At one stage, he disappeared from the function. Scott Dobbie and John Chiene left before the party ended. As he climbed into his car Chiene showed Dobbie his new car phone, on trial from British Telecom. They joked about trying it out over the weekend, just for fun. Chiene mentioned he was going to be at Brands Hatch for the motor racing on Sunday and Dobbie could try calling him there.

Scott Dobbie was soon glad that his boss had installed the car telephone. He went out on Sunday morning to get the newspapers, and over breakfast came across an article in the *Sunday Times* Business Section by Ivan Fallon. From the first line it was clear what the argument was: 'Ernest Saunders, as the world now knows, has performed one of the great wonders of the modern commercial world.' Fallon noted that the Guinness share price depended on Saunders being allowed to free the potential of his brands and achieve cost savings: 'To do it, Saunders needs an unfettered hand and there is just a possibility he won't get it'. Fallon described the original intention to set up a holding board and two subsidiaries: 'The key man was to be the the august Sir Thomas Risk, governor of the Bank of Scotland and Distillers' principal banker. On paper and in the heat of battle that sounded fine. Events since have changed the perspective, however . . . the company is in a mess and tougher action is urgent. Lord Iveagh's willingness to step aside should permit Saunders to assume the role of executive chairman; no "rent-a-chairman" would be needed.'

Now the awful truth was dawning on Dobbie. He could see how Saunders was cleverly outmanoeuvring his opponents by getting his view out through the media first. It was a trick that had been used to outwit the hapless John Connell on the weekend of the crisis Distillers meeting in January. Perhaps that was why Saunders had disappeared from the party on Friday night — he knew when the *Sunday Times* deadline was and had gone off to call up Ivan Fallon. Dobbie reached for his own phone and dialled John Chiene's car number; Chiene was waiting in a jam of vehicles trying to get into Brands Hatch. It was the first call on the new car phone. Dobbie blurted out, 'John, he's leaked the story.' Chiene was astonished at Saunders' audacity; only on Friday he'd been telling the Guinness man he was finished if the press got wind of the boardroom squabbling.

At his Glasgow home Alf Young was also reading the *Sunday Times* Business Section with interest. He'd heard whispers that all was not well at Distillers. Fallon's piece confirmed Young's suspicions and he immediately travelled to Edinburgh to the offices of the *Scotsman* where he was Business Correspondent. He got hold of Charles Fraser on the phone who confirmed some of the background to Saunders' plan to be executive chairman. Fraser told Young how seriously he viewed the apparent breach of undertakings made in a formal Stock Exchange document. He stated on the record that 'undertakings to two individuals are of much less consequence than undertakings in a Class One circular accepted by all Distillers shareholders — it speaks for itself'. Even though Risk was tight lipped, Young had enough for a story. The first independent media shots in what was to become 'the Risk Affair' were fired the following morning in the *Scotsman*. Charles Fraser may have regretted speaking on the record; on Monday he was called by Thomas Ward who'd seen the story in the *Scotsman*. Ward claimed that millions of pounds had been knocked off the value of Guinness shares and the company were going to sue Fraser for it. It was typical of Ward; rough, ruthless, bullying and threatening. It certainly frightened Fraser.

The Scottish newspaper reading public were being told one thing over their breakfast tables on Monday 14 July. Anyone reading *The Times* that morning was getting a quite different impression. 'It appears that the Bank of Scotland, through its Governor, is demanding more of the group's banking business than the Guinness board believes is justified. Furthermore, friction between Mr Ernest Saunders and Sir Thomas has been increased by Sir Thomas's insistence on the role of "Scotland's voice" in the planning and decision making which will reshape and streamline Distillers' operations.'

Risk, throughout the Monday, resolutely refused to comment despite the flood of press enquiries into his office at the Bank of Scotland in Edinburgh. This appears to have been a mistake as it allowed the Guinness version of events to percolate into more newspaper columns than just *The Times* and the *Sunday Times*. Risk could only marvel at the bare-faced cheek of the Saunders-inspired publicity. As far as Sir Thomas was concerned there'd been no friction between himself and Saunders because there'd been no opportunity for any to take place. And there'd certainly been no discussion of the role of the Bank of Scotland at his three meetings with Saunders since April. Each time he'd been too busy trying to persuade Saunders to honour the commitment to setting up the new joint board. That day, Guinness confirmed that Sir Thomas Risk would not be appointed chairman and that the board structure that has been proposed in the takeover documents was being scrapped.

The suggestion that Risk had demanded business for his bank seems to have been put out in good faith by the Guinness PR men. One insider remembers being summoned by Thomas Ward who was brandishing a letter which he said was written by Risk. Ward read out the letter which contained a request that the Bank of Scotland be appointed official bankers to the new group. The letter was written on blue Bank of Scotland notepaper, but the observer could not actually see the text or the signature at the bottom. But there was no reason to suspect anything and it was taken as read. Later Sir Thomas Risk denied ever sending such a letter. It is likely the letter had been written by a bank executive who'd been asked to quote for extra business.

On Tuesday 15 July, Risk decided he must do something to defend himself. He was not used to public relations or image making; as Governor of the Bank of Scotland he'd hardly ever dealt with pressmen. The Bank's official PR advisers were the London firm of Good Relations, run by Anthony Good. He contacted Good and asked for advice about a statement to release in response to the claims by Guinness. That afternoon Risk made his first public pronouncement, which was brief: 'I do not know the reasons for this decision nor on what issue Guinness has been unable to reach agreement with me, as stated in their announcement yesterday. Press speculation that it has to do with demands made by me in relation to the banking business of Guinness is wholly without foundation.' He was reluctant to say anything further when pressed by journalists. At this stage he hoped that the Department of Trade and other authorities would want to talk to him. He didn't want to personalise the issues if there was going to be an official investigation.

Coincidentally, Anthony Good was also advising another aggrieved party, Wood Mackenzie. John Chiene had decided that enough was enough once the row over Risk had hit the newspapers. On Tuesday 15 July Woodmac resigned as brokers to Guinness, losing in the process one of their biggest clients. Charles Fraser also announced that he'd have nothing further to do with Guinness and would give up his position as Scottish lawyer to the company. The other advisers were still pressing Saunders to appoint the proposed board. But Cazenove and Morgan Grenfell remained in the pay of Guinness. With the news of the row out in public the Guinness share price was coming under pressure. Ironically, after months of trying to keep the price up, the Risk Affair knocked 40 pence off Guinness in just a week.

If Saunders thought the shockwaves from the Risk row could be contained within his own coterie of followers, he was in for a nasty shock. He'd already had informal discussions with Bank of England officials about his plans. When the news broke publicly on the Monday Robin Leigh-Pemberton entered the fray. The Governor of the Bank of England was already well briefed with regard to Saunders' grand design. He had earlier invited Lord Iveagh to meet him that afternoon to discuss the boardroom changes. But it was Saunders in his new capacity as

chairman and Ward who made their way across London to the
City for a chat with the Governor. Perhaps it was no
coincidence that Saunders had replaced Iveagh that very
morning. Even so Saunders got a carpeting. Later in the week
Saunders had a one-and-a-half-hour tongue lashing from the
Scottish Secretary Malcolm Rifkind. He was profoundly
concerned that Saunders might go back on pledges that had
been made to locate the Head Office in Edinburgh.

Whatever compromises were made by Guinness, they did
not prevent Ernest Saunders from achieving his main goal for a
time, the leadership of an international drinks empire. Sir
Thomas Risk and Charles Fraser were not brought back into
the fold or even consulted. There was no contact from the
Stock Exchange either with them, or Wood Mackenzie. It was
strange indeed that the authorities did not even bother to find
out the opinion of as eminent a financial man as the Governor
of the Bank of Scotland. Moreover, the phone call that Risk
had expected from the Department of Trade never came.
Senior sources within the Scottish Office have since indicated
that the DTI were 'within an ace' of an inquiry. Why it never
occurred is a mystery. Alf Young, seven months later,
speculated about intervention from Number 10 Downing
Street. He received a vehement denial from Malcolm Rifkind.

Risk was, in the words of one observer, 'gravely
embarrassed' by the sequence of events. But, rather more
seriously his standing in Scotland had considerably diminished
as many people felt he'd been gullible in agreeing to join the
Guinness bandwagon. Later, of course, his critics would eat
their words. An Edinburgh broker remembers Risk as 'having
been duped into accepting a job which at the end of the day he
was never going to be given'. But Risk was fated to suffer more
than mere embarrassment. The full weight of the Guinness
public relations machine was turned against him. He and
Fraser were painted in the English press as 'little Scotlanders'
who were insignificant but interfering.

The slurs on his character verged on the slanderous.
Anthony Good had frequent calls from journalists repeating
claims made by the Guinness camp. Risk was described as
'past it, bureaucratic and very difficult'. One scribe from the
Daily Mail was present at a briefing at the Good Relations
office in London and repeated a suggestion that Risk was head

of a Scottish masonic mafia. Anthony Good informed the journalist that Risk was in the building and asked whether he would be interested in meeting him. The journalist was introduced to Risk and Good challenged him to repeat some of the rumours he'd heard. The journalist shuffled and squirmed and then asked Risk whether he was a freemason. Risk denied it and pointed out that, logically, he could not therefore be part of a masonic mafia.

There are a number of people who have argued that Risk and Fraser should have dug their heels in and refused to budge until the spirit of the offer document was upheld. One former Distillers director puts it thus: 'Tom Risk is a very respectable and respected and very able chairman of the Bank of Scotland. But I think he should not have handed his cards in so rapidly. He should have sounded the alarm bells.' But Risk believed he'd set the alarm bells ringing after the first meeting with Saunders in May. It was up to the City's firemen to take responsibility.

It was never clear whether the 'City' did understand the issues at stake. The Stock Exchange expressed concern but accepted the position advocated by Cazenove and Morgan Grenfell. They proposed that a new board should be created with suitable non-executives from the business world at large to act as a healthy check to the power of Saunders the chief. The search was now on amongst the great and the good to find the right chaps for the job. Then it would be left to the shareholders to decide. It was a neat solution, but it could be said to have smacked ever so slightly of buck-passing.

Labour Trade spokesman John Smith raised the matter in the House of Commons and pressed the Secretary of State, Paul Channon, for a statement. Channon was embarrassed again as his family firm's reputation was dragged into the political ring. Smith wrote to him complaining about 'a coach and horses being driven through regulations'. Smith also wrote to Sir Nicholas Goodison, chairman of the Stock Exchange, arguing that promises made in a takeover document were being broken, and that the affair showed the City unable to regulate itself. Goodison replied that there were grounds for an investigation under the Companies Act if statements were made in bad faith but noted that 'there were occasions, however rare, when a Board finds it necessary to depart from the precise terms of intentions stated in Listing Particulars'. Then, argued Sir Nicholas, the variation should be put before the shareholders.

While Paul Channon took flak from the Labour benches, a former Tory Cabinet Minister was working furiously behind the scenes to cobble together a solution agreeable to Saunders and colleagues as well as the Department of Trade and the Stock Exchange. Lord Iveagh had engaged the services of the merchant bankers Lazard Brothers to advise on the composition of the new board and the proposal to put to shareholders. The chairman, Sir John Nott, former Defence Secretary, headed the effort to smooth the path for Guinness. There was some difficulty finding willing candidates for the non-executive positions on the new board. But on Wednesday 13 August the names were announced. There were to be five outside directors: the chairman of Tesco, Ian Maclaurin, the boss of Vickers, David Plastow, Anthony Greener, who ran Dunhill Holdings, and Sir Norman Macfarlane, the prominent Scottish businessman who ran the Clansman companies. Another director 'with strong Scottish ties' was to be appointed forthwith. The five non-executives were to be given the power to hire and fire the chairman and vice chairman. The new board structure was described in some quarters as unprecedented.

The details of the full composition of the board were not revealed until the following week, on Friday 22 August, in a circular to Guinness shareholders. After a lengthy preamble about the need to create a great new British company the circular finally got round to explaining why Sir Thomas Risk was not to be chairman. The two-tier board had been dismissed because it was 'too unwieldy and unresponsive to provide effective direction and control'. Then what everyone had been waiting for: 'Since April, certain members of the Board have held discussions with Sir Thomas Risk. These discussions covered various matters, including the manner in which it was felt that the Company should be run. In the light of these discussions and the situation at Distillers, the Board of Guinness concluded that it would not be in the best interests of the Company and its stockholders for Sir Thomas to be elected chairman.' When the circular finally reached Sir Thomas he wondered what these discussions were supposed to have been. He could only remember a couple of lunches when Saunders had already made up his mind about being chairman.

Despite the lengthy discussions with the Stock Exchange and the DTI and the services of Lazards, the circular seemed to be lacking in consistency. Changes being proposed would need alterations to the Articles of Association of the company and therefore Special Resolutions at a meeting of shareholders. These resolutions need a 75% majority. The non-executive committee was being vested with special powers to remove the chairman if necessary. And Lord Iveagh was being accorded the new title of President. These changes needed Special Resolutions. But shareholders were being asked to vote on Ordinary Resolutions with only a 50% majority needed. If this was an oversight in the heat of the moment it was an amazing lapse by the authorities and advisers who'd vetted the documents. Alternatively Saunders and his allies may have felt they couldn't risk proposals needing a 75% majority vote.

In the flurry of excitement over the circular there had been one further victim of Saunders and Ward. Bill Spengler had been hoping for an executive role in the new company ever since the end of the bid in April. Indeed, in the presentations to the City institutions prepared by Bains, Spengler's name had been inked in alongside Saunders. To begin with Spengler was heavily involved with selling the merits of a Distillers/Guinness merger. He had been gradually eased aside in the latter stages, but had been promised a position on the new board when it was finally established. In the summer Spengler was invited on to the board of the Commonwealth Games when Robert Maxwell became chairman. Spengler had been given no formal executive role over the summer but was led to believe he'd be number two to Saunders. He'd even been used to do some of Saunders' dirty work in sacking old Distillers people and telling former boardroom colleagues they were no longer needed. But the day before the circular was released he was told by Thomas Ward that there was no room for him on the board. Spengler quit immediately, the last survivor of the old Distillers board.

The stage was set for the dénouement of the Risk Affair. On Thursday 11 September Guinness shareholders made their way to the Mount Royal Hotel in West London, near the Guinness headquarters, for the Extraordinary General Meeting. Those of them who had bought the *Daily Mirror* that morning found an editorial urging them to back the management talents of Ernest Saunders. It may have been the first time that the *Mirror* had ever commented on a shareholders' meeting. But the proprietor was Robert Maxwell, who had an interest in the outcome of the meeting. He was a shareholder in Guinness through various trusts and pension funds. Maxwell appeared at the meeting in his shirt sleeves and took the microphone as most people were taking their seats. He launched into his pro-Saunders speech and had to be interrupted by the Guinness chief who thanked him politely but informed him the meeting had not officially opened. Security was so tight that most shareholders were still in long queues waiting to get into the hall and the start of the meeting was delayed.

The so-called President of the company, Lord Iveagh, told the meeting of how the board had reached the view that a constructive relationship could not be reached between Risk and the management. The first speaker from the floor was Jonathan Lyons, son of Sir Jack. There followed speeches of lavish praise for Saunders until Graham Knox rose to his feet. Knox had said before the meeting that he was going to criticise the whole business of the board changes. He'd been encouraged by Stock Exchange and Bank of England officials to speak his mind. They'd all seemed antagonistic to Saunders. In the event his was to be the only voice of protest. Knox was head of investment at Scottish Amicable, a major financial institution based in Glasgow. But he suffered from the deficiencies of having a beard and speaking with a Scottish accent. To the predominantly English audience he seemed just like another moaning, nationalistic Scot.

Knox and his team at Scottish Amicable had supported Argyll for their Guinness shares: 'One of the things that I really didn't like about the Guinness proposals was their board structure — the two tier board farce was clearly never going to work. I take with the most enormous pinch of salt Saunders' statement that when he got inside Distillers he found things were worse than expected. Everybody from Land's End to John O' Groats knew things had to be done.' Knox sat down to timid applause after delivering his prepared attack on Saunders' failure to honour commitments. Next up was another

Scot who congratulated Saunders wholeheartedly on beating the Edinburgh mafia. Saunders seemed mighty pleased but the speaker, Raymond Gillies from Milngavie near Glasgow, pressed on with a sweeping denunciation of the Scottish establishment. As giggles broke out around the hall Saunders looked uneasy, and then had to interrupt and thank Gillies for his contribution. To experienced observers of the Scottish financial scene Gillies was a well-known eccentric with a long-standing grudge against the Royal Bank of Scotland. Some wondered how he came to be sitting at the front of the gathering alongside the institutional shareholders. 'Was this just a brilliant coincidence or was he part of the machine?', mused one observer.

After further speeches in praise of Saunders the meeting drew to a close. Saunders announced the results of the count of the proxy votes, which showed a 10–1 majority in favour of the resolutions. Knox appealed for a full poll of those present in order to register his protest vote. There were two seconders to the demand but Saunders arrogantly brushed it aside. He had triumphed by a huge margin and routed his critics. Saunders was the king and his courtiers revelled in his reflected glory.

Graham Knox proved to be the only fund manager who spoke out; the rest, despite the anger before the meeting, remained silent. Representatives of the huge Legal and General and Prudential funds spoke in praise of Saunders. Some of the Scots may have been wary of the fact that the Distillers pension fund was about to be put out to tender by independent management. One cynical participant remembers the meeting as a 'triumph of stage promotion over justice'. Another observer remembers the meeting as 'very efficiently stage managed . . . those people must now really be biting their tongues because they lost the opportunity to say in the City you still have to honour your bond'.

After the meeting Sir Thomas Risk, who had not been present, made another statement to the media. He said it was not right that shareholders should be regulators and that the City should find a better way of monitoring takeover documents. The people being asked to monitor the conduct of Saunders and his boardroom colleagues were the fund managers, often relatively junior employees of their companies. These professionals knew that their jobs depended on backing the right investments. They knew that if Saunders had to go the Guinness share price would suffer so it was clear that short term financial considerations would dictate their votes. An Edinburgh broker present at the meeting points to possible conflicts of interest: 'A lot of fund managers don't seek publicity for their organisations because it doesn't go down too well with the trustees who may be part of the management of the company. And the managers may not like their name being brought into it because they have a trade relationship with Guinness or Distillers.'

The Risk Affair was important to Scotland, if not to the London financial players. Stockbroker Thorold Mackie sees the dumping of Risk and Fraser as 'a body blow, a complete and utter body blow'. By giving his name to the proposed merger between Guinness and Distillers, Risk certainly swayed many floating voters amongst the Distillers shareholders. James Gulliver was to discover that many Scottish institutions who'd earlier pledged support to Argyll changed their minds when Risk and Fraser's names were added to the Guinness offer package. The suspicion that Guinness might not go through with pledges to establish a Head Office in Scotland worried politicians and business people alike. Having a major company headquarters is a major boost to a city through providing work for professionals and smaller service companies. The prospect of losing the HQ of Bell's and Distillers to Mayfair appalled most Scottish observers. Cynics remembered how Carole Saunders had been pictured house-hunting in Edinburgh in March. She had told James Gulliver at a chance encounter at a cocktail party during the summer that she wasn't sure where to look now, but thought it should probably be near Heathrow.

Yet the Risk Affair wasn't just a Scottish issue. To the English, Welsh or Irish the principles were the same. The City was being tested on its powers to regulate. Saunders, again, had got his own way and by-passed the City. The scale of his victory at the meeting at the Mount Royal Hotel must have further convinced him of his immortality. His motives for dropping Risk can only be guessed at. In September 1986 no one suspected the extent of the financial commitments undertaken by Saunders and his colleagues. He may have feared exposure if Risk got near the books. He may have found

Risk a tougher adversary than he bargained for. He may simply have wanted power. Certainly on the evening of 11 September Saunders was riding on the crest of a wave.

By that date Saunders had tamed and humiliated Distillers. What seems to anger the old Distillers directors is not so much the revelations of a share support operation since then, but the fact that they were 'had'. Shareholders were left to muse on the behaviour of the man who'd wooed Distillers with talk of a friendly merger but later carried out a hostile takeover. Said one: 'I think his subsequent behaviour shows that this is precisely what he intended to do, and of all the things that he's done, that is the biggest crime of all — it did more to ruin his own name, the name of Guinness and the name of the City than all the other things.'

CHAPTER TWELVE

THE INSPECTORS CALL

The inspectors on the doorstep on 1 December quickly sent shockwaves through the Guinness HQ. No one there knew what they were after or the purpose of their mission. They merely said they were acting under the authority of the Department of State for Trade and Industry, using the Companies Act of 1985. Ernest Saunders, from his top-floor office, vigorously protested that he had no idea why they were there, though there were suggestions put about that it was connected with insider dealing in the City and had nothing to do with the operation of the company.

The chairman managed to take some time off from his office preoccupations on the evening of 1 December to go to the Barry Rooms at the National Gallery. His wife had put on a party to show off a Raeburn picture from the Distillers collection, called The MacNab. One of the guests at the party was Roger Seelig, whose offices at Morgan Grenfell had also been visited by the inspectors that morning. All lips were sealed.

A torrent of press comment was loosed with the early-morning announcement and Saunders had to act quickly to provide responses. Saunders' response was typically to find more advisers. It was decided a public relations company that had no connection with the business should be brought in and the financial agency Hill and Knowlton accepted the task. David Wynn Morgan, the chief executive of Hill and Knowlton, may have been warned by colleagues in the field that this was not an assignment to be involved with. If so, he took no notice, but he insisted on having Saunders' word that he would not be asked to say anything to the press that was not true, and Saunders put his hand on his breast and looking him straight in the face, one chief executive to another, gave him his word. He conceded to Wynn Morgan that illicit dealings would come out in the City that were connected with the takeover, 'which was of course very hard fought and dirty', but Saunders said he knew nothing of them. Therefore he could not use Wynn Morgan for doing anything other than disseminating the truth. The public relations man was satisfied, and set up shop in Guinness headquarters, taking an office on the top floor near the Saunders den, and also near an office of a lawyer, a partner from Tom Ward's firm in the US, whom the Saunders confederate had brought in to mind his interests at Guinness. At once, the phone calls started to rain in from 7 a.m. to late into the evening, and for the month of December the word was the same: that the chairman knew nothing about nothing. At the same time as Wynn Morgan was brushing off the press, the law firm Freshfields was coping with the inspectors. They were going the rounds of Guinness directors taking depositions. The more closely involved parties had to make depositions that were on the record, others were merely noted and would not be used as evidence.

For three weeks Guinness employees could only speculate on the possible reasons for the inspectors' visit that Monday morning. They will not have been reassured to hear that Schenley Industries had acquired a 5% stake in the company in April that had not been declared, but such breaches of Takeover Code were not going to bring the company down. Then the news got worse, when on 18 December some evidence started to come into the press linking Guinness managers with the disgraced *arbitrageur* Ivan Boesky. They read in the papers that $100 million had been put Boesky's way just a few weeks after winning the bid.

Things did not look good. It was not clear what the purpose of this massive investment was. Moreover, the shareholders had not been told of the investment though it turned out the sum was calculatedly just below the level where disclosure was required. People who wanted to support Saunders thought it looked just like bad judgement, but others talked of possible pay-offs for dealings by the arb in the Distillers bid.

Ivan Boesky had been exposed and disgraced as an insider trader less than a month before. The financial markets in New York and London were still reeling from the shock; what scared them was the thought of who Boesky might have shopped in his chats with the officials of the US Securities and Exchange Commission. The association of Guinness and Boesky on the front pages added to the stench of scandal. Quickly links were made between the American inquiry into Boesky and the presence of the Department of Trade and Industry inspectors at Guinness. It has since been established that the DTI moved as a result of prompting from their US counterparts, dusting down the file that had been opened at the time of the Risk Affair. But at the time Saunders was dismissing any links between the Guinness investment and the confessions of Ivan Boesky. He was also becoming more excitable, according to observers who saw him in action during those days, but he never lost his cool.

Now Saunders was looking around for ways to explain the arrival of the DTI. He attended a lunch at the *Financial Times*, a guest of honour at the invitation of the editor. It was held in the splendid dining room at the top of the building with a magnificent panoramic view of St Paul's Cathedral. Geoffrey Owen, the *FT*'s editor, sat between a tired-looking Saunders and Olivier Roux. After the meal, where Saunders did not touch a morsel, the editor suggested to the guest of honour that he might like to address a few words to the company. 'You obviously want to know what this is all about,' said Saunders. 'Well, I will give you the facts, as far as I know them. It all goes back to the beginning of the bid for Bell's. The investigation is motivated for purely selfish reasons, by the Scots mafia in Perth.' In these terms Saunders spoke for an hour and three quarters, with minimal pauses. He spoke at length on the Risk affair, saying how Risk had come between Guinness and its merchant bank. It was a performance that impressed the cynical journalists, who for a moment began to find credible some very far-fetched reasoning. The journalists left with the impression of a man who still believed himself in charge.

Inside Guinness, the strains were beginning to tell. There had already been arguments between Saunders and his trusty lieutenant Olivier Roux about what evidence to give to the Inspectors. Roux had tended to side with Freshfields, who applied the high standards of probity. But on 19 December Saunders dispensed with the services of this firm of lawyers. According to Olivier Roux, Freshfields were replaced because 'Mr Saunders found Freshfields unsympathetic.' Saunders brought in the firm of Kingsley Napley, the well-known solicitors whose expertise is in the criminal law. David Napley, the senior partner, had made a name for himself when he conducted the defence of Jeremy Thorpe. Picking this sort of firm now indicated that the armoury was being strengthened for a major fight in the courts. With his ally in discussions with the inspectors ousted, Roux decided his time also had come. He left the building the same day, and did not return to work at Guinness again. From now on, there would be a feud between Saunders and Roux which would flair up in newsprint and in courts of law, fuelling the fires of the controversy with sensational allegations.

Sir Alex Fletcher, Argylls former advisor, and former Trade Minister, was by now alleging he was the target of those who felt he was partly responsible for the DTI investigation of Guinness. Fletcher was regularly appearing in the media commenting on the affair as it was unfolding. On 18 December he appeared on Channel Four News. When he returned to his Edinburgh flat the next day, it had been burgled. Nothing was taken and it was not a messy break-in, but Fletcher was convinced he had been targeted by somebody who was trying to put the frighteners on him. Unpleasant memories were revived of the Distillers bid burglaries.

Good cheer was lacking at Guinness that Christmas; the inspectors had not gone away and despite protestations of innocence from Ernest Saunders, the belief was growing that the rot was deeper in the fabric than anybody was admitting. The worms started coming out of their holes on 29 December, when a dispute arose between Guinness and a one-time investor in the company, the banking firm Henry Ansbacher. The City was shaken by the affair. But it washed over Mr Saunders, Olivier Roux and Thomas Ward. Saunders was by now taking a well-earned rest in Switzerland skiing, Roux was back in his native France for the New Year, and Thomas Ward had gone to his Washington bolt-hole. Only Brian Baldock was in the country to give direction from the top. For the public relations people it was exceedingly inconvenient, because the press had realised that smoke was clearing and the fire becoming more exposed. It was not even a happy holiday for Saunders. The chalet to which he and his wife had retreated had been too noisy and Ernest needed some peace, so Carole left him over there, apparently 'up a mountain', while she came home and manned the telephone. He was now incommunicado.

The day after the Ansbacher dispute became public, Morgan Grenfell handed in its resignation as merchant banker to Guinness. The leader in aggressive tactics for winning takeovers now realised that for once it had gone too far, and what is worse been caught at it. With Morgan's went its main and much-publicised practitioner in the corporate finance department, Roger Seelig. The bank's compliance officers effectively handed Seelig a pistol and left him to do the honourable thing. He was told he could be a liability and was attracting too much unfavourable publicity. What's more, the firm had to be seen to be acting. Seelig's resignation was an opportunity for the many City folk who had become envious of Seelig's success to take a swipe at the whizz-kid. The damage limitation exercise involved pinning as much mud on Seelig and a collective washing of hands. For Seelig it was a devastating blow after years of devotion to his company and his art. In fact, it is now widely accepted that the Bank of England had already moved in and, under pressure from the Chancellor himself, wanted heads to roll as a means of diffusing the criticism building up in parliament and the country.

On Sunday 4 January 1987 Ernest Saunders returned from his holiday to a situation which was fast deteriorating. The non-executive directors appointed to the company after the Risk affair wanted to tackle him with the latest on the Ansbacher share operation, and the main Guinness investors at this time, Warburg Investment Management and Prudential, were also looking for assurance. The non-execs met Saunders on the Monday. By now, speculation was intense, said an insider, that Saunders was guilty. People were also noticing a growing lack of rationality about his decisions. He was protesting his ignorance more and more frequently, and there was some even talk of advancing megalomania. On the Tuesday of that week, when the clouds were growing much darker, Saunders went out and ordered for himself a new Daimler, with two car telephones to boot.

Any remaining hope that he could survive was in the end dashed by his colleague Olivier Roux. On 5 January a letter outlining his role and the role of Ernest Saunders was received by David Napley. The so-called 'Roux letter', said one insider, positively 'fingered' Saunders. It also indicated that he was being very co-operative with the authorities. The solicitor promptly circularised the letter to the Guinness directors. The die was cast. The following day Saunders met fellow directors for 'informal discussions'. It wasn't clear if this was a full board meeting and the press hounds couldn't even establish where the meeting was. That evening Channel Four led off their Seven O'Clock News with a story saying that Saunders would resign within the hour. At regular intervals the programme would cross over to an increasingly desperate-looking reporter standing on the pavement in Portman Square. Other television crews, radio reporters and journalists milled around outside the glass doors. Shortly after 8.30 p.m. Brian Baldock, who by now was making all the statements on behalf of the board, emerged to say there was nothing to say. Saunders lived on.

Friday 9 January 1987 started ominously for the chairman and chief executive of the country's fifteenth-largest public company. The *Standard* newspaper in London carried an interview with Jonathan Guinness, a non-executive member of the board and a merchant banker with a small firm, Leopold Joseph, saying that he thought it might be time for Saunders to stand down. It indicated a serious change of heart by the Guinness family, who had hitherto supported the man who made their investment in Guinness worth something after years of decline. Jonathan Guinness then seemed to lose confidence in his comment, and he wanted to retract it. But later in the day, Jonathan Guinness saw the Roux letter, and that convinced him the game was up. Saunders' faithful allies Brian Baldock, Vic Steel and Shaun Dowling also saw the tide turning against the man to whom they owed their positions on the board. The executive directors conferred by phone with the non-executives, and, having taken the temperature of the board, which by now was boiling with rage at the way they had been deceived all along the line, summoned Saunders. The meeting was at 6.30 p.m. It did not last long. Saunders was told either you go, or we do. He asked for an hour with his wife, and retreated for air to his company suite at the Inn on the Park hotel. At 9 p.m. he returned to tell his fellow directors that he would 'stand aside' for the duration of the DTI enquiry. Said Saunders to his public relations adviser 'I am only leaving temporarily. I will see you again soon.'

An obituary was played out for Saunders by the last remaining member of his fan club, Ivan Fallon, in the *Sunday Times*. Fallon asked for him to be judged fairly by a City that he now perceived were out to get their prey. It was a remarkable piece of loyalty, albeit in hindsight misguided, by a journalist who appeared to have Saunders' ear at critical moments. Scorn, and worse, have been poured on him by people ever-so-clever-by-half who have had the benefit of hindsight. Colleagues, however, admire his consistency.

Saunders never again entered the executive suite at Guinness PLC. Events now moved swiftly. On 11 January Sir Norman Macfarlane, who had led the group of five non-executive directors appointed after the Risk affair, was appointed acting chairman. He had good Scottish credentials and ran a company, Macfarlane Group (Clansman), which was known for its sticky tape, but it also printed the labels for Distillers bottles. He was described at the time as less aggressive than his predecessor, but mercifully more tactful.

The spotlight now turned on Olivier Roux. All weekend journalists besieged his flat in the up-market Holland Park area of West London. He must have silently cursed the fact that his number and address were listed in the phone book. All the journalists got was 'no comment'. But on the Monday, late in the afternoon, he announced his resignation as a director. He had been caught up, so many believed, in a game played under different rules and by more cynical operators than he was equipped to handle. It was a very hard schooling for the young man who joined Guinness at the age of 32, and was now only 36. He spoke afterwards about being 'dead tired' at the end of the bid, and barely able to make a decent assessment of all the decisions and actions that were being taken around him.

The curtain finally came down on the career at Guinness of Ernest Saunders on Wednesday 14 January. The board had got cracking on finding out exactly what went on and they instructed Price Waterhouse, their accountants, to dig deep into the papers. Now the directors had before them the result of the accountants' findings. It turned out there had been a £200 million share-support operation responsibility for which led, via Roux and Saunders, to Zurich and Bank Leu. Once again pressmen clamoured at the glass doors of 39 Portman Square. Once again they had to wait until the evening for news. It was Lord Iveagh who emerged into the glare of the television lights to read out a prepared statement. Hemmed in by pressmen Iveagh announced that Ernest Saunders was to be dismissed from his executive position. It was a poignant and stressful moment for the man who'd remained in the shadows while Saunders was at the controls of the Guinness machine. Iveagh had suddenly become the bearer of news, the role that Saunders had relished in his time. The board also demanded the resignations of Dr Arthur Furer of Bank Leu and of the American lawyer and fixer extraordinaire, Thomas Ward. Kingsley Napley were dispensed with in favour of the more traditional corporate law firm of Herbert Smith.

Saunders was disgraced but hadn't lost his PR touch. During these weeks a campaign of leaks mostly through the *Sunday Times* set a new agenda for the public understanding of the Saunders affair. An attempt was made to smear Sir Norman Macfarlane. Letters were printed which claimed to show that Saunders had offered him the top job at Bell's during the Guinness bid for the whisky maker on one condition. He had to persuade General Accident, where he was a director, to sell their stake to Guinness. Macfarlane hastily denied that he had shown any interest in the Saunders proposal. In another issue the ashes of Peter Tyrie's defection from Bell's to Guinness in the middle of the bid were raked over and found still to be smouldering. There were whispers that Raymond Miquel was getting his oar in. Roux was also a victim of the leaks and smears. A statement purporting to have been agreed by him but which was later revealed as being the testimony given to the then Guinness solicitors Kingsley Napley was published without his approval. This was said to be the 'Roux letter' sent earlier in the month and was published as such in the *Sunday Times* but this was quickly denied by Roux.

The week beginning Monday 19 January will go down in the annals of banking as the one when the brash takeover strategists found their chickens coming home to roost. The Bank of England, itself under pressure from the Treasury and the Chancellor, was now waving the big stick. In the same week that Morgan Grenfell wrote to shareholders telling them that everything was under control, two of its top men had to quit. On Tuesday 20 January Nigel Lawson demanded action. The victims were the £300,000-a-year chief executive Christopher Reeves, and £200,000-a-year corporate finance boss Graham Walsh. The City's morale had reached its lowest ebb. There was an irony in the resignation of Graham Walsh. It was an open secret that he and Roger Seelig, the ultimate canker in the Morgan's wound, were not on speaking terms, and there was no question that he would know of the ins and outs of Seelig's multifarious deals. Later in the week, the flamboyant Lord Spens, whose responsibility for the Ansbacher 'deposit' was now paraded before him, announced his resignation.

While the banking heads were rolling, details emerged about mysterious fees paid immediately before and after the bid for Distillers. A now infamous invoice list outlined a total of £25 million worth of payments. As usual it was leaked to various friendly sources in the media before being officially revealed in a letter to shareholders. Gerald Ronson's name was dragged out into the open. He immediately sent back his £5 million cheque to Guinness, with the line that 'I did not focus on the legal implications of what had occurred, nor did it cross my mind that City advisers and business people of such eminence should be asking us to join in doing something improper'. Few of the City people to whom Ronson refers believe he is quite so disingenuous as he suggests. An attempt was also made at the same time to turn the heat on Cazenove, following a remark in Ronson's letter where he stated that he was introduced to Guinness by a representative of an 'eminent broker'. The *Financial Times* were convinced enough by this remark to suggest that Cazenove was implicated. This provoked a denial from the blue bloods. It was later reported that it had been Tony Parnes, the half-commission man from Alexanders Laing and Cruickshank. Parnes' links with the brokers were severed later in the month. Sir Jack Lyons also lost his job at Bain and Co, the management consultant, after it emerged that he'd been paid £2 million for unspecified services to Guinness.

The blood-letting seemed to have ended. The toll of victims was impressive: Roger Seelig, Christopher Reeves and Graham Walsh, the top dogs of a top merchant bank; Ernest Saunders, Olivier Roux, Thomas Ward and Arthur Furer, the brains behind Guinness; Lord Spens, prominent merchant banker, Tony Parnes, prominent though less acclaimed broker, Sir Jack Lyons, unseen tycoon with contacts in the Tory Party. Who else should follow? It was painfully obvious that one player had not come up with any sacrifical victim — Cazenove.

THE AFTERMATH

As Guinness and Morgan Grenfell licked their wounds the wrath of the press was directed at one of the City's most prestigious but most secretive institutions, Cazenove. Fellow brokers and banks involved in the bid for Distillers had made sacrifices, so why not Caz? There were angry demands for victims to be thrown on the funeral pyre from Cazenove. Some of the vitriol aimed at the famous brokers may have been generated by others whose careers now lay in tatters. But it was clear that Cazenove had some sort of case to answer.

Gerald Ronson may have been playing on the mood of the party when he mentioned his contact with 'eminent brokers'. It seemed to many observers to be an obvious code for Cazenove. But the exposure of Parnes quickly scotched that line of attack. The flak was now turned on David Mayhew who most of the City assumed had been Caz's member of the Guinness 'inner cabinet'. Although in reality it's doubtful whether there was such a cabinet, it was a convenient way of looking at the team who plotted the takeover of Distillers. Only the solicitor Anthony Salz, of Freshfields, had held on to his job apart from Mayhew. The Wood Mackenzie men had resigned months before, Seelig, Roux, Saunders and Ward had all gone and the backroom boys, Sir Jack Lyons and Tony Parnes, had been unmasked. But Mayhew took the punches on the chin and didn't flinch. He knew he had the support of his superiors. Cazenove did not want to add its own people to the firing squad, for to do so might imply guilt.

But if Cazenove wouldn't hunt out the scapegoats from within its ranks, it knew it would have to break silence. Traditionally Cazenove shunned publicity, and City journalists knew they'd never get a quote from the gentlemen partners in their modest offices tucked away behind the Bank of England. Cazenove had invisible pulling power and had stayed independent while other brokers were swallowed up in the scrambling for position before Big Bang. But two poisoned darts had penetrated the protective carapace around the blue-blooded broking firm. The partners of Cazenove felt deeply wounded by Gerald Ronson's revelations. The second blow, which prompted retaliation, was hearing the firm's name besmirched in the House of Commons. Labour spokesman Robin Cook claimed that Cazenove had purchased 20 million Guinness shares on 6 May, the same day as the £7.6 million was paid to Henry Ansbacher. He accused Caz of paying back members of a concert party who'd bought Guinness shares on a temporary business. What's more, Cook suggested that Caz were now so powerful that the Stock Exchange couldn't control them.

So at last, on Thursday 29 January, Cazenove's were stung into a public statement. In the first sentence they noted the 'intense interest' surrounding the Guinness bid for Distillers: 'we have decided to depart from our practice of refraining from public comment'. Cazenove revealed that they'd appointed their own solicitors, Simmons and Simmons, to conduct an internal investigation of possible breaches of the law and the Takeover Code. The main finding was that 'nothing in their inquiries had led them to believe that Cazenove was involved in, or aware of, any illegality'. Then there was a rap over the knuckles for not checking out the links between Schenley and Guinness. The statement proceeded to defend Cazenove's actions when the Guinness share price was rising during the bid — 'we judged that it was due to the market's perception of the chances of Guinness winning the bid'. Then the matter of the deals involving supporters of Guinness shares — 'we cannot know the full scope of the dealings in Guinness shares during the bid period. It is clear that a very significant number of transactions took place without our involvement.' Robin

Cook's accusations were denied; apparently 'the 20 million shares were issued by Guinness to Cazenove Nominees as part of the bid in exchange for Distillers' shares'. And finally to the future of David Mayhew; was it in any doubt? 'No, nor has it ever been. That should be obvious from the above.' And so the book was closed: Cazenove retreated back into its privileged hideaway and slammed the door.

Slowly the pressure eased on the City's elitist stockbroking firm. Anthony Forbes and David Mayhew lived to fight again. The critics pointed out that Cazenove were so reluctant to dump one of their own because they are a partnership rather than a company. As one City banker observed: 'In a partnership one really does have unlimited liability and collectively it is therefore much more important to present a solid front.' Others wondered why the Big Guns had not directed their fire at Cazenove. The Chancellor, Nigel Lawson, and Robin Leigh Pemberton had made Morgan Grenfell pay dearly; they'd lost their three top men and also paid a heavy price commercially (Seelig was rumoured to have been bringing in 25% of corporate finance profits). Because Morgan's was a public company the impact of the resignations was felt acutely. For a while there were rumours that the takeover kings would themselves fall to a hostile bidder. But no such crisis for Cazenove, no ticking off or washing of dirty linen. Soon it was business as usual.

The £25 million invoice list which had thrown up the names of Gerald Ronson, Ephraim Margulies and Sir Jack Lyons (through his company J. Lyons Chamberlayne), now began to absorb the attentions of those city journalists with amateur sleuthing tendencies. The race was on to find the names behind the names on the list. Quickly Zentralsparkasse und Kommerzialbank was tracked to Austria and a sheepish Viennese bank manager confessed to buying Guinness shares and offered to pay back his fee. One mystery name Cifco baffled the journalists; a company of that name was traced to Bombay which provoked angry denials from a local manager. It was later revealed that Cifco is Swiss and the manager Charles Rosenbaum is a friend of Ephraim Margulies. Attempts to find out more about Rudani Corp of the Dutch Antilles, who'd submitted an invoice for almost £2 million, fell on stony ground. It was reported later that the deal had been arranged by Roger Seelig.

But the biggest puzzle was the name of Marketing and Acquisition Consultants Limited, registered in Jersey. They'd apparently received £5.2 million. This figure was soon to be repeated as frequently as other famous numbers, for example the Ansbacher £7.6 million, the £25 million invoice list, and the £50 million Bank Leu deposit. Within hours of the publication of the list the lines were red hot to the picturesque port of St Helier in Jersey. Instant company searches had revealed that one of the directors of Marketing and Acquisition Consultants(MAC) was a Michael James Dee. Soon his secretary was coping with a barrage of calls from London. Even Mr Dee's elderly mother was bothered by phone calls at midnight as the relentless search for the missing Guinness millions gathered momentum.

Dee would reveal very little when he came to the phone. He admitted to being a nominee director acting for a client and confirmed that the missing £5.2 million had reached Jersey. But no, he couldn't speculate why the money had been paid. Dee said he was angry that neither the Department of Trade Inspectors nor any official of Guinness had yet been in touch — perhaps they were letting journalists do the hard work. But most newspapers discovered little more.

As the City journalists ran up large phone bills investigating the bizarre collection of companies in Jersey, Switzerland, Austria and the Dutch Antilles, the new boys at Guinness were trying to sort out the future of the company. Sir Norman Macfarlane was trawling the brewing industry for a new chief executive to replace Saunders. In the meantime he won points in Scotland by calling the first board meeting of the new Guinness to be held north of the Border. On Tuesday 10 February the directors converged on Edinburgh at the smart Distillers headquarters near the Murrayfield rugby stadium. Some of the new non-executives were taken round the local bottling halls; for most of them it would have been their first visit to the great whisky centres. Sir John Nott had also made the trip to Edinburgh and was seen slipping into the building. Lazards were playing an active role in shaping the new Guinness. The meeting decided on a successor to Saunders, although the decision was not announced until the following week.

The heir to the Saunders kingdom was an altogether different style of businessman. The sober-suited Old Etonian Anthony

Tennant joined the ship from Grand Metropolitan where he'd been in charge of brands such as Bailey's Irish Cream and Crofts sherries. Earlier in his career he'd been part of the team which devised the slogan 'sssscchh . . . you know who'. Tennant's appointment was no surprise. He was worthy and had the right qualifications; one City analyst remarked that 'the City is not looking for a charismatic figure in the mould of Mr Saunders'. Hamish McRae in the *Guardian* suggested that Distillers could end up better run than it would have been by Saunders or even Gulliver but 'would it not have been much easier to hire Mr Tennant in the first place, rather than go through the rigmarole of a contested takeover battle?' Alongside Tennant was a new finance director, altogether a more radical choice. Michael Julien was snatched away from a key position at Eurotunnel, the consortium that was then struggling to get enough money to start the Channel Tunnel. One of their first decisions was to sell off the ragbag of retail interests built up by Saunders — Tennant made it clear he wanted to stick to the core beverage business.

With the new management in place to go out and sell the whiskies and the stout, Sir Norman Macfarlane could turn back to the more sordid business of tracking down the infamous £5.2 million. The lawyers began rattling the sabre in Jersey and initiated court proceedings there in a bid to force MAC to reveal what had happened to the money. There was little press interest at first as the lawyers from both sides got bogged down in legal wrangling. But soon the defences crumbled and the figure behind the screen emerged; it was none other than Thomas Ward. He was said to have received the money through the Jersey company in return for work done at the time of the bid for Distillers. The Guinness side claimed that there'd been a series of transactions designed to disguise the destination of the money and that it had since moved on from MAC: 'It whizzed around bank accounts like traffic around Piccadilly Circus.'

With the City speculating about what Thomas Ward did to justify a fee of £5.2 million, the stage moved to the High Court in London. Guinness began legal proceedings against Ernest Saunders and Thomas Ward to recover the money arguing that the payment had been authorised illegally without full approval of the board. On Wednesday 25 March Ernest Saunders was back on the front pages after allegations that more than £3 million of the money had passed through a Swiss bank account in his name. Saunders' lawyers told the court that he had let Ward use the account as a temporary haven for the funds but he had no beneficial interest in it. Speculation now mounted that Saunders could have paid himself out of company funds, which would have been flagrantly in breach of his responsibilities as a director. A court order freezing the assets of Ward and Saunders was granted. This included the mansion at Penn which Saunders had put on the market.

By the beginning of April Saunders was holed up in Switzerland. He was having treatment at a clinic in Lausanne after a deterioration in his health. Carole Saunders, who'd had an operation the previous year, had taken a turn for the worse and was said to be emotionally disturbed and under sedation. But Saunders continued to wage a legal battle through the High Court in London to clear his name. Lawyers for Saunders and Ward now attempted to get the order freezing their assets overturned. Guinness countered by directly accusing Saunders of benefiting personally from company funds to the tune of £3 million.

The Vice-Chancellor, Sir Nicholas Browne-Wilkinson, heard claim upon claim about the nature of payments made by Guinness during the bid for Distillers. It was easy to forget that the proceedings were simply an attempt by two defendants to have an asset freezing order discontinued. Affidavit followed affidavit as each of the former colleagues sought to discredit one another. Journalists covering the proceedings may have been confused to hear extracts read from 'the Roux letter' by lawyers for Ernest Saunders. This was the document disowned by Roux in January but which was being used as evidence against him.

At the same time there was a 'Roux Affidavit' which was the former Bain man's personal submission. Each of Roux's claims in the official affidavit contradicted Saunders' version of events. Saunders claimed to have known only about the £5.8 million fee to Gerald Ronson but Roux said the former chief executive had known about every one on the invoice list. Roux also said that Ward had submitted a £5.2 million invoice which he said was for consultancy costs in the United States. Roux had paid it, believing that no director had a personal interest.

Saunders claimed that Roux knew the money was going to
Ward. At times it seemed the court's time was being wasted in
an elaborate buck-passing operation. Roux, Ward and Saunders all knew the position with regard to the Companies Act.

The Guinness lawyers quietly dropped their accusation that
Saunders had benefited personally from any of the £5.2
million. Ward's lawyer, David Aufhauser, partner in the
Washington firm of Williams and Connolly, denied that
Saunders ever received any of this money. Two days before the
Easter holiday, on Wednesday 15 April, Sir Nicholas gave his
conclusions to the court. He emphasised that it was not his
position to weigh up evidence or give a verdict but noted that
the £5.2 million payment 'could not have been lawfully made'
under the Companies Act. He noted the conflict between Roux
and Saunders: 'There is no possible halfway house, either Mr
Roux or Mr Saunders is lying.' Sir Nicholas decided that
Saunders' UK assets should remain frozen. It was now up to
Guinness to pursue the £5.2 million through a full action in the
High Court.

Ernest Saunders came to England in person on Monday 4
May. He spent two days preparing with his lawyers, Payne,
Hicks Beach. On Wednesday afternoon he was interviewed by
Department of Trade inspectors. Later he returned to his
solicitors' offices just behind the Law Courts off the Strand.
But at ten minutes past six two detectives from the Fraud
Squad were shown into reception. They arrested Saunders and
drove him to Holborn police station. He was shown into a
police cell but later that evening twice asked to see a doctor.

The following day, Thursday 7 May, at 2.18 p.m. Saunders
was led into Court Number One at Bow Street Magistrates
Court. He was described on the charge sheet as aged 51 and
unemployed. He was wearing a blue pinstripe suit and
dark-blue crew neck jumper. He looked unshaven. Minutes
earlier magistrate Jeffrey Breen had fined a drunken vagrant.
Now he was faced with the former chairman of one of the
largest companies in Britain. Saunders was charged with intent
to pervert the course of justice and with the destruction and
falsification of documents.

Ernest Saunders leaned forward, resting his arms on the
dock as the magistrate heard the police reasons for objecting to
bail. Saunders was released on bail just before 4 p.m. after a

short adjournment to consult with his lawyers about raising up to half a million pounds. Saunders was allowed to stay at the house of his solicitor, Stephen Ralph, after giving an undertaking not to contact past or present members of Guinness.

Ernest Saunders returned to court on Tuesday 12 May. Tiny Rowland, newspaper proprietor and boss of the Lonrho company, put up bail of £250,000. Rowland had met Saunders twice before, once in Switzerland in April. He had heard from Saunders about the methods used to lobby the Department of Trade at the time of the bid for Distillers. Rowland then wrote to Trade Secretary Paul Channon enquiring why his Lonrho Group had not been shown the same favours when bidding for the Harrods store empire House of Fraser. Another sum of £250,000 was pledged as surety by a Mr Herbert Heinzel, a cake manufacturer from Hertfordshire. He said he was an old family friend of the Saunders and had been contacted in Switzerland by Carole Saunders, who sounded desperate. Saunders was bailed to reappear in the court and departed with his solicitor. Back at the offices of Payne, Hicks Beach, Saunders gave a press conference. Defiantly, he threw down a gauntlet: 'Those responsible for my current situation will be exposed.' He read out a statement to the crowd of journalists: 'I am incensed at the allegations of dishonesty and wrongdoing made against me and make it clear that all such charges are strenuously denied and will be vigorously contested.'

Now attention focussed on the Annual General Meeting of Guinness PLC which was marked in diaries throughout the City for Wednesday 27 May. On the agenda was a resolution calling for the removal of Ernest Saunders from the board (despite being sacked as chairman in January, he had never formally resigned as a director). Rumours that the former chairman would appear at the meeting to defend himself began to circulate. Journalists, television crews and photographers from across Europe and even from the United States harassed Chris Davidson and Alan Stewart in the Guinness press office, demanding interviews and photo opportunities on the big day.

In the run up to the meeting two financial transactions took place which attracted little media comment. Henry Ansbacher announced they'd sold their Guinness shares and were returning a sum of £7.4 million to the company. The question of who owned the shares was never fully resolved. Ansbacher had lost nothing, but £200,000 of the original sum deposited by Guinness had been swallowed up in dealing costs and 'losses' on the sale of the shares. Bank Leu also put 40 million of their Guinness shares on the market. They were sold to the London stockbrokers James Capel who managed to pass them to City institutions within minutes. Then the Swiss bank returned the deposit of £50 million. A Guinness spokesman was unable to confirm whether any interest had been earned on the money during its year in Zurich. The Swiss connection, which in January had been referred to by Sir Norman Macfarlane as 'in apparent breach of Companies Act requirements', was quietly wound up.

On Tuesday 26 May, Ernest Saunders was back in London closeted with his solicitor, Stephen Ralph, at the offices of Payne, Hicks, Beach at Lincoln's Inn. At 6.30 that evening Ralph rang journalists to tell them his client was sending a letter to shareholders and another to Sir Norman Macfarlane. It was a typical Saunders PR touch and ensured he would upstage the Guinness meeting the following morning. He tendered his resignation as a director and so pre-empted the board's resolution calling on shareholders to oust him. But more dramatic was an open letter to shareholders, which Saunders asked Sir Norman to read out at the meeting.

In the letter Saunders said that he'd agreed to stand aside for the duration of the DTI enquiry provided that he stayed on full pay and had his legal costs paid, but 'none of these terms have been honoured'. He explained his resignation letter to Sir Norman Macfarlane: 'I have myself concluded, and I have likewise been advised, that whilst the criminal charges, although strongly denied, remain outstanding it is not in the interests of your company that I should remain a director.' He denied that he'd benefited from any of the £25 million list of payments or knew about any unlawful share support operations. Saunders claimed that he'd had no opportunity to respond to investigations by the company which led to his sacking: 'My family first heard of my dismissal from the media.'

The letter continued with an attack on his adversaries: 'I can no longer hide the fact that I feel incensed at the lies which have been told about me by others. I am also distressed by the way in which I have been treated, particularly by my former colleagues on the Board who were my allies whilst it suited them, but now seek to make me a scapegoat. An investigation into the company appears to have turned into a personal vendetta. For my part I am content that the record of what I was able to achieve on your behalf during my five years of office should speak for itself and I will ensure that the truth behind the alleged improper activities will in due course emerge. I have always recognised that the kind of success which we achieved could not be won without making enemies. My surprise and disappointment has been to find such enemies on my own Board and among those who have so handsomely reaped the benefits of its success.'

The contents of Saunders' letter were reported on the front pages of national newspapers as the Guinness shareholders made their way to the Connaught Rooms at Holborn in central London - the meeting was due to begin at 11.30 a.m. The traditional venue for a Guinness annual general meeting is the Park Royal brewery, but for 1987 it was deemed important to find somewhere with a greater audience capacity. Some shareholders grumbled that they were missing out on the traditional Park Royal hospitality and sampling of the company's beverages. Even so, around 1,000 people turned up. Like the emergency meeting in September 1986, they had to queue up to gain admission. Some familiar faces could be seen in the crowds; Bay Green, Anthony Good, Sir John Nott but no Saunders. Security was tight and no journalist or photographer was allowed into the main chamber — more than 50 media folk were herded into a gallery above. Television crews were disappointed not to get a shot of the chairman arriving at the meeting. Sir Norman had slipped into the building before 9 a.m.

Sir Norman Macfarlane opened the meeting with a predictable preamble about the most difficult and traumatic year in the company's history. Then he announced that because Ernest Saunders had tendered his resignation as a director the resolution calling for his removal would be withdrawn. Sir Norman said he would not be reading out the letter from Saunders as 'it is no longer relevant' and it contained allegations with which the board disagreed. A cry went up from the back of the hall 'we want to hear it'.

One of the first speakers from the floor was the Labour spokesman Robin Cook, who was at the meeting because the Labour pension fund owned Guinness shares. He had warned Sir Norman what questions he was going to ask and had obtained some useful pre-election coverage in newspapers the previous day. After firing in his pre-prepared questions on how much the board had known about mysterious payments, the sale of Distillers brands to Lonrho and role of Sir Jack Lyons, Cook slipped in another on Cazenove. He asked whether Guinness thought it was right to retain the stockbroker's services. Sir Norman appeared a little surprised and replied that he could see no reason why they shouldn't continue to use Cazenove. But later it was confirmed that David Mayhew no longer worked on the Guinness account.

A number of shareholders spoke in favour of Saunders; one pointed to his achievement in increasing profits and another argued that he shouldn't have been dismissed so hastily. Another shareholder questioned the role of the auditors Price Waterhouse and said he'd be voting against their reappointment. Each contribution was greeted with hearty applause and shouts of 'here, here'. But there was equally stout applause for a speech from the floor from a former advertising manager and director of Guinness, Alan Wood. He argued that Saunders had brought shame on a 'great company and a great name'. Saunders himself was not present but, in the words of one observer, his spirit seemed to linger over the meeting 'like Banquo's ghost'.

The rest of the business of the meeting was transacted smoothly and most of the resolutions were passed unanimously. But there were a handful of votes against the formal election to the board of Sir Norman Macfarlane. He left the Connaught Rooms refusing to comment on any aspect of the meeting to journalists. But the press consensus was that he'd handled the meeting skilfully. Ernest Saunders' solicitor, Stephen Ralph, confirmed that they had begun legal proceedings against Guinness alleging unfair dismissal, and other civil actions would follow. Meanwhile the shareholders dispersed with a gift pack of the Guinness alcohol-free lager 'Kaliber'. Many were still confused at the momentous course of events that their company was caught up in. But the share price was at its strongest for many months and that was reassuring many of the doubters.

The new Guinness management has been quickly getting to grips with the demands of running a multinational drinks business. A distribution agreement with Moet-Hennessy has been reached for joint sales in the U.S.A. The thorny problem of the Dewar's trademark has vexed the new bosses. They are desparate to get back the Dewar's rights from Schenley and a full scale takeover of the US company is being negotiated.

Meanwhile Saunders' old colleagues and adversaries have been quietly rebuilding their shattered careers. They take a keen interest in newspaper revelations and most are still being advised by lawyers. Roger Seelig spends half the week in Gloucestershire and the other half at his London flat near Marble Arch. He still has a clutch of directorships and is busy with consultancy work for old clients. Olivier Roux is also a free man and is considering starting up his own business, possibly with some former Bain colleagues. He has been helping Guinness with various legal matters and is frequently at the Portman Square offices. Lord Spens is running his own investment fund, based in Mayfair. His old assistant at Henry Ansbacher has moved over to join him. Thomas Ward has resurfaced in Washington and is back full-time at his desk at Ward, Lazarus, Grow and Cihlar. He is believed to have had conversations with the American Securities and Exchange Commission, although this has been denied by his lawyers.

James Gulliver and associates are now heading a major food retailing group, in the same league as Tesco and Sainsbury. After spending more than £650 million on the Safeway supermarket chain they began to sell off their drinks interests. David Webster admits that they will never attempt a massive bid again although feels they have all 'learnt a lot'. Gulliver is still bitter that his grand hopes of reviving Scotland's whisky giant have been dashed. Argyll are poised to sue Guinness for depriving them of Distillers. The action will centre on the crucial £70 million stake which changed hands on the last day of the bid.

Raymond Miquel has bounced back into the company high life as boss of the brewery group Belhaven. He announced his return with a vengeance in May after agreeing a £100 million deal to take over the Garfunkels restaurant chain with such assets as the Deep Pan Pizza company. It's a far cry from Scotch whisky and Gleneagles, but he still orders a bottle of

Bell's when he's staying at his favourite London hotel, the Sheraton Park.

John Connell is quietly retired in Walton-on-Thames. He has made no public statement since Guinness took control of Distillers. Bill Spengler lives in comfortable semi retirement in Kingston-on-Thames. He and Connell are close and often have dinner together. And what of the man who recruited Saunders to Guinness? Tony Purssell lives a stone's throw from his former protégé's residence in Buckinghamshire. This rather unworldly, gentle character still has a well paid executive job.

He, at least, got clear before the bomb dropped.

INDEX